The
Life of Saint Monica

By
MGR BOUGAUD

Translated by
MRS EDWARD HAZELAND

Read St Monica's life. You will see her care for her Augustine, and find much to console you.—*St Francis de Sales to St Jane Frances de Chantal.*

Fourth Edition

London and Leamington
ART AND BOOK COMPANY
New York, Cincinnati, Chicago: BENZIGER BROTHERS

1900

ST MONICA AND ST AUGUSTINE

After Ary Scheffer

CONTENTS.

CHAPTER V.

CHAPTER VI.

CHAPTER VII.

CHAPTER VIII.

CHAPTER IX.

APPENDIX.

NOTES AND DOCUMENTARY EVIDENCE.

PREFACE TO THE SECOND EDITION.

The first hint of our intention to compile a life of St. Monica, a life till then unwritten, awoke, we must avow, some little surprise and much anxiety, even among our friends, who asked where the materials for such a work could be found, and what would be its interest when written. As to the materials, we had studied them for more than twelve months with ever-deepening emotion; for what more touching than that drama in which we behold a son saved by his mother's tears, under whose life-giving dew he becomes a great genius and a great saint? We therefore determined to carry out our intention, looking to God to bless our labours, and to maternal hearts for pardon, if temerity attached to our project. We have no reason to regret our decision. The first edition of this work, a large issue, was exhausted within a few weeks, and in spite of the urgent demands of the public, we have been unable to send forth our second edition until now.

But apart from this kindly welcome, clearer proofs of the divine benediction resting on our work and

1

manifested by the feelings its perusal has awakened. Since its appearance not a day passes without bringing us letters, the majority from stranger-hands, all imbued with maternal sorrow and maternal hope. For six months we have heard the beatings of these hearts, the cry issuing from the inmost recesses of these souls, and listened to expressions of gratitude so deep that it has filled us with astonishment.

Scarcely had the Introduction appeared, when a lady, one who had known severe afflictions, but who by her trials had attained a high degree of virtue, wrote, asking us for permission to print a hundred thousand copies of the same, "that many other mothers might share the consolation she had found therein." The same day, the father of a family, a faithful, loving soul, such as is rare at the present time, addressed us in terms the indulgent language of which compels us to abridge his letter. "In perusing your Preface to the Life of St. Monica, a cry goes up from every heart; accents such as these cannot fail to console many a sorrow, and heal many a broken heart. They penetrate to the very depths of the maternal soul, and suffuse the father's eyes with tears. Yes, reverend sir, I but re-echo the sentiments of every parent when I avow that we have been taken captive by your words. So true, so eloquent, so impassioned are they, that they penetrate to the inmost depths of our being, compel us to return to that path where dwell the austere but solid joys of faith, and by means of the noblest and purest affection of which man's heart is capable, rouse the dormant energy of our will. I have but thanks to offer. Service such as yours is beyond reward; but if a father's gratitude avail aught, I beg you to accept the expression of the same," &c.

Now for a mother's words. " Sir, if I reflected for one single moment on my presumption in addressing you, I should at once lay down my pen; but I yield to the impulse of a heart overwhelmed by sorrow, a heart that as yet dares entertain no ray of hope. I have just read your book, and with my tears have bathed the page where you assert that, if she will, a mother may save her son. But, sir, I am only a poor sinner. Can I, in spite of this, do as you say? I ought to be a saint, for my husband was a worthy man, called by God to endure many trials. He was betrayed, calumniated, ruined. For fourteen years I shared his tears and sorrows, and last year he departed this life, overwhelmed by deep affliction. I have one son, but alas! he was the cause of my poor husband's most bitter tears. Pray for this unfortunate child, that he may have courage to renounce his present mode of life, for which he has sacrificed parents, name, and fortune. Entreat that he may at least not lose his soul. Oh, sir, you must indeed be dear to St. Monica. Supplicate her on behalf of a broken-hearted mother who dreads lest her son should be lost."

As I write, I have more than fifty letters in sight, all bathed in tears and breathing the same spirit. I pass these over, and fix on one, which, though of a far different tone, has also deeply moved me. The

writer is a lady bearing a name of no little note;
a great soul, which, though it once fell, arose greater
than before, transfigured by repentance and by the
painful sacrifice which the love of God exacted at her
hands. After a few words as to the general character
of the book, she adds: " Shall I now describe how
deep was my emotion in perusing the pages which
give us a transient glance at the young girl who
*forgot God for Augustine, and for whom Augustine
forgot God?* For me this veiled figure wears no veil;
it is my own soul that, after struggling for fifteen
years, escaped from her trammels, finds rest in God
alone, and whose life is now spent in prayer, penitence, and love. History says nought of the graces
which were potent enough to sever her from Augustine and from Adeodatus, but my grateful soul can
tell the tale. Neither does history say that she gave
herself to God in order that her son might do so too,
and that she might enclose his soul in a network of
incessant prayers, so that should he ever learn his
mother's story, or fall himself, he might know in
what way the soul may arise from her degradation;
also that she never ceased to mourn the misfortune
of his birth. This, too, I can relate. Though my
wounds heal but slowly, I trust, whatever may be-
tide, to end my life in the love of God, a love out-
weighing all besides. Pray for me, and unite your
entreaties to mine, that our Lord would perfect His
work concerning me, a work, the completion of which
I await mid ceaseless tears and prayers, but at the
same time in peace." Then, alluding to a passage

in the book, she adds: "God in heaven, and my
loved ones, offered to God and ransomed by my
tears, almost suffice me. For what else is required
to enter heaven when repentance is rather the result
of love than of fear?"

Here are words in a far different key, those of
a young girl; one of those angels of piety, purity,
and modesty, who in large families of small means
sometimes devote themselves to aiding their mother,
or, should she be removed, replace her; and whose
young virgin-hearts, at the age of eighteen or twenty,
know all the anguish of maternity. She writes thus:
"A few days ago I read your Preface in the *Annales
d'Orleans,* and for a moment I envied the happiness
of mothers, to whom it is given to bestow a double
life, and from which happiness I myself seemed
excluded. I was about to make my plaint to our
Lord, when a note, appended to your Preface,* quite
consoled me. Yes; I, too, have my Augustines, and
very tiny ones, whom God in His mercy has proportioned to their Monica; and I felt more deeply than
ever convinced that I must devote myself wholly to
them. I regret my shortcomings in this respect,
and mourn my want of courage and hope. Had my
trust in God been more steadfast, and my tears
on their behalf been mingled with a firmer hope,
they might have been saints ere this. Also, there
are so many other souls besides these......I long to
see our holy Mother engrossing the warmest affec-

---

* See Note relative to Eugénie de Guérin.

tions of every heart." Thus did I realize that touching and intimate communion of soul with soul, of which the Rev. Father Lacordaire thus wrote in such sublime terms in the early days of his apostolate: "Then did I realize that communion in which consists the true happiness of the priest, when worthy of his sacred mission, which dispels every shadow of regret for the ties, hopes, and friendships which he has renounced for his Divine Master's sake. I beheld the dawn of affection and gratitude, evoked by no personal gifts or qualities, uniting man to his spiritual guide by ties alike divine in their sweetness and in their strength. Once initiated into this happiness, a foretaste, as it were, of the life to come, all else vanishes, and pride has no abiding-place within the soul." As for myself, I had tasted of this sweet communion of soul with soul on the publication of the Life of St. Chantal. St. Monica revealed it to me in its inner and profounder depths.

But a work of this kind does not always fall into such devout hands; sometimes it finds its way to regions essentially mundane, whence there falls on the ear accents fraught with a charm and beauty of their own. "I must confess to you, sir," wrote a mother, "that I had never considered the biography of a saint very interesting reading, and but for my son winning your book in a lottery, I might never have set eyes thereon. Heaven be praised for the good fortune which placed it in my son's hands, and inspired him to present it to me. Little did he know what would be the result of his gift, what a signal manifestation it would be of the truth that God is ever near to those who seek Him. For, sir, it is St. Augustine to whom I owe so much, seeing, alas! that I find more analogy between his perplexed and blinded soul and my soul, than between my worthlessness and St. Monica's incomparable virtue. May I venture to tell you what I think of your work? I fear lest the example you set before mothers is so perfect that none will have courage to follow it. We are so cowardly; our love to God is so feeble; and if we love our children, it is scarcely for God's sake that we do so. I thought I loved my son as a Christian mother should do, at least since the time when, by heaven's grace, having grown a little more serious, surmounting all obstacles, I placed my son in a Christian school, and so fulfilled, as I thought, all that was requisite on my part. But, sir, the example you have placed before me has totally undeceived me. Who now can rise so high? I am almost tempted to be discouraged, and wonder whether God exacts from every mother the same exalted degree of love, and if so, how we can attain it.......Rather see one's child die than sin! Though in my prayers I sometimes tell God that such is my desire, I fear lest my words should be insincere, or my heart belie my words."

Fear not, mother! you who begin to discern the divine heights of affection, and yet hesitate to climb the same, take courage! the hour is at hand when you will become a true mother indeed.

What other letters shall I cite? It is the happi-

ness of a book like this that it addresses itself to the
noblest feelings of the soul, penetrating to regions
wholly separated from us, there also awaking emotions full of hope.   One letter is from England, and
bears the signature of a Protestant minister, one
of those many souls who in that noble and religious
country are seeking for the truth.   "Allow me to
thank you for your beautiful work on St. Monica,
which I have just read, and which impresses me
the more forcibly, inasmuch as there is a striking
similarity between the impetuous Augustine and the
age in which we live. Ah! soon may it hear the
divine voice addressing to it the words, '*Take and
read;*' may the holy Scriptures lead it back to the
fold of the Church, that mourning mother whose
mission it is to persevere amid prayers and tears.
For, sir, do you not think with me that the day is at
hand when, in fulfilment of Malachi's prophecy, the
hearts of the fathers shall be drawn to the hearts of
the children?   Seven hundred millions of the human
race await the moment of our reconciliation to embrace the Gospel.   As St. Monica of old, even so let
us, by our prayers, sighs, and pious labours, hasten
the moment of their deliverance.   On the evening of
the day on which I finished reading your book, I
showed it, in a Protestant drawing-room, to a lady of
high position, (a great admirer of Madame de
Chantal,) who transcribed many pages of your work.
Every heart was moved at the thought of the woes of
the present age, towards which each of us must act
the part of a St. Monica."

I should never weary of perusing these letters, resounding with deep, true, and fervent parental love, a love on which we ground our fondest hopes for the present age: which, though its woes are indeed profound, are, God be praised, not irremediable. I will cite one other letter, the language of which is most consoling: " Allow a simple Vendean mother, much impressed by your Life of St. Monica, to thank you most warmly in the name of every Christian mother. Sure I am that none will read your book without being inspired by noble sentiments and moved to the inmost recesses of the soul, glorying in the grandeur of their vocation and in the sublimity of their influence. Yes, sir, you are right; if a mother ought to die for her child, much more should she be ready to do so in order to save his soul. Once this resolve enters the heart, sure I am that success will crown her work. I started on reading that page where you depict the mother of the Machabees, St. Symphorian's mother, and many others besides, urging their tender offspring to die rather than offend God. But, sir, why have you cited no mothers save those of antiquity? Do you deem those of the present day incapable of similar heroism? Have you no modern instances to quote?" Then, piqued by a noble jealousy, this mother relates to me the example of two or three women whose conduct amid the horrors of the revolution equalled that of the mother of the Machabees. Madame de la Roche St. André, for instance, who, when sentenced to death with her three daughters, entreated and obtained permission that the latter should mount the scaffold first, "that," she said, " I may see all I love safe." Also, Madame Saillous de Saumur, who, when led to the scaffold with her young and beautiful daughter of eighteen, noting with anxiety the attentions paid the latter by an officer of the escort, (a man known to be a profligate,) and the hesitation of her child, who, by listening to his proposals and following him, might save her life, offered the executioner a reward if he would allow her child to die first; then, when her own turn came, loosening her tresses, she drew forth some pieces of gold, gave them to the executioner, and died, rejoicing that at least her child's virtue was for ever safe.

Thus wrote the Vendean mother. She might have added the story O'Connell relates of the Irishwoman, whose son, fearing lest his aged mother, his young wife, and family, should be rendered homeless and deprived of sustenance, hesitated whether or no to vote for a measure that would prove detrimental to the liberty of his country. He was on the point of giving way, but on stepping forward to record his vote, his old mother seized him by the arm, exclaiming, "Remember thy soul and freedom's cause."

The above cited letter moved me to tears, and I said: "Yes, the present age is indeed one full of trouble and unrest; but whilst mothers' hearts beat thus nobly, there is every room for hope. Yes, our Augustines will be saved by our Monicas.

To aid in bringing about this happy result I wrote

my book, and I thank God that it has awakened an echo in so many hearts; and I am grateful to mothers who, by the intuition of their love, have discerned in my pages that which my feeble genius was unable to accomplish.

I well know that my book does not do justice to the grandeur and beauty of my subject; it also falls far short of my own ideal; but among the objections to which it may be open there is one which I repudiate: that I have said too much of St. Augustine. One of our greatest orators wrote to me thus: "Let who will assert that St. Monica's history can never be aught save the history of her son, this it is which makes it so grand and beautiful, and renders your book so unique and so original." A mother says: "Those who complain that St. Augustine has the pre-eminence in the Life of St. Monica, know nothing of a mother's heart. A mother's greatest joy is to give her children the first place; she allows them to overshadow her, but is still near to aid and to support. Their life is her life, and I can conceive no history of any mother that is not the history of her children also."

Therefore, in lieu of diminishing, I have thought it right, in this new edition, to augment the space allotted to St. Augustine, and this in compliance with the advice of one of the most zealous defenders of the Church in the present day, who, after imparting to me his friendly anxiety on first hearing of my project, adds: "Thanks to God, who has blessed your zealous, disinterested, and pious labours, my fears are exchanged for the most perfect satisfaction. The *History of St. Monica* is as well, but more graphically, written than *St. Chantal.* The style is as correct, but more vigorous. You have been equally fortunate in surmounting the difficulties of your subject, and what it refused you in breadth and variety, you have compensated for by depth and elevation. Not so rich in its surroundings and details as is the *Life of St. Chantal*, though neither depicting a religious epoch nor religious movement, your new work does less and yet more. As in Ary Scheffer's picture the figure of the mother relieves that of the son, so is it with your book. The very simpleness and exigeance of the subject will render your St. Monica a winged arrow from St. Augustine's quiver." After these kind expressions, he adds: " May I say that had you given us one chapter containing a brief and concise sketch of St. Augustine's genius and sanctity after his mother's death, on such a golden background St. Monica might have stood forth in even higher relief."

Obedient to such a master, I have essayed to write this chapter ; but to make it a " golden background" I should need the pen of the eloquent apologist who kindly gave me the idea.

This is the sole alteration I have made in this second edition, save a few touches here and there, added in compliance with kind suggestions, gratefully received.

Once more I send forth this book, which God has deigned to bless. Again may it console and strengthen, teaching mothers how grand a thing devotedness is, and also teaching them to be the saviours of the present age, and ensure their own salvation by truly and fervently loving their children's souls. A Protestant historian has said that the France of olden days was a kingdom formed by bishops. Alas! neither bishop nor priest can re-mould France of the present day if Christian mothers come not to their aid. In confiding man's cradle to a mother's care, God has confided to her nearly all.

MEURSAULT, 29 July, 1866.

INTRODUCTION.

A history such as the one I undertake to relate should not be written, but sung! For it is a poem, a poem of the most beautiful love that perhaps ever existed; a love the most profound and most tender, the most noble and most pure; also the strongest, most patient, and most indomitable; a love that during twenty-five years of tears and trials, never for an instant wearies, but rather strengthens with trial, becoming more ardent and more persistent as its obstacles increase; a love which, triumphing at last (for who could resist such love?) ends happily in a species of transport and ecstasy.

Have you ever seen Ary Scheffer's beautiful picture, representing St. Monica and St. Augustine seated on the sea-shore? St. Augustine is in the foreground, a young man about thirty years of age. His face is pale, refined, still slightly sad in expression, as that of a person just recovering from a serious illness; his eyes are dark and deep, a little lacking perhaps in softness and tenderness, but suffused with the most beautiful light; the pensive lips are closed, as those of one accustomed to mental labour. The hair is short, cut close to the head, and revealing a broad forehead, on which falls a ray of light, emblem of this powerful mind. The elbow of the right arm is resting on the knee, and the fore-arm seems lifting itself to support a wearied head but the head no longer needs support; it is erect, slightly thrown back, in order that it may gaze heavenwards. With his left hand Augustine presses his mother's hands, as though saying that if after so many errors, deceptions, and struggles, he can now raise a purified and happy look towards God, it is to his mother that he owes it all.

And this mother, how radiant is she by his side! She is in full light, whilst Augustine is still a little in shade, as befits a penitent; she is a head taller than her son, to denote that she has preceded him, and, until now, has soared higher in the paths of virtue and of love. Beneath the radiant joy suffusing her countenance, I should have liked to discern the trace of her past tears; but how beautiful are her eyes, as indeed all eyes are that gaze heavenwards; these half-open lids tell the tenderness of the loving soul, and express the pure, calm, grateful joy of a mother who has found her son! Clad in white, and enveloped in long veils, which lie like folded wings, she appears but awaiting the signal for flight, and in her present state, having led back to God her Augustine, who is now a Christian, a penitent, and on the road to sanctity, she would indeed fly away did she not clasp her son's hand in hers; this it is that retains her still; but in closely looking at these hands, more clasped than clasping, and about to re-open, we feel that this final embrace will not retain her long.

It is of this mother that I write. I would relate her story for the consolation of so many Christian mothers who weep to-day as they wept of old; to warn the younger among them who are a prey to vague disquietude, to reveal to all how divine is the strength with which God has endowed them in the interest of their children's eternal salvation; how unexpected and unfailing are the resources concealed by him in that wonderful thing we term paternity and maternity.

Leibnitz said: "We should reform the world if we reformed education;" and I say, we should reform education, children, youths, and men, and extricate the present age from the terrible religious crisis it is traversing, could we but transform mothers. And what is required to effect this? A very simple, but rare thing, wanting in nearly every mother, even in the best. I mean the consciousness of their God-given strength, and the courage to exercise it to the very utmost when the soul of their child is concerned.

Generally but very few individuals tax their powers to the utmost. For example, what thinker does so as regards his reasoning faculties? What orator is able to draw from his soul her every word? What public or private individual, what Christian, knows how to apply his whole being to any work, whether temporal or spiritual? To tax one's spiritual or mental powers to the utmost demands a painful effort, from which almost every one recoils; hence the rarity of heroes and saints. On the other hand, the misery and alarming danger of the present day is, that there are scarcely any mothers now who exercise to the utmost the divine powers attached to maternity.

I made this remark one day to a Christian mother, who was disquieted about her young son's future, and who confided to me her anxieties. I replied: "Why fear? Your son will be what you make him: good, pure, noble, generous, brave, fearing nought but God, if you possess these virtues, and know how to plant them in his soul so deep that no power shall be able to uproot them." "You believe so?" she asked me. "But think of the passions of the human heart, the pestilentious atmosphere of the age, the many dangers which a mother can neither foresee nor ward off." "Dangers a mother cannot foresee; yes, doubtless such there are," said I; "but dangers that she cannot ward off, there are none such, if she knows how to use the strength which God has given her. Even should her child succumb to evil for a moment, if the mother but will so, he will arise from the abyss, and return to virtue's path." "If the mother wills it?" "Yes, only will it." "And if I will so with all the powers of my soul, I shall save my child?" "Yes, certainly." "Ah, well, I will it," she replied, in a tone that I shall never forget. Noble and Christian mother! she has willed it, and wills it still; and though the work be not yet completed, and the child, as a feeble bark, is exposed to the storms of early life, all augurs that the will of his mother will be stronger than the winds and the waves. Such is the doctrine of the book which I now offer to the Christian public.

But before bringing forward a memorable example in support of this doctrine, I crave permission to dwell on it a little; for this doctrine, so simple, so elementary, and apart from which maternity is but a heavy burden inasmuch as it is only a powerless ministry; this idea, formerly so popular, and which caused so many a noble heart to beat with sublime enthusiasm, is one of those most ignored at the present day; and I avow that I can neither comprehend why this should be so, nor console myself for the fact.

Look at the earthly life, and behold how God has arranged so that in this respect even paternity and maternity should possess a species of omnipotence. The child is the offspring of a pre-existing affection, and one which excels all others in tenderness, depth, and sweetness. Long before making his appearance in this world, he lives in his father's thoughts, in his mother's blissful dreams, and when at last he takes his place at their hearth, he is neither a stranger nor unknown. He is the very substance of his parents; their blood flows in his veins; he bears their double likeness, so that in gazing at him his father traces on his lips and in his smile something of the charm of her who gave him birth : and the mother, in her turn contemplating the child, also perceives in his eyes and brow something of the intelligence and nobleness of him whose son he is.* And, as if these all-powerful ties were inefficient to assure efficacious protection, at the moment when the child issues, so to speak, from his parents' hearts, God inflames them with a love, nobleness, tenderness, unselfishness, and devotion, truly admirable; and since nothing would be more sad than such a love, if powerless, He adds a strength not of this world. This young man, so volatile, thoughtless, and ardent in the pursuit of pleasure, whence comes it that he is so changed? He is a father. This young girl, "yesterday she required delicate food, costly apparel, and a soft couch: the faintest breath of air incommoded her; to-day, coarse bread, a rough garment, and a handful of straw suffice her, so long as her breast affords one drop of milk to nourish her babe, and her ragged mantle one corner wherein to wrap him."† Yesterday the slightest look alarmed her; where are the armies, thunderbolts, or perils, that can blanch her cheek to-day? It is told of one who, on hearing that her son had been borne away by savages, threw herself into their midst, and by the majesty of her grief, and the august cry of her love, compelled them to retreat. Who but has heard of that other mother, who, seeing her child carried off by a lion, followed

---

* Who does not remember the admirable words addressed to St. John Chrysostom by his mother, and related by him in the first book of his work on the Priesthood? "My son, I could not turn my eyes from you, for you seemed to me the living image of my dear departed husband." (*De Sacerd.*, lib. 1, n. 5.)

† Chateaubriand, *Génie du Christianisme.*

him in her distraction, and by her very grief moved the savage beast to pity?

This strength and love are so profound, so evidently do they proceed from the very Heart of God, and from the bowels of His infinite goodness, that we may without exaggeration say that a parent's heart is the most beautiful work of His hands. All else may perish, but so long as there remains in the world one mother's heart, there will be an irrefutable proof of divine goodness; for if weak woman can do so much for her children, what will not God do for His? What miracles of generosity and power will there not issue from this ocean of boundless mercy, if but one drop of this love, placed by God in a weak human heart, can work such mighty wonders?

Therefore the Church, distrustful of all terrestrial affection, because she knows its weakness, says even to the child of the best mother: "My son, love thy mother, and forget not the womb of her that bore thee." She says to the young man and to the maiden, at the very moment that they, enraptured, approach the altar to vow an eternal love: "Children, ever love one another." The Church, who, as those old in years do, scarcely believes in the eternity of vows or the duration of earthly friendships, experiences no shadow of fear or disquietude for the most lowly mother; she counts on that maternal heart, for that love is the sole earthly love that she does not distrust. And God Himself, when He wishes to arouse our confidence, and make us comprehend the magnitude of His love for us, and consequently the certainty of His omnipotent aid, seeks no other type than maternal love: " Can a woman forget her infant, so as not to have pity on the son of her womb? And if she should forget, yet will I not forget thee."*

Behold the father and mother, such as God created them; behold the incomparable love, the indomitable strength, beneath whose shadow the children grow up in peace.

These miracles, has God wrought them but for this miserable, terrestrial life? Is it but for the transient fleeting things of time, for a life soon to be quenched in the grave, that God has made paternity so grand and noble a thing? Has He done nought for the soul? When the divine life He has implanted within, of which so many a foe strives to rob us, is at stake, can it be possible that He has left maternity an unarmed, defenceless spectator of dangers she cannot avert, of ruins she can never repair? Ah, let us not thus blaspheme the divine work. As regards the life of the body, a mother can do much; with regard to the soul she can do all; and the world would be saved could we succeed in convincing mothers of this truth.

The Count de Maistre wrote as follows to his lively and witty daughter Constance, who complained of the rôle assigned to woman in society, and desired that they should take up the pen and become authoresses: " My dear child, how you deceive yourself respecting woman's real power and mission. Neither

* Isaias xlix. 15.

the *Iliad*, *Æneid*, *Jerusalem Delivered*, *Phœdrus*, *Athalie*, nor the *Treatise on Universal History*, nor *Telemachus*, were written by her; but she performs greater things, for on her knees is fashioned the world's most precious treasure." Foremost among the divine powers attached by God to motherhood is that, not merely of forming the child's body, but the more signal one of moulding his soul.

Undoubtedly, if the father be wanting in elevation of character, and the mother be engrossed with trifles, they will imprint the same character on their child; but, given a true mother, one of those noble and faithful souls who would rather die than belie their God or their conscience, in accordance with the spirited motto of our fathers: *Potius mori quam fœdari;* and picture to yourself the influence to which her child's soul will be subjected during the nine months that he slumbers within a womb sanctified by such an affection; and during the two or three years in which, whilst tending his cradle, she awakes him to honour and to virtue; and during life's sweet spring, when the child believes in his mother, and, so to say, in none but her; also, later on, during the perilous season of youth, when, though the world deceives us, we still listen to the truth from the lips of a Christian mother; and so on through the whole of life; for so long as one's mother lives, there radiates from her heart, as from a gentle luminary, a light-giving, warming, vivifying influence. The character imprinted by such a mother on the soul of her offspring will be indelible and proof against all the assaults of the enemy. The child will either un-swervingly tread the paths of truth and virtue, or, should he for one moment deviate therefrom, he will at least preserve some vestiges of the sacred fire, some sparks of probity and honour, and in the midst of surrounding evil will experience a sadness and disquietude, that clearly prove he was made for something better; a thousand divine stigmata reveal-ing to the most careless observer that a Christian mother has been there; like those beautiful marble antiques mutilated by the Vandals, which, amid their degradation and their ruins, retain the stamp of the great master who chiselled them.

Would that I had time to unroll here the annals of Christian paternity and maternity; I should then bring forward, in order to fire the hearts of my readers with a noble enthusiasm, the two generations of great souls: those who never swerve from the path of light and virtue, and those, alas! who only attain it, as M. de Maistre says, by an *ellipse,* which brings them back to the spot whence they started;* and in both the one and the other you would see how profound is this divine character when imprinted on the soul by a true mother. Who moulded St. Ber-nard? Who made him so pure, so strong, and so inflamed with divine love? His father, Texelin; his saintly mother, Aleth. And St. Chantal? Ah! she was motherless; but she had, shall I say, a father, a mother, or both at once, in that incomparable magis-trate, President Frémyot. And St. Symphorian, to

* De Maistre, *Soirées de Saint-Pétersbourg,* tom. I., p. 87.

whom did she owe her heroic life and death, save to her intrepid mother, Augusta ?

How utter the name of Origen, that great yet tender genius, without beholding his venerable father, Leonides, bending over his cradle, and reverently kissing his child, as the temple of the Holy Ghost? And St. John Chrysostom, whose noble thoughts and magnanimous resolves were due to his courageous and sublime mother? And St. Athanasius, St. Ambrose, and St. Gregory the Great; and later on, St. Louis, St. Edward, St. Francis of Assisi; and in modern times, St. Francis of Sales and St. Theresa? One need cite all the heroes and all the saints, for there is scarcely one to whom God did not give, in a father or mother worthy of him, a precursor fitted to prepare him for his lofty destiny. And if the shades of history do not always allow us to discern the venerable hands that have moulded his soul, I do not hesitate to affirm their existence; just as when I see a statue by Michael Angelo, or a picture by Raphael, it matters little whether they bear the artist's signature or no. I look at them, and through the obscurity that veils their origin, and which at most conceals but a mere name, I hail the genius which has conceived them, and which alone could have given them birth.

It was said long ago by a writer, brilliant and profound, in spite of his apparent levity : " *Fortes creantur fortibus et bonis.*"—The strong spring from the strong; the good are created by the good.* And holy

* Horace.

Scripture, irradiating this beautiful thought with heavenly light, expresses it still better: "*Generatio rectorum benedicetur.*—The generation of the righteous is blessed." To the honour of Christian mothers this will be always true.

As for those souls, so beautiful also, who, ere refinding the path of light, remain an instant in darkness, but who are sad, uneasy, and restless, because they have wandered from the truth, and from their mother's teaching; to them I present in this volume such an example that I deem it useless to cite any other. In it we shall see how this divine character is imprinted on the child's soul, and how impossible it is even for the most violent passions ever to efface it when it has been imprinted by a true mother.

But, O mothers! to influence thus deeply the soul of your child, how great must be your sufferings! The pangs of childbirth are nothing in comparison, and this is just, inasmuch as that which you have to fashion is the grandest thing the world contains. An author, on completing his book, said: "I have just concluded my task, which has been written during the silence of seventeen nights. Still shuddering at the suffering it has cost me, I gaze at it with anxiety, and wonder whether the world will heed my words." O mothers! can you say as much? Do you shudder at the recollection of the sufferings you endured in forming your child's soul? Will the world be able to say of you what St. Augustine said of the admirable mother whose life I now lay before you: "She suffered more in begetting me to truth and virtue than she suffered in giving me birth"? This is the first lesson contained in my book, and I feel persuaded that in the sad times in which we live it will neither be inopportune nor devoid of interest.

It contains a second lesson, likewise very important, and the necessary consequence of the first one. Of what avail for God to endow mothers with power to imprint a sacred character on their children's souls, if at the dawn of passion He did not invest them with a second power, omnipotent and infallible also,—the power of efficaciously protecting their children, and snatching them, if they will, from every peril? Is not this the reason why God has made this admirable law, that when the young man ascends the scorching summits of the hill of life, the father descends the same; that when the young girl is about to taste of life's enchanted cup, which at sixteen seems synonymous with happiness, the mother has quaffed it even to the dregs, and has learnt the hollowness of the world's vanities and illusions, at the very hour in which her children are in danger of being dazzled by the same? Why is it so, save that they may learn from lips whose sincerity they will never question, the sole words capable of disabusing them of their illusions?

Is not this the reason, too, why God has endowed parents with a kind of intuition, enabling them to discern the real dangers which await their child, and the road whereby he may avoid the same? Is it not that the child may be directed aright on his perilous journey that God has rendered paternity so holy a thing, and that He has subjected so many fathers to those sublime contradictions which daily meet our gaze, which we cannot define, and which awake both smiles and tears?

I know a magistrate, an honourable, amiable, and clever man, but one who had rarely used his intellect save to rail at holy things. I went to see him a short time ago, and found him with his charming little daughter of eleven or twelve years old sitting on his knee, whom he was preparing for her first communion. He was hearing her say her catechism, and as I entered he was just explaining to her the meaning of the word mystery, telling her that there were mysteries everywhere, in nature, in society, in man especially, and therefore it was not to be wondered at that there were mysteries in the Divinity; and so delighted was he at the quickness with which his little child had caught the meaning of her lesson, that he repeated to me her answers, and some of those remarks that fall so sweetly when they proceed from children's lips. On beholding this charming scene, I thought of Diderot taking his daughter to catechism at Saint-Sulpice, and explaining to her each chapter; of another, who shall be nameless, for he is still living, who forbids his children ever to enter his study, lest their gaze should be sullied by the papers lying on his table. He is willing enough to corrupt the world, but he is a father, and he will not sully his daughter's mind. Sublime and touching contradictions, occurring continually in days such as these! Too often the *man* is frivolous, sceptical, impious, a railer at holy things; but the *father* is always holy. God has willed it thus, and that for the children's sake.

But especially at the hour of their children's danger has God placed within each parent's heart that invincible strength of which I have just cited such noble examples. Thanks to divine goodness! whatever sufferings mothers have endured to save their children's temporal life, they have done more to save their souls. They have suffered to spare them suffering; they have cast themselves into the lion's jaws; have braved hostile armies; have spent whole days, nights, and weeks by their child's sick bed, without food or sleep. This I have seen them do, and I have wondered more at their love than at their strength; they have laid down their lives on their children's behalf, and what more can one do for those one loves? Yet I repeat that they have done a thousand-fold more to save their children's souls. To die for those we love, is not the highest sacrifice. We can do more than die for our loved ones; a mother's greatest martyrdom consists in giving up her children's life; in holding truth, virtue, honour, true beauty of soul, her child's eternal life, in such high esteem, that rather than see these holy things tarnished or withered, she would see her child die.

I know not who the philosopher was who on asking himself the question, "What is man?" gave this sublime reply: "Man is a being capable of yielding up his life in the cause of justice." The Christian mother is a more wondrous being than this. She is capable of giving up her child's life in the cause of justice; who so intensely loves justice, truth, that is to say, God's indwelling presence in her child's soul, that rather than He should quit the sanctuary where she herself has placed Him, she would see the material tabernacle break and disappear. What say I? She is a being who, when persecution breaks out, and evil is in the ascendant, rather than see her child's eternal happiness imperilled, and thus lose him for ever, hesitates not one moment to hand him over to the executioner, preferring to see him dead than sullied. Behold what a wondrous spectacle our Lord Jesus Christ has exhibited to the world in creating the Christian mother.

Scarcely had He appeared here below, than we see lowly women taking their little children on their knees, and mingling austere lessons of faith with kisses and caresses, say: "My child, I would rather behold thee lying dead at my feet, than ever see thee commit one mortal sin."

Sublime creature! What she has said she has also done. Behold her as the mother of the holy twins of Langres, descending into the dungeon where her little children were imprisoned for the faith, and going from one to the other, with a countenance beaming with joy, exclaim: "Oh! of all my glorious ancestors, not one has conferred such splendour on my name as that which the immortal honour of your deaths is about to do."

Then again, as the mother of St. Symphorian of Autun, who, learning that her son was sentenced to be beheaded for Christ's sake, and that he was already being led to martyrdom, trembling lest in the early bloom of his sixteen years he should for one moment regret bidding adieu to life, ran to meet him, and as soon as she caught sight of him, cried: "My son, look up to heaven; they do not rob thee of thy life, they but give thee a better one in its stead."

Then again, as did St. Denise, she stands at the foot of the instrument of torture, by her looks sustaining her dear child amid the agonies of the blows inflicted; and then, when life was extinct, she carried away his little lacerated corpse, burying it with songs of Christian joy mingled with a mother's lamentations.

And if looks and exhortations did not suffice, if supplications and tears were needed, we behold her fall at her child's knees, conjuring him to die courageously for his mother's sake; as that heroic mother of the Machabees, who, though born before our Lord's advent, was already consumed by the fire which He was about to kindle upon earth. After she had encouraged her six eldest children to die, and with grief in her soul, but serenity on her brow, had at the death of each received that incurable wound which the loss of a child inflicts, when it was the turn of her seventh son, a child of thirteen, her Benjamin, trembling lest his courage should fail, she cast herself at his knees, and pointing to her breast, exclaimed: "My child, remember that for nine months I bore thee in my womb, and that for three years I nourished thee at my breast; for my sake fear not the executioner, but die courageously, as did thy six brethren." What a mother's agonies at such a moment as that must have been, no pen can tell, nor yet describe the sufferings of a Symphorosa, a Felicia, and many others who followed in their train. One feels that an eternity of bliss, with their children folded in their arms, is the due of such mothers as these.

Undoubtedly it is but rarely that God demands such sacrifices. But it is none the less true that she who is incapable of sacrificing her child's temporal life is no Christian mother; and that she who hesitates to sacrifice herself in order to save her child from acts of sin and cowardice, is a degenerate parent, and unworthy the noble name of mother. But when she has resolved to give up all, time, ease, even her child's life, rather than see him stained by sin, can it be possible that her child should perish? The storms of an evil age may bear him away; he may be driven before the tempest and drift from his moorings; but perish, never! His anchor fails not. Do you know where it is? In his mother's hands, therefore nought can sever him from it. This truth stands prominently forth in the following touching story, and I venture to promise myself that no mother will end its perusal without learning how to hold,—when the tempest is fiercest,—the anchors which will save her children's frail bark from foundering. And yet, necessary as it is to remind mothers of the double power God has given them of moulding and shielding their children's soul, if this book contained no other lesson, I should perhaps never have written it. I wished to draw attention to a higher doctrine, and reveal to mothers a more important secret, too much ignored at the present day, which constitutes the august grandeur of Christian paternity, and is also its greatest aid in critical times.

Never shall I forget the emotion I experienced when I first attended the deathbed of a young man. I can even now see the father pacing the room, speechless and sad, overwhelmed by that tearless grief that is so injurious in its effects; by the deathbed sat the poor mother, whose sobs, repressed during her son's agony, at last broke forth. I was sitting at her side, my heart rent with grief, but speechless, for I knew not how to console her. I well remember that during the long silence, such as ever follows poignant sorrow, (for at such times what can one say?) I asked myself how it was that God, who is goodness itself, could permit such things, and inflict such cruel wounds on a mother's heart? I learnt the answer to my question two years later, when in the same chamber, and, alas! at the foot of the same bed, I aided that mother in her dying moments, and was startled by hearing these words, almost her last: "I am going to join my child." Light broke in upon me, and I then saw that this life is not all; and that if, in order to elevate and purify souls, and render them rich in virtue, God sometimes severs loving hearts, it is that He may reunite them in a region where their mutual affection will be deepened, and parting will be unknown. Trembling with emotion, I closed that mother's eyes, and many a time since then, thinking of her and her son, both vanished from our gaze, both now reunited in heaven, I ask myself what trace remains of their painful wound? Scarcely a memory, and who can tell but that this memory is itself a happy one?

But allow me to say there is another deathbed, beside which I cannot think that God will leave a mother powerless. Suppose that, instead of being parted from her child for a day or for years, a Christian mother beholds him on the point of being lost to her for eternity; picture to yourself a holy mother, one loving God above all else, seeing her child fall away from God, and become the object of His eternal hatred: is it possible that at the moment when the terrible separation is about to be accomplished, she can do nought to save him? I do not appeal to the sacred writings for a reply; I listen to the voice of reason, of common sense, above all to the voice of my heart. which cannot be more tender than the Divine Heart, and I say with certainty: No; that is not possible; God has not left a mother powerless at such a moment. It must be that somewhere within the most divine part of her soul, in the profoundest depths of her maternal love, He has hidden something, I know not what; some deep impulse; a cry, a tear, or a sob, which, though every mother may not be able to give it utterance, (as it was not every mother who could utter the cry which melted the heart of the Florentine lion,) is nevertheless there, and which, if it but proceed from the soul, as it surely will do where reigns the two-fold love of God and of her son, will infallibly save her child's soul. This is my belief.

Yes; when, in order to reclaim her erring son, she has exhausted counsels, warnings, and reproofs; when there seems nought else that can be done, she has still one resource left, and that the most mighty power of all,—her tears. Let her pray and weep; within those depths where the heart of the mother and the Christian meet, let her search until she finds a certain tear, made expressly by God; and behold! her child is saved. We daily see young men who have abused all their opportunities, whose life has been one scene of ignominy and vice, returning to the paths of virtue, and that because of their mother's tears.*

Holy Scripture is also in harmony with these consoling thoughts. In the days of your deepest

---

* What I say of mothers, I say, to a certain extent, of wives, daughters, and sisters, and will cite one touching instance, that I may enlist in the noble crusade of prayer all souls worthy of entering those ranks. Who has not heard of that charming brother and sister, too soon vanished from this world, Maurice and Eugénie de Guérin? Maurice, led away by the dissipations of Paris, had for an instant forgotten the God and the faith of his childhood. What did his sister do meanwhile? She trembled for him; she groaned and prayed. "Maurice," she wrote, some time after his decease, "I believe thou art in heaven. Thy own religious sentiments and the infinite mercy of God inspire me with this confidence. Must not God, so good, compassionate, loving, and paternal, have had pity for His returning son? There are three years of thy life that grieve me. Would that I could efface them with my tears! I placed all my hopes in thee, as if thou hadst been my son. I was less thy sister than thy mother. Dost thou remember that when we were speaking of my grief at thy dear soul's errors, I likened myself to Monica weeping for her Augustine? How earnestly have I entreated God for thy salvation! A saintly priest said to me: 'Your brother will return.' Oh yes, he did return, and then left me for heaven,—for heaven, I hope."

sorrow, read the story of Agar banished from Abraham's tents, fleeing to the desert, and leading her child by the hand. Overhead is the scorching sun; her feet tread the burning sand; her child, parched with thirst, groans, and is at the point of death. She stops a moment, and looks anxiously round for help. The horizon is one blaze of fire: nowhere can she find that drop of water for which she would give her life. Then, filled with despair, seeing death approach, she lays her child down beneath a palm-tree, and departs, saying: "I will not see the boy die." But soon, (for she was not far off, and though she could not see him die, she wished to behold him still,) when the unhappy mother hears her son's sighs growing weaker and weaker, mad with grief, she falls on her knees and utters a cry,—what cry I know not, but it reached the Heart of God,—and at the same moment a well of water sprang up at her feet, as if God intended to show us that He cannot withstand the sorrow of one who entreats for her child's life. How much more surely then will He give ear when she weeps over an erring, guilty one, who is in danger of eternal death.

But it is specially in the New Testament that this consoling lesson stands forth with more marked tenderness and love. Have you observed that the Saviour's loving Heart was never deaf to the cry proceeding from a parent's heart? When the centurion, for instance, came to Him, saying, "Lord, my son is dangerously sick," what does the good Master reply? "Go, thy son is healed." Jairus and his wife throw themselves at His feet, weeping, (they had lost a child of twelve years of age, that pleasing time when waning childhood and approaching youth lend so sweet a charm;) our Lord, moved with compassion, leaves all, follows them, enters the house, and taking the child by the hand, restores her to her mother. It is true that He did not instantly grant the request of the Canaanitish mother; He feigned indifference, but only that a still deeper cry of faith might issue from her heart; and when that cry has gone forth, He exclaims: "O, mother, great is thy faith; go, thy daughter is healed." Who has not read the touching story of the widow of Naim? She does not go in search of our Lord, does not even see Him; but overwhelmed by grief and blinded by her tears, follows the bier of her only son. It is Jesus who beholds her, who, touched by her grief, draws near, and stopping the bier, says, "Weep not, O mother," and gives her back her child. Why did our Lord multiply such miracles as these? That He might make mothers understand the august power He has entrusted to them; that He may teach them to utter that cry which He cannot resist: and consequently make them resolve never to be discouraged, whatever storms assail their children's youth, but follow them with their tears, and lead them back to God by their own prayers, sufferings, and self-sacrifice.

But, so important is this lesson, so deeply must it be graved on the soul, that these examples, touching though they be, might have proved insufficient. A still more abundant light was needed in order to enkindle in maternal hearts the fire of unquenchable hope, and for this end God resolved to give the world an example which it could never forget.

We shall therefore behold a young man, trained by the holiest of mothers, whose tender years were most lovingly, vigilantly, yet strictly guarded; one, gifted with a genius of the highest order, and a heart even superior to his intellect; consequently one whose spotless childhood should have been succeeded by the happiest and purest youth; and so it would doubtless have been had his education been confided solely to his mother. Unfortunately she was married to a madman, for what other term can be applied to a man who, as careless of his son's virtue as he was of his own, unreasonable and despotic in his wishes, appeared for fifteen years to make sport of his child's innocence, willingly exposing him to every kind of peril! Victim of his father's rashness, we shall watch this poor youth fall from one sin into another, a prey to every storm that rends the heart; and, after being but too easily drawn aside by the tenderness of his affections, freeing himself from that first chain, ennobled, if vice can be ennobled, by a certain degree of honour and an inviolable fidelity; then fettering himself with new ties, wholly ignominious, passing sixteen years of his life in the most lamentable slavery.

Then, as mental darkness is ordinarily the just punishment of ill-regulated affections, after first quenching, and then openly abjuring the faith of his childhood, we shall see him tossed by every wind of doctrine; enamoured, but soon dissatisfied, with ancient philosophy, and rightly so, since it offered but shifting sand, on which his lofty intellect could erect nothing stable. After this he falls into the meshes of a seductive, vile heresy, and for nine years vainly seeks the rest it could never afford; then, weary of so many fruitless efforts, despairing of the truth without ceasing to love it, discouraged, sad, and sick at heart, he sinks into the lowest abyss of all, that of absolute doubt; and heart, conscience, genius, all are on the verge of destruction; and instead of being Augustine the saint, he is in danger of becoming a sophist, perhaps a Libanius, or at most a Symmachus.

But, wondrous sight! Arrived at that point where all seemed lost, we shall behold him suddenly resume his flight, at first slowly, like a wounded eagle, then quickening his speed, and soaring aloft; beating his wings at the dawn of the light, hailing the newly-found truth with cries of the most sublime eloquence, or rather, with tears and sighs humbly receiving that beauty, always ancient and ever new, which he had known and loved too late; and from the abyss of passion and of doubt soaring, victorious at last, to the loftiest summits of divine light and love.

And when you seek for, or question him as to the cause of this wondrous conversion, there is but one reply,—his mother's prayers, tears, and groans. For after having moulded her son's heart as no mother had yet moulded a child's heart, when warned of the dawn of passion in Augustine's soul, she had, for his sake, gained her mother-in-law's heart, converted her husband, and purified, alas! too late, the noxious atmosphere of his home; and after having followed him to Carthage, Rome, and Milan, joining the most energetic course of action to the most tender and winning words, seeing all was in vain, and that her son, deaf to her entreaties, was falling from abyss to abyss, she resolutely turned to God, and one day, when the danger was most imminent, there issued from her soul, as from that of the unhappy Agar, a cry so profound and so touching that it moved, as such a cry ever will move, the very Heart of God, and He gave her back her child. She died of happiness, bequeathing to all mothers, who weep as she wept, the secret of her own consolation. It is this side of St. Monica's history that I desire to record, if God, who has graciously inspired my design, will deign to bless and guide my pen.

I may perhaps be asked where I have found the materials for such a history. I rejoin: is it credible that God works such wonders only to leave them in the shade, and kindles such lights but to hide them under a bushel? He Himself has prepared an historian worthy of St. Monica, and who else could this be, save "the son of so many tears"? Augustine loved his mother passionately, spoke of her incessantly, and has embalmed her memory in almost every work that issued from his pen. More than twenty years after her death, his locks silvered by arduous labours and penance rather than by advancing years, the moment having arrived when divine love, which had broken down every barrier and inundated his soul, would seem to have destroyed all other love, his mother's name, his mother's memory, would suffice to move his heart and fill his eyes with tears, even when in the pulpit. Yielding to the charm of these souvenirs, he would discourse of them to his people at Hippo, and his sermons, where one would hardly have looked for such allusions, are full of words of touching beauty, bearing the impress of filial gratitude, and the two-fold mark of genius and of sanctity. It is needless to say that nowhere has he spoken of his mother so fully, with such heartfelt joy and deep emotion, as in his *Confessions*. And yet, in perusing this work we feel that St. Augustine does not tell all. A species of modesty restrains his pen, and in several passages it is evident that he designedly veils the halo surrounding her, lest a ray of the same glory should be reflected on his own brow. But the heart divines that which he withholds; tradition indicates it, and the Church often hymns the same. She who is herself a Mother, and knows not how to speak coldly of her children, has celebrated St. Monica's memory with eloquence peculiar to herself The spouse of our Lord; saints; doctors; pontiffs; virgins; celebrated writers; and orators of renown, have each in their turn praised her throughout the long flight of ages, in words worthy of being known. These gems I have gathered, and now present them as an offering to Christian mothers.

The idea of this work did not originate with me, but with one to whom I owe much, a great and holy bishop, who for many years has shed much light and peace upon my path, and who, among other gifts, which I treasure in the secret depths of my heart,

has taught me to apply my soul to the science of
true greatness, which is nought else but true sanctity.
Those who have read the *Life of St. Chantal* will
not need to be told that I allude to St. Francis of
Sales. In studying his writings I have been struck
with his devotion for St. Monica, and the tender
enthusiasm with which she had inspired him, and
proofs of this will be found in that history. We will
only say that he speaks of her in every page of his
writings; that he gives her as a model to women
living in the world; to wives, mothers, and specially
to such as have Augustines for their sons. That
when he desired to form Madame de Chantal to that
degree of perfection which God demanded from her
he gave her no other patroness, but desired her to
fix her gaze constantly on St. Monica during those
first years of widowhood when she was learning
to be a saint, even whilst in the world; and she
it was whom he gave her as an example when he
wished to turn her thoughts aside from the religious
life at an epoch when her children were too young to
forego a mother's care. Need I say that later on,
during the brilliant and perilous youth of Celsus
Benignus, when she beheld him forming those friendships and engaged in those duels which made her
tremble for his soul, St. Francis de Sales reminds
her more frequently and in more touching terms
of St. Monica? On the walls of her cell, by the
side of the Mater Dolorosa, which he had given
her, and which hung beneath her crucifix, he desired
her to suspend, and frequently contemplate, the

image of that afflicted mother, on whose heart was reposing the son she had saved by her tears. And also, which is not so well known, that when he had quitted this terrestrial scene, leaving the Venerable Mother de Chantal alone with her sorrows and anxieties,—a foundress' anxieties and a mother's griefs,—one day, when the latter were pressing heavily upon her, (for it was reported that Celsus Benignus was in danger of being executed, as the Duke de Boutteville had been, on account of his unhappy and incorrigible propensity for duelling,) St. Francis of Sales issued, as it were, from his tomb, in order to persuade her to re-peruse the Life of St. Monica. At least, while kneeling weeping at the foot of the altar, she heard a voice, which she recognized as that of her sainted father, saying to her : "Read the Eighth Book of St. Augustine's *Confessions.*" And in studying these wondrous pages, in which St. Augustine is seen saved by his mother's tears, she had a presentiment that she too would save Celsus Benignus by dint of prayers, tears, and self-sacrifice, which also came to pass, as will be seen in the above-mentioned life.

This suffices to explain my reasons for writing the present book, and to acknowledge the debt of gratitude I owe to the amiable and holy bishop who inspired me with the idea. If St. Francis de Sales supported, comforted, and strengthened so many weeping mothers by citing St. Monica's example, why should not this same example produce the same fruits now? The world was in a sad condition then; the reformation was rending the bosom of the Church; scandals were multiplying; open and secret apostasy was filling every heart with fear; every mother trembled; and in order to reassure, console, and teach them that there is no peril that a mother cannot avert from her child, St. Francis of Sales bid them: "Read St. Monica's Life; you will see what she did for her Augustine, and many things which will console you."

The world is not much happier now than at the close of the sixteenth century; the dangers are scarcely less imminent; a change of principles has been accompanied by a change of manners. The atmosphere with which our young men are surrounded is impregnated with sophisms. The hearth is threatened; the cradle is no longer safe. Never perhaps have wives and mothers, worthy of their mission, been called to such important duties. Will they permit me to tell them, not with the authority of St. Francis of Sales, nor with his charm of language, but at least with a heart which understands and can sympathize with their sorrows: Read St. Monica's Life; learn from this wife and mother how to pray and weep as she did; never to lose hope, and never to be discouraged; and remember that if the young men of the present day are in such imminent danger, it is because their wives and their mothers do not weep as they should weep.

EM. BOUGAUD,

VICAR-GENERAL OF ORLEANS.

ORLEANS,
Vigil of All Saints, 1865.

HISTORY OF ST. MONICA.

CHAPTER I.

BIRTH AND PARENTAGE—EARLY YOUTH—MARRIAGE.

332—353.

The road leading from the ruins of Carthage to those of Hippo, and passing by ancient Sicca Veneria, traverses one of the most beautiful countries in the world. The ancients extolled its fertility, and we have lately seen a few touches of the pickaxe suffice to re-cover it with gardens of olive, groves of orange and lemon trees, with roses, vines, and rich harvests. As little effort was required to bring to light, for they were scarcely covered by the sand, innumerable monuments of the most beautiful Roman art, fragments of statues, shafts of pillars, sarcophagi covered with inscriptions, ruins of theatres, baths, temples, Roman roads, all the vestiges of a high state of civilization. Then, after travelling for some hours, surrounded by this renaissance of nature and these beautiful ruins of art, we in thought go back to that time when nature and art flourished simultaneously,

ınd re-people these vast horizons with that haughty
race which in the persons of Hamilcar, Hannibal, and
Jugurtha, caused the fortunes of Rome for a moment
to waver in the balance; and who, later on, touched
by divine grace, after spurning all other yokes,
accepted that of our Lord Jesus Christ: gave Tertullian, St. Cyprian, Lactantius, Arnobius, St. Augustine, and among virgins and martyrs, St. Perpetua,
St. Felicitas, and so many others, to the Church, we
feel that we tread one of those fruitful soils where,
as Virgil sang, the rapid growth and beauty of the
harvests is surpassed by that of the inhabitants.

About midway along this road, not far from the
famous battle-field of Zama, and on the declivities of
two hills which greet the rising sun, and are shaded
by clusters of olive trees, stands a simple village,
called by the Arabs of the present day, Souk-Arras.
The few white houses of which it consists occupy
part of the site where stood the ancient Roman city
of Tagaste. The remaining portion, which is of considerable extent, covers the adjacent table-land, on
the surface of which extensive ruins lie sleeping in
the sun, half buried in sand, and overshadowed by
acanthus, locust-trees, and beautiful angelicas. At
the foot of this plateau extend vast meadows, watered
by many refreshing streams which empty themselves
into the Medjerda, the ancient Bagradas of the
Romans; beyond, lie barren sandy tracks, still un-
reclaimed from the desert, and the horizon is bounded
by a forest of cork-trees, behind which is the sea
with its storms and calms.

On those unknown hills, for notwithstanding the beauty of its site, Tagaste is alluded to by no writer of antiquity save Pliny, who only mentions the haughtiness of the race inhabiting it; on those hills, with their vast and brilliant horizon, God placed the cradle of the Saint whose life I am about to relate.* It seems that in selecting such a spot, God was already thinking of St. Augustine; for him was formed this lofty plateau, towering as an eyrie above the vast surrounding plain; but He also made it St. Monica's birthplace, in order to show us that in a mother's case God has her children in view in all He does, even in the selection of the spot where she first opens her eyes to the light.

It was the year of our Lord 332. For eighteen years St. Silvester had guided St. Peter's bark, and twenty years previously to the time to which we allude, Christianity had been established on the throne in the person of the Emperor Constantine, the conqueror of Maxentius.

The Church was emerging from the catacombs; and as nature after a long winter suddenly starts to life beneath the sun of May, so the Church, her three centuries of affliction and sorrow ended, was about to give birth to many of her most illustrious children. St. Monica and St. Jerome were born the same year; the one at Tagaste, the other at Strido in Dalmatia. St. Gregory of Nazianzen was in his fifth, St. Basil in his fourth, and St. Gregory of Nyssus in his third

* There is no doubt as to Souk-Arras occupying the ancient site of Tagaste. Proofs of this will be found in the Appendix, No. I.

year. St. Hilary of Poictiers and St. Martin of Tours were a little older; the one just entering on his sixteenth year, and preparing for baptism: the other on the point of being ordained priest. St. John Chrysostom, and St. Paulinus of Nola, were not yet born, but the pious maidens for whom God had reserved the signal honour of giving them birth, were in their retirement unconsciously preparing themselves for their great mission.

St. Athanasius was the only one of this brilliant galaxy that had already reached to man's estate. Though scarcely twenty-seven, he had just ascended the episcopal throne of Alexandria, where he was destined to remain for nearly half a century, erect, invincible, bearing the brunt of every attack, as if to afford those great men whom God was then sending into His Church leisure to arrive at maturity.

It was at this time, during the brief interval intervening between the death of those martyrs who had lost their lives in the local persecutions which even Constantine could not prevent, and the birth of the doctors, that there appeared in the bosom of a Christian family, (the abode of peace, honour, and virtue,) a child highly favoured, inasmuch as she was chosen of God to be the mother of the greatest doctor of that age, the mother of St. Augustine. She was named Monica, a name that no saint had borne till then, and which was about to be rendered by her such a touching symbol of hope and consolation. Her father, whose name is unknown, and her mother, who appears to have been called Faconda,* were devout Christians.†

It is not easy to ascertain their exact rank. They belonged, apparently, to one of those noble families, such as we see in revolutionary times, who, though poor, still retain somewhat of their former splendour; numerous servants, but straitened means; noble connections and relationships, but withal leading a life more and more retired, and this as much from necessity as from principle. Twenty years before, when nearly the whole of Tagaste had been seduced by the teaching of Donatus, St. Monica's family had remained staunch in the faith: this but increased their isolation, and the misfortunes of the empire accelerated their ruin. It is true that Constantine's accession had seemed to promise them, together with all the ancient and rich provincial families oppressed by taxation, some degree of relief; but this hope was now waning, and as Constantine's efforts were as vain as those of Diocletian, St. Monica's parents foresaw that of all their ancient splendour, they could bequeath her nothing but a memory and a name.‡

---

* Such is the general tradition in all the orders of the Rule of St. Augustine. She is called Faconda, or Facundia, in all the Augustinian Liturgies.

† *Confess.*, lib. IX., cap. viii.

‡ This is to be gleaned from a careful study of the *Confessions*, and the collating of several important passages, such, for instance, which speak of a numerous staff of servants in St. Monica's home, (lib. ix. cap. viii. ix.) their intercourse with the most distinguished families, and their noble connections, (St. Augustine's Letters, 39th in the first Benedictine edition.) St. Augustine's allusions to the smallness of his own patrimony, and the poverty of his family, (*Serm.* 356) must not be

4   s. m.

It is doubtless to these circumstances, and to her early training, that St. Monica was indebted for her contempt of this transitory world, and her intense love of eternal things.

But St. Monica, in alluding to her early training, not only praises her mother's zeal, but also gratefully mentions the care bestowed on her by an old servant, to whom her childhood was entrusted. This servant had been nurse to St. Monica's father; had borne him aloft on her shoulders, as young mothers are wont to do;* and after watching him grow to man's estate, and being present at his marriage, she, in virtue of her age, purity of manners, and the relation in which she stood to him, became attendant, or rather, second mother to his children. Zealous, prudent, austere, somewhat given to scolding, but devoted to her young mistress, a genuine type of those old domestics whom Christianity was beginning to exhibit to the world, and who were not the least beautiful of her creations, she surrounded with most watchful care the cradle where lay such holy and glorious destinies.

Guarded from every danger, the object of so many tender cares, never did child give fairer promise. When quite a little thing, she would, when unobserved, go alone to the church,† seeking a quiet corner, and standing there with joined hands and

taken literally; such expressions were prompted by humility. It seems to us that St. Monica's family was noble, but ruined, as were all the other noble families of this epoch.

* *Conf.*, lib. IX. cap. viii.

† *Breviarium canonicorum Regularium Ordinis sancti Augustini.* Paris, 1523; 16mo, in black letter. *Ad prim. Noct., lect. i.*

modest down-cast eyes, found such a charm in conversing with God that she would forget it was time to return home. When she did return, timid and embarrassed, because it was late, and because she had gone out alone, she was severely corrected, and sometimes flogged : but neither blows nor reproaches elicited a single murmur, much less did they diminish the affectionate gratitude she cherished for her nurse.*

Sometimes also, when playing with her companions, she would suddenly disappear, and then would be found at the foot of a tree, motionless and absorbed in prayer. She often arose secretly at night, then, kneeling on the ground and folding her tiny hands, would recite, with a spirit of recollection and fervour unusual in one so young, the prayers her good mother had taught her.† It seemed as if, in these moments of intimate communion, God intended to familiarize her from her infancy with the divine science of prayer, of which, later on, she would make such wonderful use ; thus early did He train her in the use of that powerful weapon with which she was to gain such striking victories.

Another trait in St. Monica's character was her love of the poor.‡ When at table, she would often hide a portion of her own bread, and when no one was watching, would post herself on the threshold of the door, seeking for some poor person on whom to bestow it.§ There were two classes to whom this

* *Boll. 4 Maii.*
† *Breviarium Canonicorum Regularium, etc. ad prim. Noct. lect. ii.*
‡ Ibid.   § *Boll. 4 Maii.*

pious child was most warmly attached; poor travellers, and the indigent sick. She spied out the former as they were approaching her father's hospitable roof, seated them on a bench, and, though so young, would claim, according to ancient usage, the honour of washing their feet. The latter she was accustomed to visit, and lavished on both such services as a child of her temperament and years could render.*

At the same time St. Monica was noted for her sweet and peaceful disposition. When playing with her companions, a word from her sufficed to appease their little quarrels. There was so much repose in her countenance, voice, and manner, that, unconsciously to herself, she imparted it even to her elders, making others participate in her own peace.†

To these heaven-sent gifts, whereby God was already fitting her to become the mother of a saint, were joined other virtues, the growth of which was due to her nurse's constant and careful supervision. St. Augustine says: "Wisely severe in correction, admirably prudent in instruction, she trained her early in the sternest virtues. However thirsty the child might be, she was never allowed to drink anything, not even a drop of water, between meals," in order to inure her to sobriety, penance, strength of soul, and spirit of self-sacrifice, without which there can be no true Christian, spouse, mother, or saint. "Thus didst Thou fashion her, O my God," exclaims St. Augustine; "and neither her father

---

* *Boll. 4 Maii.*

† *Brev. Heremit. Divi Augustini.* i vol. 1475, black letter.

nor her mother surmised what she would one day become. But Thou didst prepare her cradle in the midst of a faithful family, one of the best regulated in Thy Church, where, under the guidance of Thy only Son, she grew up in that fear of God which is the beginning of wisdom."*

Amid this promising dawn of virtue there was visible in St. Monica, I do not say a blemish, but one of those light shadows permitted at times by God in order to render His saints more humble and more vigilant. As is customary when initiating young girls in the duties of housekeeping, this pious child was allowed to draw the wine for the day's consumption. "Now," says St. Augustine, "it happened sometimes that, before filling the flagon, she would put her lips to the edge of the vessel into which she had drawn the wine, not from the love of wine, for, on the contrary, she was rather averse to it, but from mischievousness and the delight children take in doing what is forbidden, a delight that soon vanishes before the weight of authority.

"But whereas by slighting small failings one gradually falls into graver ones, it happened that from daily adding drop to drop, she ended by drinking nearly a little cupful. Where was her wise old guardian all this time? What of her strict prohibitions? And what possible remedy for a failing concealed so carefully, hadst not Thou, O Saviour, been watching over us? Her parents were absent,

* *Confess.*, lib. IX., cap. viii.

but Thou, ever omnipresent God, who rescuest souls even by the instrumentality of the wicked, didst save her. And how? A maid-servant always accompanied her to the cellar, and was consequently an unreproving witness of her transgression. She it was whose cold and cutting sarcasm was the invisible instrument wherewith the divine hand cut this gangrene to the quick. For, quarrelling one day with her young mistress, she reproached her with this failing, and with the intention, not of correcting, but merely annoying, insolently called her a wine-bibber. Stung to the core, Monica blushed, and seeing the heinousness of her transgression, condemned herself severely, and never repeated the offence."* It is asserted that she then resolved never to drink anything but water. However this may be, we find that her fault, as in the case of most saints, was attended with the most happy results; it was the source of penitential tears, humility, and self-distrust, and, unconsciously to herself, thus early prepared her to guard with the most tender vigilance the glorious cradle which would one day be entrusted to her care.

About this time, that is, in the year 348 or 349, Monica witnessed an event which made a deep impression on her at the same time that it filled her with profound joy. Tagaste, as already said, had fallen a prey to the Donatist heresy, and this had involved her in many troubles during the last twenty years. So formidable and constant had these com-

---

* *Confess.*, lib. ix., cap. viii.

motions grown, that the emperors were compelled to interfere, and Constantius issued an edict prohibiting the public profession of that heresy. Many cities returned to the Catholic faith, and among them the people of Tagaste, whose return was so prompt, unanimous, and sincere, that it was evident that fear of the schismatics had alone prevented their taking this step long before. St. Alypius says that a few years later it would have been vain to seek for a happier city, or one more obedient to the holy see, than was Tagaste.*

St. Monica was probably about sixteen at the time her native city escaped from the thraldom of a fanatical party which had robbed it of its religious freedom. It was doubtless with joy and deep enthusiasm that she witnessed the return of Tagaste to the true fold; and if, as some think, this was also the august moment of her baptism and first communion, she must indeed have experienced one of those profound and strong emotions which leave a lasting impress on the soul.

The gifts with which nature had endowed St. Monica, developed with her growth. One who certainly was best capable of judging, and who would never have praised even his mother at the expense of truth, has tenderly eulogized her accurate, noble, and quick intellect, affirming often that it bordered on genius. Later on we shall behold her conversing on the deepest religious and philosophical

---

* August. Ep. 48. Labbe, conc., tom. ii., cap. cxxxvi.

questions, St. Augustine and his friends grouped around her, "thinking," he says, "that we were listening to the teachings of some great man." This wonderful intellect was already giving signs of its existence; her thirst for learning was insatiable, and when quite little she would leave her playmates, in order to follow the conversation of her elders, specially that of the educated and thoughtful. She would sit for hours at the feet of her grandmother, a woman venerable for her years and her faith, whose touching recitals, (for she had been the contemporary of martyrs,) filled the pious maiden with deep enthusiasm.*

To these intellectual gifts, with which God had endowed her for St. Augustine's sake, were associated still higher qualities,—an untiring gentleness united with rare firmness; unruffled calmness, persevering and courageous disposition; a heart inclined to tenderness, and yet full of energy. In brief, one of those richly endowed natures one sometimes encounters, where the rarest harmonies are mingled with the most startling contrasts.

It is not so easy to satisfy the legitimate curiosity of our readers respecting the external gifts with which St. Monica was endowed. It seems that she was fairly tall, and very beautiful. At least, when about eighteen or twenty, faith, piety, modesty, love to God and man, so enhanced her beauty, that one of the earliest chroniclers of her history declares it

---

* *De plurimis claris mulieribus*, a Fr. Jacobo Philippo Bergomensi, Ordinis Heremitarum Divi Augustini; 1 vol. folio, 1493, black letter.

passed description, and this we can readily conceive. We may say of the beauty of the saints, that which holy Scripture says of their peace of mind: "*Exsuperat omnem sensum.*" It is a beauty above all other beauty, and passing all understanding. The psalmist compares it to that of the temple, in that it raises the soul to God.*

Monica's personal charms were enhanced by her modesty. Her parents, proud of her beauty, as is generally the case with parents, even the most Christian ones, spared no pains to adorn it. But she gently and firmly refused the precious scented tissues in which they wished to clothe her.† She had learnt from those grand doctors of the African Church, Tertullian and St. Cyprian, the value of simplicity and modesty, and the difficulty of preserving a spirit of mortification and self-sacrifice beneath a costly garb. Her favourite dress was the plain, full, white robe, with neither fringe nor border, such as was then worn by young Christian women, and which is so often met with in the paintings in the catacombs.

Such was St. Monica's early youth : a lovely dawn heralding a still brighter day. When just on the verge of womanhood her hand was sought in marriage. Her parents gave their consent, and, by one of God's incomprehensible designs, this young virgin, whom we should have expected would follow in the steps of St. Agnes or St. Agatha, or who, if remaining in the world, would seem predestined to form a happy

---

* Ps. cxliii. 13.   † Boll., 4 Maii.

marriage, was bestowed on one apparently the least worthy of aspiring to such an alliance.

Patricius was a native of Tagaste, and although nothing is known respecting his birth, he probably belonged to an ancient and noble family, one of even higher rank than St. Monica's. At least, such is the conjecture of the ancient writers with regard to this marriage. Patricius was not endowed with much of this world's goods,[*] and his position in Tagaste was probably a less important one than some historians have surmised. He was a curule, that is to say, one of the city magistrates; but it was compulsory on all persons possessing twenty-six acres of land, to serve as magistrate; and this office, usually but an insignificant one in small towns, had become so onerous, in consequence of a law obliging the curials to collect the taxes at their own risk and supply the deficiencies in the same from their own purse, that none were ambitious of the office, for the people had nothing wherewith to pay, and the needy treasury would accept no excuses.[†] Ruined, or on the eve of ruin, but of noble lineage and ancient family, such seems to have been Patricius' position.

As regards his personal qualities, St. Augustine

---

[*] *Confess.*, lib. ii., cap. iii.

[†] Possidius, in his *Life of St. Augustine*, says positively that Patricius was a curial, or decurion, *i.e.*, that he belonged to those magistrates to whom the colonial and municipal towns were entrusted. They formed a kind of municipal council, *Curia Decurionum*, and their decrees are signed D.D., *Decreto Decurionum*. Candidates for this office were not to be under twenty-five, and must hold more than twenty-four acres of land.

assures us that the heart of Patricius was larger than his fortune,* and this proved to be the case. But these qualities, which we shall see gradually unfolding beneath the gentle hand of the angel whom God was about to give him as companion, not only were almost wholly obscured, but buried and stifled, as it were, by the most ignominious and pernicious habits. First, the fact of Patricius being a heathen, living, as he did, in the fourth century, (the Council of Nice had just been held,) at the moment when such men as Athanasius, Paul, and Anthony were flourishing, proves him to have been either profoundly indifferent to questions of the most vital import, or strangely blinded, perhaps by his secret passions. So indifferent was Patricius in matters of religion, that eighteen years' union with a saint scarcely roused him from his lethargy; he was alike heedless of vice and virtue, and in order to gratify his own pride, frequently exposed his son's virtue to corruption, and his temper was more violent than anything we of the present day can imagine.

It was nothing unusual to see St. Monica's young married friends and relatives bearing on their faces traces of their husband's brutality. This was of such general occurrence that it hardly awoke any remark, so harsh were the manners of African society, which Christianity had not as yet had time to transform.* Still every one trembled on hearing that Monica was about to be married to Patricius, for he was

---

* *Confess.*, lib. ix., cap. ix.   † Ibid.

reputed to surpass all others in violence and in brutality.

But this was only a part of St. Monica's bitter cup. In order to be worthy of her, and enjoy a mutual happiness, her husband should have known that holy Christian love which filled her heart; the reserve, modesty, delicacy, mutual respect, and all which makes the honour, charm, and sanctity of marriage. Up to this time Patricius had led a very irregular life, and one marked by many shameful excesses, into which we shall see him relapse, alas! almost on the very morrow of his nuptials.

Nor was this all. As St. Monica was but twenty-two, and Patricius nearly double her age, this discrepancy, added to the difference of mind, heart, character, tastes, and principles, presaged little chance of happiness, but much of sorrow, solitude of heart and mind, and in consequence of this, exposure to many perils and temptations, unless she proved herself sufficiently heroic to bear her sorrow nobly, resist temptations, and perhaps even dissipate the shadows which dimmed her life.

In studying these facts we involuntarily ask how it was that St. Monica's parents could consent to such a marriage; for life has burdens enough without intentionally adding to their number, and it is a dangerous experiment to count on poor fragile human nature's heroic qualities. Moreover, as they were Christians, and pious Christians, they must have known what marriage was, and how irksome its bonds were when uniting individuals unsuited to each other;

and that to marry a pious girl to a thoughtless libertine, is to crown her with thorny roses, and sentence her, young as she is, to a life-long martyrdom. The ancients had a punishment akin to this: they chained the living to the dead, and shut them up together.

Had our saint's parents thought of all these things, which faith, and, in its absence, reason, experience, or their own heart should have taught them, they would have shuddered, and probably have never taken.the course they pursued. But I know no case in which even Christian parents allow themselves to be so easily blinded and misled, as in the marriage of their children. Patricius was a pagan, thoughtless, unprincipled; but Monica would convert him. He was violent and angry, but good-hearted; his manners loose, but he was no longer young, and the heyday of passion was over; moreover, he was of good lineage and ancient family, loyal, upright, and honourable. What more was needed?

This is the way in which marriages are arranged; or rather, this is the way in which a young girl is vowed to a life of sorrow, the harder to bear, inasmuch as her tears must be shed in secret.

As for Monica, she probably knew very little of the real state of things. She believed in her mother, trusted to her father's judgment, and, as the majority of pious young maidens, when she gave her hand to Patricius at the foot of the altar, she did so principally as an act of obedience.

There are authors who assert that St. Monica held this marriage in great aversion; that she humbly and affectionately remonstrated with her parents,* but that, obliged to yield, (for God had ordained that she should purchase with bitter tears the honour of being St. Augustine's mother,) she consoled herself by thinking of the good she might effect in that poor soul, and sacrificed herself heroically by marrying him. One thing is certain: after praying, and receiving in return treasures of faith and generosity, (for no prayer is ever lost,) she, whether ignorant of, or resigned to her fate, appeared at the altar so radiant with virtue that all present were touched by the sight.

"Who," exclaims an ancient writer, "shall describe this holy maiden as she appeared at the foot of the altar, when pronouncing the sacred vows that were to bind her to her husband! What saintly modesty! What beauty of soul irradiated her brow, and chastity without compare!"† Only those who were present can realise a scene which language fails to describe.

* *Breviarium Canonicorum Regularium Ordinis S. August., ad primum Nocturnum tertia lectio.*

† Boll., Maii 4.

CHAPTER II.

A NON-CHRISTIAN HOME.—ST. MONICA'S GENTLENESS AND PATIENCE.—GOD CONSOLES HER BY PERMITTING HER TO BE MOTHER OF THREE CHILDREN. AUGUSTINE'S EARLY TRAINING.

355—369.

There is nothing so sad as the early days of an ill-sorted union, each day of which sees some cherished dream fade and vanish as leaves before an autumn gale, revealing the asperities and difference of character, the conflicting tempers and the harsh realities of life, so that unless supported by faith and by love to God, discouragement must inevitably ensue.

Until then St. Monica had never dwelt but in a Christian home, and knew nothing of those homes where God reigns not supreme, and where unbridled passion renders life one continued storm. Her mother-in-law was still living, and, as if all conspired to render her position as painful as possible, circumstances compelled Monica to inhabit the same home. A heathen, like her son, she resembled him both in temper and in character; was imperious, violent and peevish, and moreover, jealous with a mother-in-law's jealousy. The maid-servants were worthy of their employers, and as no other way of injuring their young mistress lay open, they resorted to calumny, and this in order to please St. Monica's mother-in-law.

A young wife of Monica's years would have found such a position a trying one, even if sure of her husband's love and protection; but how much more trying when each day revealed the abysses separating her from Patricius. The latter could not sympathize with his saintly companion's mode of life. Her prayers wearied him, her alms appeared excessive; he thought it strange that she should visit the poor and sick, and hold slaves in esteem. At every step our saint encountered the thousand obstacles described by Tertullian as invariably besetting the path of a Christian wife of a non-christian husband. This keen observer says: "How can a Christian wife serve God if her husband is an unbeliever? When she has to attend the services of the Church, he will require her to meet him at the baths earlier than usual; on fast-days he will hold a banquet, and if she wish to leave home, he will make excuses that the servants have no leisure to accompany her. Will such a husband permit his wife to go from street to street visiting the brethren in their poor hovels, or allow her to rise at night for the paschal solemnity, or approach that holy table so much inveighed against by the heathen, or permit her to glide into prisons for the purpose of kissing the martyrs' chains, and washing the saints' feet? If she wishes to relieve strangers and travellers, granary, cellar, all will be locked."*

* Tertull., *Ad uxorem.* lib. ii., cap. iv.

This was daily St. Monica's sad experience; a lot to which she would have resigned herself had not her purity of heart been endangered. "But alas!" continues Tertullian, "will not the pagan husband expect his Christian wife to conform to many pagan customs, to deck and tend her person, and yield him that kind of affection on which the divine blessing does not rest?"*

Monica early experienced this, and, young and innocent as she was, she was astonished to see how weak is the heart of man when untouched by divine grace. But she did not allow this sight to discourage her. Instead of losing heart, as many Christian women do; or quitting the conjugal roof, as Fabiola, a noble Roman lady, married to a cruel heathen much resembling Patricius, had just done; Monica, taking a loftier view, understood that God had confided this poor soul to her care, that she might try to heal, convert, and enlighten him. Of what avail is marriage, its dignity, its graces, and its close ties, unless it be for the reciprocal illumination of two souls? Of what avail is natural affection, where God bestows it, and that supernatural affection which He never refuses, and which is intended to perfect and transform that other love, save that it may itself be the illuminator? Let him who is in the light give light to him that is in darkness! Let the strong help him that is weak in the faith, says the Apostle. Let the living raise the dead! Should this demand groans,

* Tertul., *Ad uxorem*, lib. ii., cap. iv.

tears, and life itself, such a martyrdom is worthy a
Christian woman's every effort!

St. Augustine does more than reveal to us this
noble thought of his mother's: he tells us, in a few
lucid words, the course she pursued in order to ensure
success in so difficult an undertaking. " Modest and
wise, submissive to God and her parents, she yielded
a respectful obedience to the husband selected for
her; and as she ardently desired to win him for Thee,
O my God, she strove to impart to him, by the beauty
of her own conduct, a revelation of Thee which should
touch his heart."* That is to say, she used neither
word, argument, nor reproach. In lieu of preaching
virtue, she practised it. She strove to be gentle,
humble, patient, modest, and devoted; sure that if,
instead of talking about the truth, (no difficult matter that,) she practised it in her life, the day would
come when Patricius, no longer resisting, would
yield to such a discreet, gentle, and true light. But
much time and heroic virtue were necessary to
accomplish this. Monica's resolution was taken.
She well knew her husband's weaknesses and infi-
delities, but never spoke to him on the subject. She
suffered in silence and wept in secret; but knowing
how vain it is to expect fidelity to a creature from
one who loves not God, she contented herself with
ardently entreating for her poor husband that faith
and divine love which alone can render man chaste.†

When in his fits of passion, she preserved the same
lowly, gentle, prudent silence, prompted by real affec-

* *Confess.. lib. ix., cap. ix.*   † Ibid.

tion. Of what avails it to speak to a man who is beside himself? She would therefore wait until his anger subsided, and then, taking advantage of the return of reason, and those moments of tenderness by which all violent but warm-hearted men such as Patricius strive to obliterate the pain they have given, she would, privately, and with great delicacy, proffer a few words of explanation, and even of tender remonstrance, which were generally well received.*

This gentle manner, this talisman, consisting of silence and abnegation, were recommended by her to all her friends. When, with faces disfigured by their young husbands' ill-treatment, they came to confide their troubles to her keeping, she smilingly replied, " Beware of your tongue;" and they felt she was right, for though her husband was the most violent tempered man, he never struck her. He might start with rage, and threaten her, but he never did more, for her gentle gaze always restrained him.†

And not only did she keep him within bounds, to the admiration of all at Tagaste who had known Patricius prior to his marriage, but in pursuing this method faithfully and patiently, she gradually acquired a beauty in her husband's eyes, of the dawn of which he was himself unconscious. Her gentleness, delicacy, and the countless little proofs of her faithful love, stole into the heart of Patricius, where they made an impression, the depth of which he only learnt later on. His affection for Monica, whom, in

* *Confess.*, lib. ix., cap. ix. † Ibid.

spite of his shortcomings, he loved, imperceptibly
underwent a change. It acquired elevation and
nobleness, and a new and unwonted feeling of respect
mingled therewith. "She daily acquired fresh beauty
in his eyes," says St. Augustine, "the beauty of
virtue, and this was already winning her husband's
love, and admiration also."*

It was amid these sorrows and hopes, the latter
vague and distant, that in order to console Monica
and endear Patricius to her, in spite of his want
of fidelity, and also to render the home where she
was destined to suffer so much, supportable and even
dear, God permitted her to taste a happiness, next to
self-consecration to God perhaps the greatest that
earth knows, the happiness of becoming a mother.
Whilst still in the bloom of youth, Monica beheld
herself the mother of three children, in whose endearments and smiles she found some alleviation to
her sorrow.

Her eldest-born, the celebrated St. Augustine, first
saw the light on November 13th, 354, his mother
having then attained the age of twenty-two. It is
said that some time prior to his birth heaven revealed
to Monica the wonders he would one day effect, provided she trained him in the fear of God. And we
must admit that a careful perusal of the *Confessions*
seems to confirm the idea of some mysterious presentiment, unless, (and this would be more touching
and wondrous still,) the depth of her anxiety and the
earnestness of her prayers for Augustine during his

* *Confess.*, lib. ix., cap. ix.

wanderings, the tenacity of her hope, and the certainty she seemed to have of her son's conversion, sprang only from her deep faith in God and her ardent love for Augustine.

Her second child, Navigius, was gentle and pious, widely differing from his brother, knowing neither his deep repentance nor his sublime ardour, and who, without soaring so high in virtue, has bequeathed the Church a memory which, though its outlines are but faint, is nevertheless not without charm. Navigius was well informed, but timid, retiring, and of very delicate health; one of those gentle beings who flit across the scene of life, living rather for others than for self. Twice or thrice he will appear in the course of this history, always side by side by St. Monica, whom we may say he never quitted, but was her tender consoler and faithful guardian even unto the end, and specially so during the sad days of Augustine's wanderings in the paths of error. He appears to have been the father of St. Augustine's young nephew, Patricius, subdeacon of the Church at Hippo,* as well as of the saintly doctor's two nieces, who in early life took the veil as spouses of Jesus Christ.†

We therefore see that St. Monica's second son was the source of but little anxiety and much consolation.

Augustine and Navigius were not the only children, (to use the former's sublime expression,) whom Monica "conceived in her womb, to temporal, and in her heart, to eternal life." She had a daughter also,

---

* Sermon 336.   † Possidius, xxvi.

whom it is thought she named Perpetua, after one of
the most renowned African saints, the celebrated
martyr of Carthage. Unfortunately we know less of
this third child than of her brother Navigius. In
piety she resembled her mother, and, like her, entered
the marriage state, but soon becoming a widow, and
apparently a childless one, she withdrew to her
brother Augustine's house, where she resided until
his ordination; "after which," says Possidius, "he
would permit no woman, not even his own sister, to
tarry beneath his roof." She then entered religion,
and became superioress of one of the convents
founded by St. Augustine, from her cradle to her
tomb exhaling such a sweet odour of virtue that
the great doctor always bestows on her the appella-
tion of saint.* Altars erected to her, and also
to Navigius, are to be found in Rome and many
other places, where they were, and still are, invoked
as saints.

Such was St. Monica's family. The father a
pagan; the mother-in-law and servants doing their
utmost to render Christian training impossible, but
all in vain; St. Monica's three children are ranked
among the saints, as if God intended to show us what
a genuine mother can do, even when unsupported,
and how blessed those children are who owe their
birth to one in whose heart dwells the love of God,
and where reigns every virtue.

Monica would have found happiness, or at least
consolation, in her little family, had not a grief, more

* St. Augustine's Letters. Letter 24th.

bitter than any she had yet known, mingled itself with her joy, and poisoned her life. Patricius succumbed more and more to his evil passions; neither the intellectual beauty nor the loving heart of his saintly spouse, nor his marriage vows, nor the birth of his three children, had power to restrain this fickle soul; and in spite of Monica's tears he began openly to abandon himself to the most disorderly habits. Words fail to paint the agony inflicted on a Christian wife and mother by such a course as this; it is the martyrdom of soul mentioned by St. Ambrose, not less agonizing and excruciating than bodily torments, and none the less severe for being endured in the silence of home.*

But nothing could induce our saint to swerve from the line of conduct she had marked out for herself. Abandoned by her husband in the very flower of her age, Monica, then about twenty-seven, and in the fourth or fifth year of her married life, seeing all her early hopes vanish, redoubled her fervent trust in God, and still persevering in her silent, discreet, and gentle behaviour to her husband, devoted herself wholly to her children.

All mothers love their children; but who shall tell the depth of love that fills the heart of her whose married life is one scene of sorrow and desertion? Who paint the anxiety and vigilance of those who, in giving birth to their children, know that they are about to launch them on a treacherous, dangerous sea, the more perilous to their innocence inasmuch as

---

* *Sancti Ambrosii opera.* tom. II., p. 497.

they will find no protectors in their fathers ? This is the sight about to unfold itself to our gaze in the following narrative, and which would be even more interesting did not a dense veil conceal the early years of Navigius and of Perpetua. Let us, then, though unwillingly, take leave of these two children of our saint, and concentrate our attention on Augustine's infancy and early years.

Need we say that Monica did not defer her child's education until he had acquired the use of speech ? She did not even wait until his birth, but at the first intimation of the happiness God had bestowed on her, she withdrew into solitude, and having gathered from the pious books which were then her constant study that it was in her power to sanctify and, as it were, baptize her child in the love of God during those long months in which they led one and the same existence, she redoubled her vigilance, piety, and purity of heart, so that the little soul which would take its bent from her should receive nought but holy impressions. Naturally anxious as to her new responsibility, she raised her eyes to heaven, and, fearful lest she was wanting in the knowledge and love requisite for such a work, began to offer her child to God with all the ardour of which she was capable. " St. Monica," says St. Francis of Sales, " consecrated the great St. Augustine before he was yet born, and by frequent dedications of him to the Christian religion, and to the service and glory of God, as he himself testifies of her, when he says that 'he had already tasted the salt of God in his mother's womb.' "*

That touching expression, " *ab utero matris meæ,*" "from my mother's womb," recurs perpetually in the *Confessions.* If Augustine learnt to love Christ Jesus; if there is a single fibre in his being that vibrates with love for God and for the truth; if even in the midst of his wanderings any spark of honour remains; if he is naturally averse to all that is low, coarse, and transitory, he is never weary of telling us that he acquired it *ab utero matris meæ :* as if to make us comprehend how great the beauty, elevation, and sublimity of his mother's thoughts and feelings during those nine months.

So soon as he was born St. Monica had him carried to the church, and since it was not then the custom to baptize new-born children, as is seen in the history of Constantine, Theodosius, St. Ambrose, St. Martin, St. Eusebius, and many others, she wished him to be at least enrolled amongst the catechumens, viz., those who were candidates for baptism. Meanwhile, until the time arrived when our Lord would take full possession of that temple which, after a moment's pollution, was destined to become so beauteous, the cross was graved on the brow, and salt, symbol of the faith, was placed on those lips which would one day be such sublime interpreters of the same.†

No fear that a mother such as Monica would allow her child to be nourished at a stranger's breast. She

* *Introduction to the Devout Life,* part iii., chap. 38.
† *Confess.,* lib. I., cap. xi. *De utilitate credendi,* cap. i.

would have dreaded lest any strange, worldly, or perhaps even sinful influence, might counteract her efforts in the task, the full difficulty of which she well knew. She fed Augustine at her own chaste breast; there he enjoyed " the delight of being nourished with his mother's milk."* With it she made him drink in the name and love of Jesus; and he who had already received in his mother's womb so profound an impress of faith, enjoyed the additional blessing of receiving, amid the caresses showered on him in his cradle, a second impress no less mysterious and more profound than the previous one. Happy those children who are trained simultaneously for heaven as well as earth, and who, in opening their eyes in this world, read faith, purity, honour, and virtue on their mother's brow.

St. Augustine has described this his early happiness, in a few words full of interest. "Whence came I, O my God, on entering this dying life, or living death ? I know not. What I do know is, that on my entrance there Thy loving arms received me; this I learnt from my father and from my mother, in whose heart I reposed for a brief moment." And after this delicate allusion, he adds: " After this I was the recipient of a second grace, that of enjoying the sweetness of my mother's milk. For this I bless Thee, O my God, for it was not she who filled her breast. Thou didst provide this nourishment for me, proportioning my appetite to my requirements, and inclining my mother to satisfy the same. Love

---

* *Confess.*, lib. I., cap. vi.

prompted her to impart liberally what she had received in such plentiful abundance, and by an admirable law, in ministering to my happiness she ministered to her own.......And together with this milk, which I found so delicious, my heart enjoyed the greater happiness of lovingly drinking in the name of Jesus Christ.......This I have learnt since then, for at that time, ingrate as I was, of what was I capable? Of feeding at my mother's breast, enjoying happiness, weeping when I was in pain, and nothing more."*

However tender the care Monica lavished on her infant child, it was but the prelude to the more important work with which God had entrusted her. Her first care was to mould Augustine's conscience. Soon the hour would arrive when he must pass from his mother's tuition, and be exposed to the pernicious influence of his father's example; and when, bidding adieu to his mother's tender care, he would find himself in a vortex of corruption, and surrounded by corrupting influences, from which he could not escape uninjured unless his conscience were of the highest order.

In order to mould his conscience, Monica incessantly placed the groundwork of the faith, the clear, pure light of Scripture, before her child's eyes. Among other lessons there was one she loved to transmit to him, even as it had been transmitted to her by her own forefathers: the contempt of earth and of all finite, transitory, things. She constantly

* *Confess.*, lib. I. cap. vi.; lib. III., cap. iv.

directed his gaze heavenwards, endeavouring to grave in that young heart an impression so deep that nothing should ever efface it. We know how she succeeded. That acute sensibility, ever craving for a happiness this world can never bestow; that deep, mournful feeling of dissatisfaction which gives such a touching, even human beauty to St. Augustine's soul; those sublime ejaculations, "Thou hast made us for Thyself, O Lord, and our heart cannot rest until it rests in Thee;" all this Augustine learnt from his mother's lips and early lessons.

Not only did Monica daily strive to inspire her son with a contempt of earth, she also endeavoured to inspire him with love by constantly telling him of the Divine Love, of the Incarnation, of our Lord's poverty and hardships, all endured for love of us; of the cross to which His bleeding limbs were nailed in order that He might prove to us the greatness of His Love.* How deeply such words as these, proceeding from such saintly and impassioned lips, must have sunk into Augustine's tender, loving soul! So profound was the impression, that even amid all the errors and passions of youth Augustine could never forget that radiant and touching figure of our Lord "who by humility abased Himself to the level of our pride." We shall note hereafter that he would lay down the finest writings in disgust if the name of Jesus Christ were absent.†

---

* *Confess.* lib. I. cap. xi.   This shows us the character of St. Monica's early lessons.

† *Confess.* lib. III. cap. iv,

At the same time, in order to render his conscience perfect, Monica strove to inspire him with an aversion to sin, and to all that sullies and degrades the human heart; and with that self-forgetfulness which leads a mother not to shrink from humiliating herself in order that she may preserve her child from evil, she told him of her own transgressions. She gave him a full and detailed account of the danger to which she was exposed in her childhood, of the cellar, the little cup, the servant's reproaches, and the harsh name bestowed on her, the whole of the touching story which we have thus learnt from her own lips; happy if at this price she might succeed in inspiring her son with a horror of sin, however venial it might be, and a determination to avoid all dangerous occasions, however trifling they might appear.

In these familiar conversations, her little son seated on her knees, she taught him the vanity of earthly things, the exceeding greatness of Divine Love, the hideousness of vice, and the aversion in which all evil must be held. These lessons he never forgot: in vain did he try to stifle the voice of conscience, that even though unhappy, he might be at peace; that voice could not be silenced; he bore the arrow in his heart, knowing no respite to his pain until that day when he returned, penitent and vanquished, to recover peace, honour, self-respect, purity, and joy, in the God of his childhood, and the God of his mother.

There is one incident of Augustine's early childhood which reveals (in spite of the father's incredulity,) how deep were the faith and piety of this childish heart; and also, in spite of her own prudence and tact, how difficult and delicate a position Monica's was.

We quote the following graphic description from the *Confessions.* " When still a child, I was suddenly seized with such violent pains in the stomach that my life was despaired of. Thou, O Lord, who even then wast watching over me, Thou knowest with what ardour and with what fervent faith I begged to be made partaker of the baptism of Thy Son Jesus Christ, my Lord and my God. I urgently entreated it at my mother's hands, and from Thy Church, my mother also."* Such was Augustine at the age of seven or eight. He is dying in intense agony, but thinks of nought save God, his own soul, and eternity.

His mother's conduct is, perhaps, still more worthy of admiration. "My mother," says St. Augustine, " was moved to the inmost depths of her being." And why so? did she fear losing her son? Yes, doubtless, for she was a mother. "But, O Lord, Thou knowest she was more anxious for my soul than my body. Her pure heart yearned to make me partake of eternal life by procuring my baptism. Full of anxiety she ran urgently demanding it, that I might be cleansed from my sins, and profess my faith in Thee, O Lord Jesus."†

In view of this ardent faith of both mother and child, we are surprised to learn the following. St.

* *Confess.*, lib. I., cap. xi.   † Ibid.

Augustine adds: "Meanwhile my pain ceased; and as my life was no longer in danger, nothing more was thought about my baptism," which, indeed, was not administered till twenty years later. Or rather we should be surprised, and rightly so, did we not, despite Augustine's delicate and discreet silence on the point, gather enough to discern the hand of Patricius here. So long as Augustine was in danger, Patricius would not thwart Monica. He was too indifferent to religion, and also too honourable and generous a man, not to respect the religious scruples of his dying child; neither did he wish to add to Monica's grief at losing her son, the thousand-fold more poignant grief of beholding his eternal salvation imperilled. But so soon as the danger was over, Patricius' indifference and paganism re-assert their sway, and at the father's desire, Augustine's baptism is deferred.*

Monica said nothing. She knew that words would avail nought with Patricius; and since the Church tolerated this custom, no other way being open to her, she resigned herself in silence. In addition to this, the lamentable tone of society, the schools, books, theatres, and games of the day, from none of which could Augustine be entirely shut out, reconciled Monica to a certain extent. For, seeing that the social atmosphere was so vitiated, that unless he fled to the desert and refused to learn to read, as

---

* *Breviarium secundum ritum almæ Ecclesiæ Arosiensis. In festo sancti Augustini. Ad Matut. secunda Lectio.* 1 vol. 12mo, black letter, without date; the approbation is dated 1504.

St. Anthony had recently done, it was almost impossible for a young man not to succumb to the surrounding dangers; and if it were true, as St. Paul has asserted in words that make the hearts of Christian mothers tremble with alarm, that faults committed after baptism are graver, relapses more serious, stains more difficult to efface, why be in any hurry to administer baptism? Why not defer the reception of this all-powerful grace until the day when Augustine, supposing he should for a brief moment wander from the truth, returned to the paths of faith and virtue. "This was my mother's view," says St. Augustine, "and knowing the temptations, storms, and tempests, that awaited me, she consoled herself by the thought that in lieu of exposing the image of Jesus Christ to their fury, she would but expose the unformed clay on which that image was one day to be imprinted.*

But whilst resigning herself to the only course left open to her by her husband, Monica felt it henceforth her duty to watch over Augustine's soul with ever-increasing vigilance. Taking warning from the danger he had just incurred, gladdened and encouraged by the religious ardour he had manifested, she resolved not to lose sight of him for a single instant, and withdrawing herself more and more from the sad pleasures of the world, constituted herself his angel guardian and his visible providence.

This was not all. In order that nothing might

* *Confess.,* lib. 1., cap. xi.

hinder her in this important work, St. Monica applied herself more sedulously than ever to win the hearts of her husband, mother-in-law, and servants, and perchance one day even associate them with herself in her grand undertaking.

Her mother-in-law was the first to yield. She was a haughty, imperious woman, whom the false reports circulated by the slaves had prejudiced against Monica. Her daughter-in-law's gentleness won the day, and gradually disarmed her of her prejudices. St. Augustine says: " She was convinced of the untruthfulness of the reports, and without saying anything to Monica, went to Patricius, and acquainted him with his servants' malicious conduct. He was extremely angry, had the servants flogged, and his mother gave notice that if any one, thinking to please her, should calumniate her daughter-in-law, they should be rewarded by a similar punishment. As may be readily supposed, the slaves held their tongues, and St. Monica henceforth lived in lasting harmony with her mother-in-law.

The slaves had been silenced by terror, but Monica strove to silence them by love; she won their hearts, and became henceforth the object of their faithful, tender care.

Monica's winning gentleness was felt beyond the immediate circle of her own home. St. Augustine says: " Thy faithful servant who, thanks to Thee, gave me my life, had been endowed by Thee with one most precious gift: animosity and dissension

fled at her approach."* She became the confidante
of the entire neighbourhood; all troubles were
brought to her. If any one hastened to her still
burning with resentment at the ill-treatment they
had received, she would listen patiently, for none
excelled her in soothing anger, and making peace
between those who were at variance. She was a
proficient in the art of silence : every confidence was
held sacred, and she never repeated any remark, unless
such as was calculated to soothe resentment or afford
consolation. " There is one virtue my mother possessed," continues St. Augustine, " which would
appear to me of little value, had I not learnt from sad
experience how many there are who not only act the
part of tale-bearer, but aggravate the wounded feelings
of the sufferer by exaggerations and additions.
Merely abstaining from repeating irritating remarks
is of small avail, unless one endeavours to heal the
breach by kind words. This was my mother's practice,
because she was taught of Thee, O God."†

She exhaled the sweet odour of peace ; her house
resembling those sanctuaries at whose thresholds
silence keeps her guard, and whose peace imparts
itself to all who bring their burdens and their sorrows
there.

Her husband was the chief object of her loving
solicitude. He was a pagan, she desired to convert
him ; he was a father, and she hoped to secure his
co-operation, or at least ensure freedom of action.

In a few charming words St. Augustine has de-

* *Confess.*, lib. IX., cap. ix.   † Ibid

scribed his mother's skill and tact in surmounting the serious difficulties of her position. " At that epoch I was a believer, so was my mother, and the whole household, save my father."* This is a description of a home of the fourth century; the present day, alas! can furnish many a counterpart.

Listen to the following words: how true, beautiful, and consoling they are. " Nevertheless, however powerful my father's example, he could never destroy my mother's influence over me, nor shake my faith in Jesus Christ, in whom he believed not."† And thus will it ever be; when the mother is a believer, and the father not so, the child will not hesitate for a moment; his mother's faith will be his faith.

Monica, knowing that this state of things might not always continue, that the reign of the passions was at hand, and that they would find the youth more ready to obey their voice on account of his father's pernicious example, knowing also how plastic is the heart of childhood, lost not a single day. " She taught me," says St. Augustine, " to honour God above all else, even above my father; to listen only to His voice, and to give Him my heart's best affections."‡

" It is true," he adds, " that she was full of loving, tender consideration for her husband. As she was obliged to run counter to his wishes sometimes, and also oppose him in matters of faith, she served him with the greater sweetness and humility. More en-

---

* *Confess.*, lib. I., cap. **xi.**　　　† Ibid.　　　‡ Ibid.

lightened and virtuous than her husband, she always kept in the background, rejoicing to call herself his servant; and whatever sacrifice such conduct involved, was amply repaid by the permission she obtained to train her child in the school of Jesus Christ. To this her whole time and energies were devoted; her life was summed up in two words: God and her child." To train the one, contemplate the other, and love them both, sufficed her. What other consolation could she need?

But alas! how soon does maternal anxiety mingle with maternal joy; how soon the moment arrives when the child must be entrusted to stranger hands. Young as St. Augustine was, it was time for him to commence his studies, and St. Monica, fearing lest his intellect should be cultivated at the expense of heart and conscience, was in no hurry to part with her child; she therefore confided him to masters residing in Tagaste, whose duty it was to impart to him the rudiments of learning, under his mother's superintendence.

One would have supposed such brilliant genius would have developed with marked rapidity, and that, as regards intellect at least, such a child would have fulfilled his mother's fondest hopes; but it was far otherwise. The first thing discernible was an insurmountable laziness and invincible repugnance to study.* It seemed to him an odious, uninteresting task to learn to read and write, and to be told over and over again that twice one are two, twice two are

* *Confess.*, lib. I., cap. xii.

four.* Grammatical studies were not more captivating, and with the exception of Latin, which he learnt from his cradle amid caresses and endearments, and the Punic language, which he loved as being his mother's and his own native tongue, he could never overcome his aversion to the study of languages. His instructors, knowing what such a nature was capable of, tried the effect of threats and chastisement. But severity only increased his dislike to study, and made him have recourse to falsehood and little acts of cunning, in order to deceive his parents and his teachers.†

Alarmed at this first dawn of evil in Augustine's soul, and conscious that some other spur than that of fear was needed, Monica led her son to " some servants of God," " men of prayer,"‡ that they might enable him to surmount his aversion to study, by a higher motive than that of fear. St. Augustine says: " They taught me to consider Thee, O Lord, as a sublime being, who, though invisible to mortal sight, art nevertheless able to aid us. Therefore I began to implore Thee as my support and refuge in trouble, and though of such tender years, fervently entreated Thee that I might not be flogged at my lessons. Alas! Thou didst not always grant my prayer, but this was for my good; and every one, my parents

---

* *Confess.*, lib. I., cap. xiii.   † *Confess.*, lib. I., cap. xx.

‡ *Homines rogantes te.* Not men of prayer, as these words are often rendered, but men given to prayer, evidently referring to priests, for it appears there were, as yet, no monks in Africa.

included, made light of my punishment, which, though trifling in their eyes, was a source of great fear and pain to me."*

Unhappily, Augustine's aversion to study was not his only failing; in spite of his natural timidity and reserve, pride and an inordinate love of approbation and desire to excel became apparent in him, also an intense love of sports and pastimes. He says: " I deceived my parents and tutors by many a lie, and made them disconsolate by my love of play, shows, and acting. I robbed my parents' cellar and larder, either to satisfy my own greediness, or for the sake of having wherewith to repay the children whose society I thus purchased. At my games I would win by unfair means, for the sake of triumphing over my companions, but would not allow myself to be cheated, and if I surprised my playmates in the act of cheating would overwhelm them with raillery and reproach. If I were the accused I would indignantly deny the charge rather than plead guilty."† In brief, the old pagan blood inherited from Patricius began to boil within his veins.

Augustine was not devoid of good qualities. He loved truth, feared dishonour, was kind, tender-hearted, grateful, and affectionate. With noble impulses, keen and grateful appreciation of kindness, and full of love for his mother,‡ what would he become? Which would win the day, the pagan blood inherited from his father, or the Christian qualities

---

* *Confess.*, lib. I., cap. ix.

† *Confess.*, lib. I., cap. xix.   ‡ *Confess.*, lib. I., cap. xx.

his mother had mingled therewith ? Or rather, what would he have become had not a sacred and powerful influence surrounded him from the very dawn of his existence, and had not Monica's ardent prayers and watchful care redoubled as dangers thickened around her son.

In the midst of all this anxiety our saint was compelled for the first time to part from her child. Augustine was growing up, and such a small town as Tagaste afforded but few educational advantages. Besides which, Patricius, proud of his son, who, in spite of his laziness and his aversion to study was a child of much promise, had just resolved that, no matter at what pecuniary sacrifice to himself, or regret on his own and Monica's part at the approaching separation, his son should receive a suitable education.

Six leagues from Tagaste was a town called Madaura, the birthplace of Apuleius,* a town possessing a certain degree of intellectual culture and taste. Its fine Forum, enriched by statues of all the heathen divinities, was also surrounded by schools of repute.† Thither Monica conducted her son, parting from him amid maternal counsels and tears, but happy that he was so near that she would be able to hasten to him at the first sign of danger; little dreaming that the evil from which she had so sedulously shielded his

---

* Now Madaourouche, seventeen and a half miles from Souk-Arras. Ptolemy speaks of it as *Maduros*. In a notice on Numidia, mention is made of a Bishop of Madaura, *Mataurensis episcopus.*

† St. Augustine's *Letters*, 16, p. 28.

cradle, but symptoms of which she had so lately discerned, would so soon break forth, and inflict such swift and serious injury on the beloved child from whom she had so recently parted.

CHAPTER III.

AUGUSTINE'S YOUTH.—THE CRISIS OF THE PASSIONS COMMENCES.—CAUSES, PROGRESS, AND CHARACTER.—GOD CONSOLES MONICA, AND FURNISHES AID TO AUGUSTINE, BY PERMITTING PATRICIUS TO TAKE THE FIRST STEP TOWARDS EMBRACING CHRISTIANITY.—HE ABJURES PAGANISM.

368—370.

"I will relate my past errors, and the voluptuousness which sullied the beauty of my soul; not because I love them, but in order that I may ever love Thee, O my God, and because love for Thee incites me to recall the transgressions of my youth with sorrow and bitterness of heart, that by so doing I may rejoice the more in Thy goodness and mercy."*

In this lowly and sublime language does St. Augustine commence the record of the dawn of passion within his soul, and which arose secretly and silently at Madaura about 368, gained the ascendancy two years later at Tagaste, in 370 and the following year,

* *Confess.*, lib. ii., cap. i.

and ended so sadly in Carthage in 372, in a most disgraceful defeat succeeded by a humiliating servitude of fifteen years duration. But we must let him describe, in his own eloquent manner, the cause of this crisis, its progress and fatal consequences, and see how bitter may be a mother's grief.

Augustine went to Madaura about the year 367, at which time he was in his thirteenth or fourteenth year. We cannot clearly ascertain whether his brilliant genius had already revealed itself at Tagaste, but no sooner had he mastered the rudiments of learning, and made acquaintance with the grand sources of eloquence and poetry, than all was changed. His aversion to study vanished. His genius awoke at the perusal of Virgil, Homer, Cicero, and Ovid. The works of Virgil impressed him deeply, the description of Dido's sorrow moved him to tears; if forbidden to read Virgil, he wept, and wept if allowed to peruse his pages; so powerfully did those writings affect his exquisitely sensitive and tender soul that he could with difficulty tear himself from them.

He seems to have cared less for Homer. "This sweet liar," he says, "was not pleasing to me in my childhood." Not that Augustine's genius failed to discern the difference between Virgil and Homer, and how far the latter exceeds the former in grandeur, natural sublimity, expression, and force; but as he himself tells us, the difficulty he experienced in understanding Greek embittered the sweetness of those fables. and marred his enjoyment of those ingenious.

charming, beautiful fictions of the greatest of poets.*
Perhaps, too, Virgil's exquisite tenderness, no less
deep that Homer's, but couched in more modern
language, was more to Augustine's taste. Be the
reason what it may, Virgil was his favourite, not
only then, but through life. Terence, Plautus, and
Ovid were perused by him with varied emotions; he
revelled in their sweetness, drank in the beauty of
their imagery, and their poison too, for, alas! there
is poison in those golden cups.

In order to develop the faculties of the youths of
that day, it was the custom to make them render in
prose Juno's ardent and impassioned words, or
Dido's heart-rending cries. The prize was awarded
to him who best portrayed the wrath, plaints, and
passions of those imaginary beings, and whose de-
scriptions were the most life-like, eloquent, and natural. Here Augustine bore away the palm; his fellow
students' plaudits and his masters' eulogiums made
him conscious of his success, which success also became
the ruin of his innocence. Incited by the praises
lavished on him, he strove to experience those guilty
passions in order to delineate them the better, and as
they were still dormant in his own heart, not content
with reading those poets who had described them the
most graphically, he began to frequent the theatres,
in order to witness the scenes his masters had described, interpreted by word and gesture.

Even now that eighteen centuries of Christianity
have tempered the effect of those glowing images,

* *Confess.*, lib. i., cap. xiv.

how much caution is still requisite to guard the innocent heart of childhood from being too deeply impressed thereby! What then must the perils have been in those days, when there were neither expurgated editions nor Christian teachers, and the stage undertook to be the exponent of that which it was beyond the teacher's art to express! Christianity was emerging from the catacombs, but had not as yet been able to purify the literature or the schools of the day, so that Christian and pagan youths received the same education, and though this was a matter of universal regret, custom prevailed over paternal anxiety and maternal tears. "O fatal torrent," exclaims St. Augustine, apostrophizing usage, "wilt thou not cease? How long will thy impetuous force sweep away the children of Eve into that vast and perilous ocean which even those whose brows are signed with the cross can scarcely traverse in safety? Have I not read in those books the story of Jove, the Thunderer, and the adulterer. Not that Divine Power could ever be allied to such infamous corruption; but they have armed a guilty mortal with avenging thunders, so that we might be induced to imitate his crimes. Have not I myself heard a Terence introduce a debauched youth on the scene, pleading the example of the gods, and exclaiming, ' A god, and what a god! has allowed himself this enjoyment, and shall a poor mortal such as I am be ashamed to follow his example! certainly not!' And yet we remunerate such teaching. The forum is open to its professors! The law leaves them unchecked, and they are awarded private and state salaries! And yet it is patent to all that such teaching is calculated to make men guilty of the same vices!"

"Not," continues St. Augustine, with that good sense and moderation which, although we are apt to overlook the fact, are an essential part of genius, "not that I condemn the language employed by poets and orators. Their words are as rich and precious vases, but I disapprove of the impure wine these inebriated teachers offer us in those golden goblets, which we are forced to quaff under pain of punishment, and without the liberty of appeal to a sober judge. And yet, O my God, I who now survey my past years in Thy presence, I willingly learnt those lessons, and, unhappy one, even took pleasure therein."*

It is easy to imagine the impression such books and exhibitions must have produced on a youth possessed of such extreme sensibility, such perilous tenderness of heart, not yet baptized, absent from his mother, and having none to shield him from these grave dangers, save masters " more inebriated than himself." " What wonder," he exclaims, " that I was allured by these vanities, and that wandering far from Thee, my God, I lavished my affections on creatures; seeing that the guides provided for me were men who would have blushed to employ a solecism in narrating a good deed, but who gloried and delighted in the applause elicited by the eloquent description of their debauches! Poor, unhappy child that I was, thus early was I exposed to the dan-

* *Confess.,* lib. I., cap. xvi.

gers of life, and sad were the combats I had to sustain."*

And soon indeed did the poison begin to circulate in Augustine's veins. Still in the flower of his youth, his fourteenth year barely completed, at the dangerous and charming age, when the heart begins to expand, but withers also as a flower, he was conscious of an unwonted feeling of unrest. " My sole dream was to love and be loved. But," he humbly adds, " I outstepped the limits of chaste, pure friendship, where soul loves soul. The gross vapours of carnal affection and youthful passion so darkened my heart that I could no longer discern between legitimate affections and guilty love. Thus did the devouring fire begin to rage within my heart, and the waves and storms of passion plunged me in the abyss of shameful sins."†

By degrees his mind was filled with evil imaginations. He was keenly alive to the spur of sinful desires, and as there was no one at hand to moderate their force, they increased in strength, and exposed Augustine to the greatest danger. " Whilst still but a youth," he says, " I began to thirst for guilty pleasures, and felt no shame in spending my energies on the pursuit of them. My soul began to lose her beauty, and I became hideous in Thy sight, O my God ; but this did not check me in the pursuit of self-gratification, nor make me less desirous of winning my fellow-creatures' applause."‡ But his natural timidity and reserve led him to conceal his vices, and

* *Confess.*, lib. I., cap. xviii. et xix.
† *Confess.*, lib. II., cap. ii. and iii.   ‡ *Confess.*, lib. II., cap. i.

none of his friends or fellow-scholars had the slightest suspicion of the storm raging within.

Meanwhile Augustine's renown increased daily. His mind, secretly affected, but not yet totally ruined by evil, appeared day by day more beautiful. His eloquence began to manifest itself, and every one prognosticated that when his faculties attained their full development, he would eclipse the most illustrious rhetoricians. Patricius was delighted at these tidings; and as he had previously parted with Augustine in order that the latter might enjoy the educational advantages of Madaura, he now resolved to make a final effort, in order that he might conduct him, not to Rome, for such a step as that was beyond his means, but to Carthage, at least, where he would find schools, teachers, libraries, a numerous and select society of youths, and, in fine, all that was requisite for his intellectual development.

Unfortunately Patricius' means were small, and in spite of his generous intentions and paternal pride, time and economy were necessary in order to effect his purpose. Therefore, at the close of 369, when the vacation commenced, Patricius made up his mind to recall his child, and keep him at home for twelve months, during which time they would be able to realize sufficient money for the long and expensive journey. So Augustine returned to Tagaste. With what joy his mother welcomed him may easily be divined. She knew nothing as yet to dim her happiness, and whilst proud and happy at her son's genius and success, as mothers ever will be proud and happy

at their children's success, she was at the same time
the humblest of women; and believing him still
innocent, could imprint a confident and happy kiss
on that youthful brow.

Had Augustine been innocent and pure, or had he
courageously avowed all to his mother, this break in
his studies might have proved beneficial by bringing
him again within range of Monica's influence, and by
preparing him the better to withstand the perils of
Carthage; but having resolved to conceal everything
from his mother, nothing could have been more
deplorable than this return home, inasmuch as the
enforced idleness to which he was condemned, the
want of all occupation, the protracted reveries which
ensued, the void in his affections, all concurred to
hasten the crisis. "In the sixteenth year of my
age," he says, "domestic reasons having necessitated
my return home, the impure desires which hitherto
had but germinated within my soul now grew with
startling rapidity."

And as nothing weakens the love of God, and
renders the thought of Him so distasteful to the soul,
as passion does, the voice of conscience began to wax
fainter and fainter. "As a just punishment for my
faithlessness, the noise of my chains rendered me
almost deaf to Thy voice, O my God, and as I had
deprived myself of Thy aid and strength, the ardour
of my passions increased." And then, in language
wholly untranslatable, he tells us his heart was aglow
and seething with evil desires, which, brooking no
restraint, carried him away on their ardent waves,

making him turn a deaf ear to that divine voice to which he gave heed " but too late," and drawing him farther and farther away from God.*

In honour of her by whom that heart had been so carefully moulded, we must add that Augustine was not happy amid his guilty pleasures. From the very first he experienced bitter remorse and unrest; he sought peace and happiness, but found even pleasure elude his grasp. On awaking from his guilty joys he was overwhelmed with self-abhorrence. " Thou, O Lord, didst embitter all my pleasures, that I might seek that happiness which never palls, nor brings remorse and sorrow in its train."† Yet he would not commence that search, but remained, tossed by the waves of passion, " in proud dejection and unquiet weariness.‡

By forgetting God, Augustine sought in vain for happiness and liberty. That brilliant meteor, by which youth is so easily misled, is as deceptive as it is seductive. " I imagined myself free," he says, " while in reality I was but forging my own chains, and rivetting them more and more tightly still." " Such," says Bossuet, " was the servitude of the great Augustine, at the time when the liberty of rebels was his."§

He often betook himself to prayer, and raising his fettered hands to heaven, entreated to be rendered virtuous, but trembled lest his prayer should meet

---

* *Confess.*, lib. II., cap. ii.   † *Ibid.*   ‡ *Ibid.*

§ Sermon for a Clothing. *Complete Works*, edition Gauthier, vol. **vi.** p. 188.

with an immediate response. His supplication was: "O Lord, give me chastity and continence;" in a low' voice adding, "but not yet, not yet, O Lord." Guilty and miserable as he was, conscious of his malady, yet shrinking from being healed, the burden of corruption under which he groaned became more and more unendurable.*

Such was the sad condition of Augustine at the age of sixteen. Three or four years had sufficed to destroy St. Monica's work; a fact which would surprise us, were it not easy to demonstrate the cause of the same. The indifference of a father who as yet, having no religious convictions, cared little about his son's morals, provided that he succeeded in his studies and excelled in rhetoric; the want of prudence in Augustine's masters, who fostered his imagination and his susceptibilities, but neglected the necessary safeguards which reason, conscience, and religion alone could afford; the perusal of dangerous books and the frequenting theatres, a more dangerous practice still; guilty friendships, doubtless then already in process of formation; in fine—we do not say this in a spirit of censure, but in compassion for a pious mother who, having an infidel husband, was unable to train her son according to her own wishes, and was herself often exposed to tyranny on the part of her husband—the absence of all religious aid at a time when such succour is indispensable; neither baptism, confirmation, confession, nor Holy Eucharist, at that terrible moment when awakening passions afford their

* *Confess.*, VIII., cap. viii.

7   S.M.

vanquisher so many opportunities of triumph, or hurl their victim into a deep abyss: surely this suffices to explain the inutility of St. Monica's efforts, and the apparently evanescent character of the work she had laboured so arduously to accomplish. That work was not really destroyed, for the character impressed on a child's soul by the hand of God, and by a Christian mother, is not so easily effaced; and if the hurricane of passion for an instant dim the sacred flame of conscience, it is all but certain that the flame will only be dimmed, but not extinguished, if it has been enkindled by a Christian mother. At this time, as if God, who was watching so tenderly over mother and son, wished to provide consolation for Monica, and aid Augustine, by furnishing him, in the person of his father, with an example which might afford him some degree of encouragement, Patricius took the first step towards becoming a Christian.

Patricius and Monica had been married seventeen years, during which time the latter had allowed no day to pass without labouring with unfailing discretion to effect her husband's conversion. In so doing she had displayed the gentleness, patience, and exquisite tact pertaining to truly Christian women. She had said but little, had never sermonized, but had loved and prayed much. She now began to see some signs of the long-wished-for realization of her hopes. Time, always on the side of those who know how to wait, had come to Monica's aid. The hey-day of passion being over, Patricius was better able to discern the vanity of idols, and the sweet odour of Jesus

Christ which emanated from the heart of his saintly spouse. For a long while he had resisted his convictions, resolving never to yield. For a still longer time he had been irresolute, halting, and on the point of acting according to the voice of conscience ; then resolving that the morrow, at latest, should witness the accomplishment of his purpose ; anxious, above all, to conceal his hesitation from St. Monica, who guessed all and said nothing, only redoubling her prayers. At last, truth having won the day, Patricius told his pious spouse that he was resolved to abjure paganism.

With what joy must Monica have welcomed these tidings ! What happiness to see her husband become a Christian, at the very time when Augustine, just entering his sixteenth year, would stand in need of more vigilant and efficacious protection. She thanked God with heartfelt fervour, with tears entreating Him to strengthen Patricius in his newly-formed resolve, and to hasten the day when she should see him enrolled among the catechumens.

The catechumenate was the Christian noviciate. Before being admitted to holy baptism in an age when, paganism being still rife, apostacy was to be dreaded, adults were arrested an instant at the threshold of the Church, that it might be known whether the step they were about to take was a voluntary one, and also in order to instruct them as to the momentousness of the duties they were about to undertake. Having decided on taking this first step, Patricius went to the church to make a public abjuration of paganism, and an open profession of the Christian faith. Monica accompanied him, full of joy; Augustine followed. The probable date of this event was at the beginning of Lent, in the year 370.

Having arrived at the foot of the altar, Patricius knelt down, while the bishop laid his hands on his bowed head, praying God to admit him into His family. His brow was signed with the cross of Jesus Christ, that he might begin his entrance to the Church by honouring the Saviour's humiliation. Blessed salt was placed on his lips, symbol of that incorruptness of heart which ever after must be his. From that day his name was inscribed on the rolls of the Church, and he was ranked among the catechumens.*

Had Patricius resolved on taking the second step at once, that is to say, of quickly traversing the different grades through which the catechumen had to pass, and receiving holy baptism at the approaching paschal solemnity,† St. Monica's happiness would have been complete; but this Patricius did not do.

In those times there were a number of individuals standing on the threshold of Christianity, men who were no longer pagan, for they had abjured heathenism, neither were they Christians, for although they had enrolled themselves among the catechumens, they

---

* Tertull., *De Pœnitentia.* Cyprian, *Epist.* xiii.

† The catechumenate originally lasted two years, as we see from the forty-second canon of the Council of Elvira, which nevertheless adds : *Si bonœ fuerint conversationis.* Otherwise the time of probation was prolonged ; but in the fourth century the Church endeavoured to abridge the time.

persistently refused to be baptized. In vain did the
Fathers of the Church strive to show them their
inconsistency and their danger; in vain did the
bishops, at the approach of Easter, call aloud to
them: "The great days are at hand; give in your
names, prepare yourselves for holy baptism;" nothing
could awake them from their apathy. Christians in
name, but refusing to undertake the duties of their
calling; neither was obedience to the Church's laws,
nor confession, nor paschal communion enjoined on
them, for they were unbaptized. Sometimes even
they acted with unbridled licence, in accordance with
the sad remark then so often enunciated: "Let them
sin; what matters it? they are not baptized." Believing, moreover, that baptism administered at the
hour of death would purify them from all sin and
ensure their salvation, they staked their eternity on
this hope. Each age has its peculiar temptations,
evils, and perils. This was the evil of that age.
Numbers of men succumbed to it, among the rest
Patricius;* and much time, many prayers and tears

* This abuse awoke the most energetic remonstrance on the part of
the Fathers, especially of St. Cyprian (Epist. xxvi., *ad Magn.*), of St.
Gregory of Nazianzen *(Orat.* xl.), of St. John Chrysostom, *(Homil.*
xxiii. *super Act. Apost.)* &c. The Councils threatened those who fell
into this error with the heaviest punishment of the Church. If we look
through the voluminous records of Christian epitaphs we shall see
how general this abuse was. Catechumens' epitaphs are to be met
with in Boldeti (p. 807), Bosio (p. 433), Mattei *(Mus. Veron.*, p. 480,
No. 3), Perret (pl. vi., xvi., liii.) &c. These epitaphs make mention
of catechumens of all ages : Fortunatus, who died a catechumen,
aged thirty-six, (Lupi, *Dissert.*, vol. i., p. 132) ; Perpetuus, aged
thirty, (Rossi, i., p. 109) ; Innocentius, twenty-three years old,

on St. Monica's part, were needed to persuade him, later on, when almost in the arms of death, to receive holy baptism, and make his full reconciliation with God.

But, notwithstanding its incompleteness, this first step was a source of joy to St. Monica. Patricius was no longer a pagan; he prayed to the true God; he believed in Jesus Christ; and though Monica did not yet see him kneeling beside her at the holy table they frequented the church together, were present at the early prayers and instructions, and after seventeen years of married life began to realize that unity of mind and heart with which, for the sake of their mutual happiness, they should have commenced.

In reading the description of these scenes of antiquity our thoughts involuntarily turn to the scenes enacted at the present day, in this century of ours, which in its agitations and unrest so strongly resembles the fourth century. Who of us that has witnessed similar scenes but has witnessed the same happy results? Who, seeing pious maidens giving their hands in marriage to those who viewed religion with indifference, could refrain from exclaiming, full of alarm: "O God! what will the result be?" Ten years elapse; the thoughtless one takes the first step; he does not practise his religious duties yet, but he begins to pray. Ten more years elapse, and behold!

(Vignoli, *Vet. inscript. rel.*, p. 333); Junius Bassus, forty-three years of age, (Bosio, p. 45); Stratonica, fifty-five years of age, (Corsini, *dissert.* ii., post not. Græc.), &c. It is worthy of remark that most of these inscriptions belong to the fourth century.

he is retracing the almost forgotten road to the church, where his mother led him when a child. Rarely does he die without first acknowledging and adoring Jesus Christ.

O woe of this present age! that a Christian woman must strive so long ere she can make eyes so beloved discern the heavenly light. But also, O grand and sublime benediction of the present day! beside each young man one may some day or other place a young Christian woman as his angel-guardian. Ah! let her not forget the glorious part she has to play; let her remember that she will have an angel's power, if she has an angel's patience, fidelity, delicacy, tender and watchful love, sweet silence, and persevering prayer. A charming writer has said: "The rôle of Christian women resembles that of guardian angels; they have power to guide the world, but to do this they must remain invisible, as do the angels." *

* Ozanam, *Œuvres complètes*, vol. ii., p. 93.

CHAPTER IV. ·

SWAY OF THE PASSIONS.—ST. MONICA IS WARNED OF THE DANGER TO WHICH HER SON IS EXPOSED.—HER BE-HAVIOUR.—AS AUGUSTINE WANDERS FROM THE TRUTH, THE CONSOLATION IS VOUCHSAFED TO MONICA OF BEHOLD-ING PATRICIUS DRAWN TOWARDS IT.—HIS CHRISTIAN DEATH.

370—372.

What impression the scenes we have just related made on Augustine we know not ; probably they made none at all, for there are moments when, as the prophet says, " men, having eyes, see not." At least it is certain that the impression was not sufficiently deep to arrest the course of his passions.

The moment when Monica began to win her hus-band, saw her son free himself from her control. With Patricius the passions had passed their zenith ; with Augustine it was their dawn. He succumbed more and more to their influence ; and in reading the truthful and eloquent pages of the *Confessions,* where Augustine, as a physician watching the progress of a disease, describes and analyses the progress of the unhallowed desires enkindled within his soul, we are filled with alarm, and ask ourselves, not only what will become of his virtue, for alas ! that had already perished, but what will become of his mind, heart, character, and brilliant genius. For of that unholy fire we must say, in the words of Job, "It is a fire that devoureth even to destruction, and rooteth up all things that spring."* It ruins the health, withers the affections, and quenches genius. The chaste ardour of innocent affection; the poetic visions of budding youth; the sense of the infinite; the energies of manhood; the fire of genius, tempered by tenderness and delicacy of feeling; all these are destroyed in the bud.

Who but knows that love, friendship, charity, and pity, are the first to perish amid the universal wreck, —that the heart, that delicate plant, withers even more rapidly than the intellect?† A new and more powerful succour was needed, and since the divine voice, the paternal example, the peaceful atmosphere of home, and the holy perfume of his mother's virtues, had been powerless to restrain Augustine, there must fall on those careless ears the only voice that can effect aught when all others fail. Therefore it behoved that St. Monica should be enlightened as to the real state of affairs; for Augustine had succeeded in deceiving her, and she, like so many mothers who cannot realize the fact of their son's guilt, remained tranquil, regarding him still as a mere child.

It was Patricius who dispelled this illusion, for in some things a father's eye is more quick-sighted and

---

* Job xxxi.

† Vide the fine chapter on *les deux foyers*, in Père Gratry's *Connaissance de l'âme*; or else read Père Lacordaire's admirable discourse on chastity.

discerning than is a mother's. But recently converted, and in many respects so thoughtless still, he,
rejoicing at his son's maturity, without bestowing
a thought on the dangers besetting his innocence,
came in the gladness of his heart, smiling at the
thought of a future day when he might behold himself a grandfather, to announce to St. Monica that
her son was no longer a child. On hearing it she
was much disquieted. Hitherto she had taken comfort in the thought that Augustine was still a child.
Knowing this to be no longer the case, she, trembling
at the thought of passion's dawn, not knowing but
that it had already begun to surge within his soul,
that his innocence would soon be endangered, was
seized with fear. "My father," says St. Augustine,
"was as yet only a catechumen, and that but of
late;" therefore we must not be surprised at his
viewing matters in a more worldly light than did his
saintly spouse. "But in my mother's heart Thou
hadst already begun to build Thy temple and take up
Thy abode. Therefore, upon hearing it she was filled
with deep emotion and fear at the thought of the
dangers awaiting me." * Feelings these, natural
to a Christian mother, who losing sight of her son's
physical beauty and manly strength, thinks but of
his innocence. Thanks to God, that deep anxiety
still exists in the heart of many a Christian woman
of the present day.

She sought Augustine, and whether any avowal on
his part, or her own maternal intuition, disclosed his

Confess., lib. II., cap. iii.

spiritual condition to her, her deep emotion and tears revealed her anxiety as to the state of his soul. She often took him aside, and while walking with him would speak to him of God, of his childhood's faith, of the peace and nobleness of the pure in heart, of the repulsiveness of sin, and the horror with which it should inspire us: but, although these admonitions were uttered with the heartfelt emotion so natural to a mother, and specially so when her heart is full of faith and her son in danger, her words no longer made any impression on Augustine, and as he wished to avoid all further allusions, he began to shun his mother's society, for Monica's anxious, earnest gaze disturbed him.

He would spend whole days in the pursuits of the chase, wandering alone, a prey to those varying emotions which agitate the soul at sixteen, filling it first with thoughts of deep beauty, enthusiastic reveries, then awakening the most terrestrial and sinful thoughts, tossing it hither and thither as a helpless bark at the mercy of every wind and wave. *

When not engaged in hunting, he spent his day in the society of his friends, amid games and conversations wholly unworthy of him. "What is there more disgraceful than theft? In whom is it excusable? In none, not even in the indigent man urged on by want. And yet I wished to commit theft, and did commit theft, not from want or need, but from a loathing to be honest, and a desire to sin. There was a pear-tree near our vineyard, loaded with fruit,

* *De Quantitate animæ,* cap. xxi.

neither tempting for its beauty nor its taste. To shake off and carry away the fruit of this tree, a company of us wicked youths went about midnight, having, according to an unruly custom, been playing till that late hour; and thence we carried great loads, not for our eating, but even to be cast to the hogs. Our only pleasure therein was, that we were doing what we should not do." *

To these childish escapades, which we should not cite but that they were the cause of St. Augustine's sublime philosophising on human depravity and our innate love of evil, and also that they gave birth to his profound reflections on the danger of evil friendships, which friendships often induce us to commit sins which we should otherwise never have committed alone, sinful amusements and conversations were superadded. "When I heard my friends boasting of their infamous actions, and bragging the more, the more reprehensible those actions were, I was ashamed of being behind them in sin, and rushed on headlong, not only for the pleasure of sinning, but that I might be praised for so doing. Is there aught so worthy of reproach as vice? Yet I became vicious to avoid reproach, and when nothing came in my way, by committing which I might equal the most wicked, I pretended to have done what I had not done, lest I should be esteemed more vile by how much I was the more chaste. Behold with what companions I was walking in the streets of Babylon, and how I wallowed in its mire!" †

* *Confess.*, lib. II., cap. iv.   † *Confess.*, lib. II., cap. iii.

It is easy to follow the growing anxiety that filled St. Monica's heart. Not content with confiding her fears to God in fervent prayer, she never ceased to instil into her son's ears the most urgent counsels and penetrating, powerful admonitions. On one occasion she took Augustine aside, and "with great solicitude admonished me to keep myself pure, and above all, to respect the chastity of others, and never disturb the peace and union of married life by my own disorders." *

How rapidly do the passions strengthen and develope themselves within the human soul! This amiable youth, possessing so much natural elevation of character, and so warm-hearted, with such a mother, whom he loved with a love so tender and so true, has hardly heard the voice of passion, when he turns a deaf ear to his mother, and begins almost to despise her. "My pious mother's admonitions seemed to me but the admonitions of a woman, which I should be ashamed to obey. Thus was she despised by me; or rather, it was Thy voice, O Lord, that did speak to me, and in her was despised by me." †
Then the veil fell from Monica's eyes, and she experienced a mother's first and heaviest sorrow. What tears she shed! What counsels she bestowed! What ardent prayers did she send up to heaven, entreating God to save and protect her Augustine, whom she was now powerless to protect!

And yet, twenty-five years later, Augustine, in scrutinising his mother's conduct at this critical

---

* *Confess.*, lib. II., cap. iii.   † Ibid.

juncture, after noting her counsels, prayers, tears and vigilance, is of opinion that she did not do all she should have done to save her son; that severe measures were needed; that all, even his studies and future success in life, should have been sacrificed rather than let him proceed in such a downward career. "That mother of my flesh admonished me to be chaste; but after what my father had discovered to her in me, she should have taken more energetic measures to destroy my evil inclinations, or restrain them within the bounds of conjugal affection, if they could not otherwise be cured. She did not care for this method, for fear my hope should be hindered by the fetters of a wife; not that hope of the world to come, which my mother had in Thee, but the hope of proficiency in learning, upon which my parents were too intent: Patricius, because he scarcely thought of Thee at all; and Monica, because she believed those studies would be no hindrance, but prove steps to raise me nearer to Thee. Instead, therefore, of using a wise severity towards me, the reins of my evil inclinations being let loose, I was wholly at their mercy." *

Thus does Augustine speak of his mother; and because she contented herself with weeping and lamenting over this first dawn of passion, he says that "she walked yet with a slow pace in the paths of virtue." †   O my God! what shall we then say of so many Christian women, who show such weakness with regard to their children, closing their eyes to

---

* *Confess.*, lib. II., cap. iii.   † Ibid.

their feelings, making such ready excuses for their vices, not understanding that, next to forming her child's conscience, a mother's first duty is to watch over, guard, and, be the cost what it may, preserve it from destruction!

Meanwhile, the funds necessary for the prosecution f Augustine's studies having been collected, Patricius urged his son's departure; but Monica was full of disquietude, feeling on the one hand how needful it was to remove Augustine from the monotonous, idle, and dangerous life he was leading at Tagaste, on the other hand fearing to send him alone, so far away, to a city so corrupt as Carthage then was. Nevertheless she was obliged to accede to her husband's wishes; and, a prey to anxious feeling, but striving sometimes to reassure herself that close study might perhaps prove beneficial in diverting Augustine's mind, she accompanied him to Carthage about the close of the year 370, that is to say, at the re-opening of the schools. History tells us nought of the tears she shed, nor of her tender, urgent exhortations as to purity and fidelity to the faith; nor of her emotion at parting from such a son under such circumstances; all this we can readily imagine for ourselves.

Carthage, re-constructed at the most brilliant epoch of Roman civilization, was, in luxury and riches, one of the first cities of the empire, yielding the palm neither to Antioch nor yet to Alexandria. Being of more modern date, it wore that aspect of newness which is more attractive in the eyes of the many than of the select few. It possessed a fine harbour, recently constructed by Augustus, fine quays, long, straight, airy streets, watered by fountains and thronged with people. One of these streets, the Celestial street, was filled with temples; another, the Bankers', glittered with marble and gold. Farther on, were large manufactories of precious stuffs; corn, fruit, and cattle-markets; money exchanges, the noise and bustle of an industrial and commercial city animated by the old Carthagenian spirit. The cultivation of letters was not neglected.

In taste and feeling more Latin than Greek, the intellectual movement that had its birth in Rome, found its centre and home in Carthage, even as the Grecian intellectual movement had found a home in Antioch, and especially in Alexandria. Its schools, recognised by the long white curtains floating at the door, were both numerous and renowned; grammar, rhetoric, and philosophy were taught there; all the youth of Africa, so intelligent, but so thoughtless, frivolous, and uncontrolled, assembled there, demanding a professor to-day, and to-morrow rushing into his class, maliciously or wantonly breaking all they could lay hands on. These unruly *élégants*, whose example was so readily followed by the other students, gloried in the name of *eversores, overthrowers, noisy fellows.*

To this love of letters was joined that of art: the master-pieces of Grecian and Roman art were represented in her theatres; but Sophocles and Euripides, Terence and Plautus, did not suffice her; gladiatorial combats, and combats with wild beasts were also to be met with in Carthage, and such was the people's eagerness for spectacles of this kind, and so high the betting, that these exhibitions usually terminated in quarrelling, fighting, and often in riot too. This suffices to give some idea of the morals of Carthage, for in this respect she even rivalled Rome.

Such was the city where Augustine arrived at the age of seventeen, endowed with a lively imagination, consumed by passions at present only in their bud, dreaming of that enchanted cup in which at that early age one expects to find happiness, and fully resolved to drain it to the very dregs. What were the perils of Madaura compared with the seductions of Carthage? And if the innocent Augustine so readily succumbed at Madaura, what will become of the guilty Augustine in Carthage?

He created quite a sensation in the schools; was already master of several languages; had a singular aptitude for philosophy and metaphysics, an ardent love of study, a taste for poetry and beauty of every kind, and a natural eloquence which welled forth spontaneously from the depths of his lofty, loving soul. He astonished his fellow-students and masters even, and every one prognosticated that he would one day be the glory of the Carthaginian bar.

His reserve, timidity, and retiring disposition lent him an additional charm; his countenance, daily increasing in beauty, bore that stamp of candour so becoming in natures of a superior order, and which is at once the mark and accompaniment of true talent. Such was the impression he produced on those around

8

him: but he humbly avows that inwardly he was quite the reverse; that he dreamed of glory, was ambitious of attaining eminence in the legal profession, and that the modest exterior with which nature had endowed him, and which he never lost, concealed a soul more and more intoxicated with self-love. He tells us, "By this time I was head scholar in the school of rhetoric, and this filled me with pride and self-conceit; though much more modest—O Lord, Thou knowest it!—and far removed from the ways of those whom they call *eversores.* Amongst these I lived with a shameless bashfulness, because I was not like them; with these I conversed, and was delighted with their friendship, but abhorred their doings, their *eversions* as they call them, by which they impudently fall on bashful strangers, embarrassing them and taking malicious pleasure in their uneasiness. Such were my companions in the study of rhetoric, in which, from vain and ambitious motives, I desired to excel."*

Great as were Augustine's vanity and ambition, they were the least grave of his faults; he was more diseased in heart than mind. A vague indefinable feeling of unrest had succeeded that first terrible awakening of the passions, a feeling more dangerous perhaps than any he had yet experienced. His soul, void of the Divine Presence, longed for something wherewith to appease its hunger, but knew not where to find it. He was a prey to an indefinable

* *Confess.,* lib. III., cap. iii. and iv.

feeling of disquietude. Consumed by vain desires, he had reached that perilous moment, ordinarily the fore-runner, and frequently the herald, of a lamentable fall. "I was not yet in love," he says, "but I longed to love; and this desire was so strong within me that I wandered through the town seeking out one to love, viewing those localities with disgust that promised no recompense to my search." He adds these sub-lime words: "There was a famine within me of that superior food which is none other than Thyself, O my God; and yet that famine did not cause hunger in me, for I was without any appetite for incorruptible aliments; not that I was full, but because the more empty I was, the more I loathed this kind of nourish-ment. Therefore my fainting soul, sick and full of ulcers, miserably broke out, asking solace of earthly things. I desired to love and be loved, and that with an affection that should know no bounds."*

Augustine was poor, unknown, a unit in that large city, but he was young, elegant, agreeable, of polished manners,† and therefore likely to fall into the snares in which he was so desirous to be taken prisoner. The theatrical representations in which he took such delight from the moment of his arrival in Car-thage aided his downward career. The stage had an irresistible charm for one of his ardent imagination, and of a sensibility so extreme that the perusal of a beautiful poem, or the recital of a love-inspired act of sacrifice, moved him even to tears. "These represen-

---

Confess., lib. III., cap. i.   † *Confess.*, lib., III., cap. i.

tations filled me with delight, abounding as they did with prototypes of my own misery, and fuel for the flames that were consuming me."* On quitting these scenes, so full was he of their beauty, so moved by the sacrifices he had witnessed, that his one desire was to find a heart ready to give and receive the same pleasures and devoted affection which he had seen so well depicted.

Alas! the search for this was prosecuted even in the church, for in those early days he always frequented her services; but it was only in body that he was present, or rather he went there with a heart full of passionate desires, and eyes that sought for some object that would respond to them. I know not what occurred, nor what sacrilegious enterprise conducted him to church, nor what was the chastisement God inflicted on him, for he alludes to it but very briefly and vaguely. " I also dared, in the celebration of Thy solemnities, within the walls of Thy church, to give way to a sinful thought, and drive on even there the trade of procuring the fruits of death; for which Thou didst chastise me severely, but nothing comparable to my crime, O Thou, my exceeding great mercy, my God, my refuge from the terrible ones among whom I wandered with outstretched neck, wandering farther and farther from Thee, loving my own ways and not Thine, and in love with a fugitive liberty. † "

Some authors have supposed that it was in that church, and at the foot of the altar there, that Augus-

* *Confess.*, lib. III., cap. ii.   † *Confess.*, lib. III., cap. iii.

tine encountered that which he had for so long a time
desired to find. Whatever the case, the sad fall was
not far off. "I was entangled in those snares in
which I had so long desired to be taken captive. O
my God, with what gall didst Thou in Thy kindness
besprinkle those sweets! I loved; I was loved; and
encircled by the fetters of those mournful pleasures,
I experienced burning jealousies, suspicious fears,
angers, and quarrels."* Who this young girl was
who, forgetting God for Augustine, even as Augustine
forgot God for her, captivated such a heart for fifteen
years; following him by land and sea, to Tagaste,
Carthage, Rome, and Milan; who never parts from
him until the moment of his conversion, when she
takes her leave of him, bathed in tears, and then, to
further her own conversion, enters a convent, finally
consecrating herself to God, we know not. A delicate
reserve has made Augustine conceal her name; she
appears in this history as a veiled figure. It is
probable that Augustine concealed her name still
more assiduously from his pious mother, as well as the
chain with which he had fettered himself, and which
no tears or entreaties on Monica's part could have
persuaded him to break. However, the day soon
arrived for the disclosure of this painful secret, for in
the year 372 Augustine's son was born, the brilliant
Adeodatus, to whom, later on, in the days of his
penitence, he dares apply no name save the son of
sin; but whom, in those days, in the first thrilling
moments of his guilty passion, he named Adeodatus,

* *Confess.*, lib. III., cap. i.

The Gift of God. " Such, then, was my life, if life it can be called, O my God!"*

When Monica heard of Augustine's irregularities, so profound was her grief that it threatened to overwhelm her. Her tears flowed day and night; she could not even restrain them in public, and at times the place she had occupied in church would be found bathed in tears. The Church commemorates St. Monica on the 4th of May, and this feast may be truly termed the commemoration of a Christian mother's tears, which form the key-note of the office for that day:

Anthem 1st.—This mother wept and prayed assiduously to obtain her Augustine's conversion.

Ant. 2nd.—O blessed mother, whose prayers shall one day be fully granted! Meanwhile she wept both day and night, did this afflicted mother, and interceded earnestly for her son.

Ant. 3rd.—Behold her, this widow, who knows how to weep; she who sheds such continuous and such bitter tears over her son.

Ant. 4th.—They have raised their voice, O Lord! they have cried aloud, those floods of tears falling from that holy mother's eyes.

Ant. 5th.—She wept immeasurably; this inconsolable mother.

I call this the feast of St. Monica's tears; for the whole office is in this key, and reveals (as we shall

* *Confess.*, lib. III., cap. ii.   † *Brev. Rom.* Aug., May 4.

ourselves see later on) a grief unequalled in the annals of the Church.

Monica had one consolation; she did not weep alone, for in sharing her faith, Patricius began to share her grief also. The new life was dawning, slowly, it is true, for the clouds had been dense, but the sun of virtue and the sun of faith were rising simultaneously.

In her beautiful liturgical prayers,* the Church, and St. Augustine likewise, attribute Patricius' conversion to St. Monica's prayers and tears, and also (we have already had glimpses of this) to the charm and celestial attraction of her ever growing virtues; to her patience, gentleness, and self-sacrifice; to the lowly, unvarying and pure affection with which she met his cold behaviour; to the odour of sanctity of a heart ever offering itself on behalf of her salvation. All this created an atmosphere in which, unknown to himself, Patricius had imbibed the faith. When the good, the beautiful, and the true thus become incarnate in a human being, they exercise a species of sweet, gentle fascination that is irresistible; one must either succumb, or flee.

Happily for Patricius, he yielded. Year by year he had imperceptibly altered for the better, and latterly had totally changed. The Sacrament of Baptism, which he was intending to receive, acting beforehand, made him appreciate the value of purity, the beauty of gentleness; and, sorrowing over the

* *Missa sanctæ Monicæ,* 4 Maii. *Missal. Rom. Aug. Secr.*

past, he strove to obliterate from his saintly spouse's memory the cruel sorrows he had caused her.[*]

It is the privilege of the human heart, that if it has known sorrow a whole life long, let but one drop of love appear in its cup, and all the past is forgotten. So St. Monica gathered up this precious drop, and after seventeen years of married life, their two souls were united in the bonds of that delicate and ennobled affection, which a writer of the present age thus eloquently depicts: "When one has been to a poor fellow-creature a channel of the light that has revealed to him his degradation and raised him from it, this sublime rescue from eternal death sometimes unites these two souls, by virtue of an indefinable attraction born of happiness imparted and happiness received."[†] This charm Patricius and Monica both felt; and the tender love the one experienced for the poor soul she had saved, the gratitude manifested by the other towards that dear, gentle, magnanimous heart which had rescued him, mingling together, formed, on the borders of the tomb, one of those attachments beyond the power of earthly language to describe.

We have no particulars of Patricius' death. He was taken ill, about the year 371, and conscious that his end was near, he earnestly demanded holy Baptism, and received it with equal fervour, after which he peacefully fell asleep, dying the death of a Christian, and assisted by the angel God had given

---

[*] *Confess.*, lib. IX., cap. ix.
[†] Le P. Lacordaire, *Sainte Madeleine.*

him in his wife, and who, by dint of gentleness, patience, tender devotedness, and courageous sacrifice, had reclaimed him from his long wanderings, and led him to God. Let us in thought go back seventeen years, to the time of Patricius' marriage, when nobleness, generosity, uprightness of sentiment, and even delicacy of feeling, for there were all these in the soul of Patricius, were dormant, and as it were buried so deep that no human eye, and not even he himself, could discern them; pride, anger, indifference to religion, and evil passions alone held sway there. Under Monica's sweet influence all had changed. The base passions had subsided; the noble qualities had emerged from the surrounding obscurity and risen to the surface. Light had triumphed over all, irradiating his last moments with their brightest splendour, and illumining his dying brow, effulgent with gratitude and joy. Monica was there, shedding tears of joy and sorrow. Forgetting his past severity and frailties, she mourned to lose him at the very moment when she was beginning to enjoy his love; and, consoling herself by the thought of future reunion, had a place reserved for herself in his tomb, so that she might always repose near him whose soul she had resuscitated.*

Thus did God console His servant amid the sorrow Augustine's conduct caused her. As the latter advanced on the path of evil, Patricius retraced the same. When Augustine began to wander from God, frequented the theatres, following the bent of his

* *Confess.*, lib. IX., cap. xi.

corrupt inclinations, Patricius returned from his wanderings and was enrolled among the catechumens. When, despising his mother's counsels, prayers, and tears, Augustine had fettered himself in the chains of a guilty love, and was on the eve of dishonouring that brow, over which but eighteen summers had passed, by an ignominious paternity, Patricius had demanded holy Baptism, and, renewing his life in the waters of penance, died the death of a Christian. And thus will it be throughout this history, even to the very end. Side by side with each of Monica's sorrows, will be a consolation; and this was her due, since the poignancy of her grief had its origin in the greatness of her faith, and the tears she shed over her Augustine were so profuse, because her love to God was so boundless.

CHAPTER V.

ST. MONICA A WIDOW.—SHE IMPOSES HEAVY SACRIFICES ON HERSELF IN ORDER TO FURTHER AUGUSTINE'S EDUCATION.—ROMANIEN COMES TO HER AID.—IN THE MIDST OF HER HEAVY SORROWS SHE HAS A GLEAM OF HOPE IN BEHOLDING AUGUSTINE'S FIRST GROPINGS AFTER TRUTH.

372—375.

St. Monica had accomplished her first God-given work; she had been seventeen years in accomplishing it; for although a certain degree of obscurity envelopes the whole chronology of this history, the year

371 is assigned as the date of Patricius' death, at which time Monica was about thirty-nine.

In studying the lives of the saints, one thing is worthy of note, and naturally recurs to mind at the present moment; nearly all the great saints have outlived their husbands, as St. Monica, St. Paula, St. Elizabeth of Hungary, St. Hedwige, St. Chantal, the Blessed Mary of the Incarnation, and many others. They enter the marriage state, and continue in it but for a brief period. They taste its joys for a moment, so that they may teach the world to enjoy them aright; then God speedily severs and destroys all that holds them to earth, as if He were desirous to have those hearts solely His; and perhaps also to afford those noble souls, in the afflictions they are counted worthy of bearing, an opportunity of attaining those sublime virtues which can be so rarely practised in the marriage state. It would seem that the happier they are, the sooner are they destined to be widows. St. Elizabeth, for example, was only twenty, St. Hedwige twenty-three, St. Chantal nineteen, when God put an end to the chaste happiness of their married life. St. Monica, it is true, was nearly forty years of age when she became a widow, but the whole of her married life had been strewn with thorns.

And yet, scarcely had she become a widow, when St. Monica began to advance more rapidly in holiness. The beautiful aspirations of her soul, fettered and cramped by marriage, freed now from all impediment, soared higher and higher in the paths of virtue and heroism.

It is uncertain whether or no she received at the hands of the Bishop of Tagaste the consecrated veil and widow's habit with which the Church clothed those who undertook never to re-marry, and who, dedicated to God, were entrusted with many important offices.*

Perhaps the desire of retaining her liberty, in order to be able to aid Augustine, hindered her from consecrating herself in this manner. It is at least certain that, inspired by a sentiment of touching fidelity to her husband's memory, she vowed in her own heart to have no other earthly spouse, resolving to live henceforth for God alone. We learn this from St. Augustine, who in giving us a few traits of his mother,

---

* For the honour and protection of widows, the early primitive Church sought to transform widowhood into a species of consecration to the service of God. St. Jerome terms it the *second degree of chastity.* (Epist. xxvi.) The consecration took place, not in the church, but in the *secretarium* or sacristy. Thenceforth the widow belonged to the Church, who in return watched over her temporal interests; this explains why some Christian widows are described as not having been indebted to the Church for their maintenance: ECCLESIAM NUNQUAM, or NIHIL GRAVAVIT. (Marchi. *Monum. delle art. crist.*, p. 98.) They were employed in certain apostolic ministrations, such as visiting the sick, instructing catechumens, &c. Hence, in their epitaphs we meet with the following expression, so startling to persons unacquainted with the discipline of the primitive Church: VIDUA SEDIT, (she sat a widow thirty years, &c.) VENERIGINÆ MATRI VIDUÆ QUÆ SEDIT VIDUA ANNOS LX. (Marini, *Iscriz. Alban.*, page 195.) On a fragment of stone is the following, met with in Boldetti, (page 452): VIDUA SEDIT. This expression alludes to the seat, *cathedra*, which the widows occupied when teaching, and doubtless many of those in the catacombs were reserved for their use. (Vide Martini, *Dictionnaire des antiquités chrétiennes.*) In St. Monica's day, this occupation had almost ceased, being replaced by the practice of other active works of charity, to which the bishop exhorted the widow in blessing her habit.

as she was at that epoch, adds: "Thou, O Lord, knowest what kind of woman my mother then was, a chaste and sober widow, giving frequent alms, ever obsequious and dutiful to Thy saints, never a single day omitting the oblation at Thy altar; twice a day, morning and evening, coming to Thy church without failing, not for vain gossiping and idle chat, but that she might hear Thy voice and Thou mightest hear her prayers;"* in fact, one of those widows alluded to by Bossuet, who, widowed and desolate, bury themselves and all earthly love in their husbands' tomb, and henceforth, alone on earth, make Jesus Christ the sole object of their affections.†

To this life-long sorrow, the more singularly touching when we remember how much she had to endure on Patricius' account, was joined another grief, which, though happily not enduring, was at this time more poignant than ever: the grief of a mother who sees her son's soul at stake, and can help him in no other way than by her prayers and self-sacrifice; and who, in order that her tears may be the more potent, and the fervour of her prayers proportioned to Augustine's needs, withdrew into solitude, devoting herself more than ever to silence, retirement, to relieving the wants of others, and, above all, to a pure, generous love to God.

She had never cared for riches, and even in the days of her youth despised worldly vanities and

* *Confess.*, lib. V., cap. ix.

† Bossuet, *Oraison funèbre de la princesse palatine;* and *Lettres de piété et de direction,* letter lxxxiii.

pomp of apparel; now she entirely renounced the same, robing herself with that severe simplicity distinguishing those whom St. Paul designates widows indeed. She practised austere mortification; took very little nourishment; her fasts were so frequent and so rigorous as to be unequalled even in those days, when corporal mortification was so courageously practised. On feast days she reluctantly broke her fast, taking food as others take a nauseous draught, so entirely did her son's transgressions, and the sorrows of her Divine Lord, fill her soul with grief.

Her manners were sweet, simple, lowly, frank, bearing the impress of Jesus Christ, and all her words were redolent of faith.*

Love to the poor was one of her distinguishing characteristics; from her earliest years her greatest joy was to wash the feet of travellers, or tend the sick in their own homes. Her unhappy marriage had thwarted, not destroyed this feeling, on the contrary, it had but augmented it; as with a source whose stream is impeded, so with Monica, after seventeen years of repression, the torrent overflowed. Not content with feeding the poor, with her own hands she dressed their wounds and anointed their sores, reverently kissing and bathing them with her tears. The poor, overjoyed with her attentions, no longer styled her mother, but servant. The first name she won by her acts of love and tenderness; the second, by her acts of heroism, and the humble, lowly offices she rendered them.†

* *Boll.*, May 4.   † Ibid.

Among this multitude of poor, afflicted, and sick, were many whom she had tended when a child; to these she devoted herself again, now that she was a widow.*

Her greatest happiness was to tend the sick in their own homes, or in the hospitals, for hospitals were already appearing in the sight of the astonished Roman empire,† and until the day when the Church should people them with those countless phalanxes of Sisters of Charity, which are a creation far more wondrous than the hospitals themselves, God inspired all Christian women with a love of tending the sick, and to widows especially the Church entrusted such duties. They served in turn, both by day and night, so that the sick were never left alone. St. Monica was most fervent in this work, passing entire hours by the sick bed, rejoicing to serve our Lord in the persons of His poor.‡

To this noble, meritorious work she united a second, then more necessary, and one, the duties of which were strongly enjoined by the bishops on all Christian

* *Confess.*, lib. V., cap. ix.; lib. IX., cap. ix.; lib. IX., cap. xiii.

† These hospitals, *nosocomia*, which were first erected during Constantine's reign, (until which time the Church, not having full liberty of action, appointed deacons and widows to tend the poor in their own homes,) differed from the hospitals of the present day, inasmuch as they consisted of an assemblage of small buildings, externally one, but within independent of each other, *domunculæ*, so that each inmate had a separate cell. (Procope, *De Ædif.*; Justinian., vol. I., c. ii.; *Hist. Byzant.*, vol. III.; Gregory of Nazianzen, *Orat.*, III. Vide the new and admirable *Dictionnaire des antiquités chrétiennes*, by M. l'abbé Martini.)

‡ *Ibid.*

women, but especially on widows, the burial of the dead. Nothing so efficaciously contributed to nurture the delicate and tender regard for the dead which the Church was then endeavouring to create in the bosom of her children, as the sight of noble and elegant patrician ladies washing the mortal remains of the poor and the slaves, enveloping them in linen and sweet spices, and even robing them in their most beautiful garments.*   St. Monica followed these noble examples, not only tending, serving, loving the poor, but also with her own hands preparing their dead bodies for the tomb, joyous and proud to render such service to our Lord in the person of His suffering members. She then followed them to the cemetery, and caused prayers to be offered for the repose of their souls.†

There was another work even dearer to her heart, that of training little orphans who ran the risk of losing the faith now that they could no longer learn it at their mother's knee. To these she tried to act a mother's part, bringing them up as her own children, and sometimes even affording them the shelter of her own roof, and feeding them at her own table. Who but discerns here the noblest inspirations of an afflicted and maternal heart? She trained these children for God in order that God might restore Augustine to her. She fostered faith, love, and conscience in these little souls, that God, in return, might

---

* August., *De Civit. Dei*, lib. XII., cap. xiii ; Lactant., *Inst. divin.*, lib. VI. ; Tertull., *Apolog.*, xlii. ; Euseb., *Hist. Eccles.*, VII., xvi.
† *Boll.*, May 4.

preserve faith, love, conscience, and re-awaken divine love in the heart of her son.*

But the most useful, delicate, and noble of all her works, to which she devoted herself wholly, and for which God had specially fitted her, was that of consoling widows and married women.† Alas! the former meet with consolation, even at the present day; but who dreams of consoling the latter, or indeed who could do so? for though no wound is more painful than theirs may be, none is so secret; however poignant the soul's anguish, the lip must ever be wreathed with smiles. How many a hearth where love has never dwelt. How many a union, even sadder still, where the flame of love burnt brightly for a brief instant, then expired, leaving in its stead nought save indifference and neglect. How many a one, envied by the world, whose heart is the home of abiding sorrow. St. Monica, knowing this from her own experience, did her utmost to console these suffering ones, and that with a marvellous success.

Such were some of the works of charity to which she devoted herself; for refreshment, (the Christian, as well as the votary of pleasure, knows what fatigue is,) she turned to the Holy Sacrifice of the Altar, that living and inexhaustible fountain of love and self-sacrifice.

Any one entering the church at Tagaste in the morning would have seen St. Monica there, absorbed in prayer, motionless, kneeling most probably in the same little corner which she so loved in the days of

* *Boll.,* May 4. † Ibid.

S.M.

her childhood, her beautiful, pale countenance furrowed by tears, but radiant with faith and love. Besides regularly attending the public services, she never failed to pay two visits daily to the church, each time spending whole hours in prayer. The sacred Scriptures were her constant study, especially the Psalms, which she watered with her tears.[*]

She had a tender devotion for the saints, and martyrs especially, often making pilgrimages to their tombs, or to the scenes of their heroic deeds. On their feasts she, according to the custom of that time, carried her little basket of bread and wine to present before their altars. She placed it on their tomb, then, after tasting of the bread and wine, and thus, according to the prevalent idea of the time, sharing in the merits and virtues of the saint, she distributed the remainder to the poor; careful not to participate in the abuses which were already beginning to bring this ancient custom into ill repute, and which eventually caused its prohibition. St. Augustine says: "Therefore, when she had brought her basket, furnished with the accustomed provisions, she first tasted, and then distributed the rest, reserving only one small cup of wine, tempered with water, for her sober palate to take a little taste thereof. And if there were more memorials of the dead that it was thought proper to honour in the same manner, the same cup served her for them all, which being now not only much diluted with water, but also hot with carriage, was by small sippings divided between her

* Confess., V., cap. ix., and Boll., May 4.

and her companions; for it was devotion she sought there, not pleasure."*

She was present daily at the holy Mass, communicating with the utmost reverence and loving fervour; God bestowing on her, both in her communions and prayers, many great graces, among others, the gift of tears. She was often lost in extatic rapture, especially on those days when the Church celebrates the great mysteries of our salvation, none of which moved her so deeply as did the mystery of our Lord's Passion. The thought of Jesus on the cross overpowered her with grief.†

One day, while contemplating in church the mystery of the redemption, and striving to comprehend the immensity of the benefits flowing from the Saviour's Passion, God filled her soul with such abundant light and love, and her eyes with such floods of tears, that, almost fainting, she hastily left the church in order to conceal the grace she had received; but it was too late: her tears welled forth in torrents. The people thronged round, trying to console her, imagining her tears to be tears of grief; but at such times human comfort is in vain. Her heart having just received one of those deep wounds which the love of God sometimes inflicts on souls worthy to receive the same, her tears, in lieu of drying, did but flow in greater abundance.‡

This is the sole trait of the kind that has been preserved; but what an horizon does it not present

---

* *Confess.*, lib. VI., cap. ii.
† *Boll.*, May 4.   Ibid.

to our view; what virtues and what union with God does it not reveal! Bitter is our regret at possessing no further details of a life that must have been so full of beauty, and this regret we shall experience more than once. What would we not give to know something of St. Monica's life of prayer; of the details of her mortifications and penances (which must have been so severe in the days of her son's wanderings); her unworldly spirit, home virtues, and self-denial. It is as though God desired to reveal nothing of the daughter, spouse, servant of the poor, and contemplative; He has only revealed the mother.

Trial did but strengthen her; and this was the case with regard to the trying circumstances in which she was involved by her husband's death. His small means, and the expenses incurred in providing for Augustine's education, left his widow in a position of great embarrassment. Monica cared little for this, as far as she herself was concerned. She desired poverty; and the poverty imposed on us by the force of circumstances is, in saintly eyes, superior to all else; but Monica was a mother, and though accepting privations herself, wished to shield her child from them. Besides, what a pity it would be for Augustine's studies to be interrupted, his future marred, and he himself compelled to return to the idle, monotonous life of Tagaste, a life destructive alike to body and to soul. She would make any sacrifices rather than allow this.

At that epoch Augustine was realizing, or rather, far surpassing his friends' fondest hopes. The success he had attained in literature was nothing compared to that with which his philosophical studies had been crowned. It was now evident that the noblest gift with which he had been endowed was neither his eloquence, admirable though it was, nor his exquisite sensibility, nor his charming, keen, and brilliant intellect. One sovereign gift eclipsed the rest; and precisely at the very moment, in the year 372, when Monica was a prey to the anxieties of a mother who finds herself unable to complete the education of her son, this gift manifested itself in dazzling brilliancy, and in the following manner.

Whilst engaged in pursuing his literary studies, Augustine had frequently heard the professor of rhetoric mention Aristotle's *Categories*, as a work so deep that only by the aid of the most skilful masters, and by means of figures traced in the sand, could its metaphysical obscurities be fathomed. Eager to make acquaintance with so extraordinary a work, and unable to wait patiently until the due time when it would be explained to him, he at once began its study. To his great surprise he found no difficulty in comprehending it; followed its most difficult problems with ease; and when, later on, he was present at the public explanation of the same, found he had nothing to learn. He read, unaided, all the works on dialectics, geometry, music, and arithmetic; finding no difficulties whatever, or rather, not until he tried to explain them to others, for then he was astonished to see how difficult of comprehension they were to persons of the greatest intelligence; only a very few minds, and those of the highest order, could follow the author, and that only afar off.[*] Though but nineteen years of age, it was evident that he would one day possess that eagle-gaze which the most brilliant light would be powerless to dazzle, and that strong and mighty wing for which no summit would be too lofty.

His true character and disposition unfolded themselves simultaneously with his genius. The waywardness and capriciousness of childhood had disappeared, and was replaced by the most winning gentleness. He grew in modesty and reserve; disliked publicity and display; shunned the wild frolics of his fellow-students; was staid in his demeanour; keenly alive to honour; and most grateful to his benefactors. Tenderness of heart was his characteristic trait.

It was now easy to judge what his external appearance would be, and what the casket that would enshrine that lofty genius. He was of middle height, of that fragile and delicate constitution and nervous temperament which, according to St. Gregory of Nazianzen, are characteristics of chosen souls; his complexion clear and transparent; his eyes piercing, but tender, sweet, and expressive. His weak voice and throat, contracted and delicate chest, denoted him as more fitted to rule by persuasion than by force; more fitted for intimate, affectionate, persuasive converse in the bosom of chosen friends, than for eloquent harangues in the midst of tumultuous

* *Confess.*, lib. IV., cap. xvi.

assemblies. His whole appearance was most graceful and distinguished.*

Had Monica been worldly-minded, these gifts and this brilliant genius would have elated and filled her with pride; but beneath that fair exterior she discerned the fearful havoc made by sin; its rapidly spreading wounds; her child's conscience and soul in deadly peril; all this overwhelmed her with the most poignant grief. Moreover, she saw that with virtue faith was declining too; the clouds that had their origin in the heart, (for it is there they ever take their rise,) were already beginning to obscure the intellect, and it was easy to prognosticate that after having forsaken the path of virtue, Augustine would deny the faith; or rather, there was no need of prediction, for he had already fallen from one abyss to the other, and to the loss of virtue had succeeded that of faith. "What, then, did my wit profit me, which was so quick in acquiring those sciences, and without any man's help understood so many knotty books, when I had so foully and sacrilegiously erred in the doctrine of piety? Far happier were the lowly and simple ones, who never strayed like me, but

---

* Such is St. Augustine as depicted in an ancient portrait, carefully preserved at Milan, representing him as he was in early youth, prior to his conversion, and at the time when he was professor of rhetoric in that city. *Il ritratto*, nous apprend un excellent juge, *celo presenta vestito in una forma, che in volgo dice* MANICHÆA, *ma veramente propria, o di quei tempi, oper lo meno de' paesi dell' Africa; nè è molto dissimile da quella chè anco ne' nostri giorni si costuma general-mente in Levante. Il colore è vermiglio tendente al fosco; la fronte stessa; lo sguardo penetrante si, ma dolce e sospeso · la struttura del corpo ristreita e gentile.* All his writings corroborate the above.

rested in the nest of Thy Church, that they might be safely feathered there."*

Monica watched the course of this terrible malady, but without yielding to discouragement. She had faith in God, and also in Augustine's magnanimous and tender heart; faith also in his vigorous, lofty intellect. Therefore, hoping that science would lead him back to God, rather than see his studies interrupted, she resolved to make the greatest sacrifices, and undergo the strictest self-denial, in order to defray his expenses in Carthage. But alas! all these were of slight avail. Monica bore this new grief as she bore many another grief, secretly and silently, when a friend of Patricius, (one of the leading citizens of Tagaste, whose name should be handed down to the most remote posterity, encircled with the gratitude of the Church and of the whole human race,) Romanien, divining Monica's anxiety, came to her relief, and with the greatest delicacy offered to assist in defraying the expenses of Augustine's education.

Romanien was very wealthy; but richer still in that he possessed a noble, generous, and tender heart, allied to a fine and noble mind.† He discerned Augustine's genius; and in order to diminish the latter's expenses, offered Monica a house belonging to him in Carthage.

How pleasant it is to oblige persons of Augustine's disposition. Throughout his writings he breaks forth

* *Confess.*, lib. IV., cap. xvi.
† August., *Contra Acad.*, lib. I., cap. i.; lib. II., cap. i. and iii.

in cries of gratitude. "O Romanien! how could I refrain from thanking thee? Was it not thou, who, when I, young and poor, was about to proceed to a distant city, in order to pursue my studies, opened to me thy house, purse, and above all, thy heart? When I lost my own father, didst not thou console me by thy friendship, counsels, and fortune? Yes, it was thou who, in our little town of Tagaste, shed the first ray of glory on my path, by publicly honouring me with thy friendship, and by offering me the half of thy house."*

This delicate generosity made even a deeper impression on St. Monica; she never forgot it; and during the thoughtless, perilous days of her son's youth, she watched over Licentius with the most tender love, and vigilant, jealous care; desiring to act a mother's part to the child of one who had acted a father's part to her Augustine.

Aided by this timely generosity; his passions partly appeased by the guilty connections he had formed; and possibly rendered more thoughtful by the death of Patricius, for in spite of the error of his ways it was almost impossible for such a heart and mind as his to be deaf to the lessons of immortality and virtue that ever proceed from a parent's tomb, Augustine resumed his studies, urged on by his mother. This eminent woman, who seems to have had a firm presentiment that science would lead Augustine back to God, (believing that whatever elevates man, draws him nearer to his Creator,) was too discreet to place in his

* *Contra Acad.*, lib. II., cap. ii.

hand the Sacred Scriptures, which at that epoch would have been distasteful to him, or the writings of the Christian apologists, which his weak faith might have failed to comprehend, but urged him to the study of ancient philosophy; and under pretence of polishing his style, impressed upon him the necessity of constant study.*

These maternal exhortations, the bent of his own genius, and the natural course of his studies, led him, about the year 373, to peruse Cicero's *Hortensius*, in which the grand orator explains and discusses the different systems of philosophy, throwing light on them all, putting aside, or rather, crushing those petty sophists who had compromised true philosophy by their subtilties, or dishonoured it by trading thereon. Turning to the teachings of Plato and Socrates, he hymned in harmonious and eloquent strains that sublime and noble philosophy which raises the heart to God, lifts it from earth, and of which Socrates has so truly said: "Philosophy teaches us how to die." Cicero is one of the three or four most eloquent men this world has ever produced, men in whom greatness of soul is united to beauty of language: for this is eloquence; the language of a soul enraptured by all that is beautiful and good. True, that in Cicero's case the outer garb is so voluminous and dazzling that the vulgar mind stops to admire it, but beneath that brilliant garb there dwells a soul far exceeding it in every kind of beauty.†

St. Augustine was in ecstasies. His feelings under-

---

* *Confess.*, lib. II., cap. iv.   † *Confess.*, lib. III., cap. iv.

went a sudden change; despising the world, fortune, ambition, success, and glory, he began to turn his thoughts to God. "The reading of this book changed my disposition, and turned my thoughts to Thee, O Lord, quite altering my inclinations and desires. The world appeared vile in my eyes, and I longed after immortal wisdom with an incredible ardour of heart. I now began to arise that I might return to Thee, O Lord!"*

Had all this happened a year sooner, what might not Augustine have become! He might have unfurled his wings, and soared upward to the Light. But at the time of which we write, his fettered soul had lost her heavenly aspirations. For not only the gospel, but Plato, whose exponent Cicero is, declares the good to be father of the Light; that the soul which aspires after God must have love as its motive power; and that this act, which he so admirably styles *the movement of the wings of the soul,* implies morality and purity of heart; and that the soul developes her wings only by the practice of virtue.†

And although Augustine had not courage to break his chains, he ardently sought for wisdom. " How intensely did I long to fly from earthly things to Thee, O my God! allured by the love of wisdom, and desiring to find it. For I was much pleased with that exhortation of Cicero; it excited, enkindled, and inflamed me, not to seek after this or that sect,

---

* *Confess.,* lib. III., cap. **iv.**

† Gratry, *De la connaissance de Dieu,* vol. I., ch. ii.; *Théodicée de Platon,* p. 51.

but to love, seek, pursue, and lay hold of wisdom itself."* This state of mind continued for several
months, and was the first of the momentous crises
through which Augustine passed in his search after
truth.

Besides the grave reason already alluded to, others
conspired to cool Augustine's ardour in the study of
ancient philosophy. A few months sufficed to make
him acquainted with the whole system of ancient
philosophy, as regards the nature and existence of
God, the soul, and the universe; what struck, and
eventually discouraged him, was the uncertainty of
all these systems. He sought for light, light in its
entirety; and found nought save a few sparks and
glimmerings; nothing decided, certain, or complete:
for all depended on the reasonings of a single individual, or rather, all depended on himself; for amid
this chaos he had to grope after the truth contained therein, thus standing to himself in the
relation of both teacher and judge. In essaying this,
he found what seemed true to-day would appear false
on the morrow; each day brought him fresh light,
and often fresh doubts too: so that, tossed hither
and thither on the waves of doubt and uncertainty,
embracing a shadow where he expected to find
truth, as a thirsty man to whom only an empty goblet
is proffered wherewith to quench his thirst, he began
to doubt whether truth existed there, or at least,
whether it existed in the degree of certainty that he
desired.

* *Confess.*, lib. III., cap. iv.

Another reason led Augustine to renounce this study. He was delighted with much that he found in these writings as regards God, the soul, the Infinite, the good, the beautiful, the true; but the most beautiful of all, Jesus Christ, he found not there. "This name my tender heart had imbibed with my mother's milk, and deeply retained it in my inmost heart. And where this name was lacking, no book, however learned or eloquent it might be, fully contented me."* The reader knows why; the fibres of his heart, while still an infant in the cradle, had vibrated in unison with his Christian mother's heart; and henceforth would respond to no name save that of Jesus Christ.

Thirsting for true wisdom, and fully persuaded that it could not be found apart from Jesus Christ, Augustine opened the Sacred Scriptures. But, alas! if Plato failed to lead him back to God, how could the Gospel do so, seeing that it demands from its students, humility, purity of heart and peace? the proud mind is unworthy of understanding its mysteries, and the troubled heart cannot do so, therefore Augustine instantly closed the book. "I opened the holy Scriptures, and behold I met with an edifice into which the proud will never enter; low in its entrances, with lofty vaultings and mysterious depths; nor was it such as I could enter into, for I would not bend my neck so low. That simple language seemed to me unworthy to be compared to Cicero's writings, for the swellings of my pride could not bear its humility, and the weakness of my sight did not penetrate into the

* *Confess.*, lib. III., cap. iv.

interior thereof. Since then I have learned that this doctrine adapted itself to little ones with whom it would have grown, but in my pride I disdained to be a little one, and imagined myself some great one."* Elsewhere, he says with yet more humility: "Learn from my experience. In my youth I tried to read the holy Scriptures: but my guilty life rendered them unintelligible to me; and as my heart was not pure, I could not fathom their depths."†

Wondrous fact this, and one which should suffice to prove the divinity of the holy Scriptures. Neither intellect, science, genius, nor love of knowledge, have ever sufficed to penetrate into the deep and tender mysteries of Christianity. Humility, purity of heart, and above all, love, are indispensable to a right understanding thereof. And this for the simple reason that they are mysteries of love, and consequently, of humility, purity, and sacrifice. Therefore we must wait until one ray of these noble virtues illumines Augustine's heart; then the book he closes now will be reopened to-morrow, and the first line he peruses will draw from his eyes those floods of tears which have immortalized his memory even more than his genius has done. But this morrow is as yet far off.

In studying Augustine's character at the age of nineteen, it was easy to perceive that he would not at once return to the true faith; to do so it was requisite that he should purify his heart, and break the guilty ties that bound him: this he had not

---

* *Confess.* lib. III., cap. v   † *Sermo* 65, *De Diversis,* cap. v.

courage to do. But it was equally easy to see that he would never return to paganism nor to purely pagan philosophy; for there are abysses into which those souls never fall who have known a Christian mother's training, and if any false teaching could for an instant ensnare him in its meshes, it would at least be one in which he would find the name, but not the cross of Christ; one that would speak to his intellect, but not to his heart. And this was indeed the case.

CHAPTER VI.

THE MANICHEAN PHASE.—FAILING TO COMPREHEND THE CHRISTIAN DOCTRINE, AND THIS THROUGH WANT OF PURITY AND HUMILITY, AUGUSTINE FALLS INTO THE SOCIETY AND ERRORS OF THE MANICHEANS.—ST. MONICA'S ADMIRABLE CONDUCT.—GOD CONSOLES HER.—IT IS IMPOSSIBLE THAT THE SON OF SO MANY TEARS SHOULD PERISH.

374—377.

There was at that time a doctrine possessing a singular charm for the minds of men. Though ancient, the exact date of its origin is unknown. It consisted of a fusion of Persian, Chaldean, and Egyptian doctrines, which, after Alexander's conquests, and the Roman expeditions to Asia, became tinged with Grecian philosophy. Who was the

author of this fusion it was difficult to say, and
indeed, very few cared to know. Whether or no, an
Arab named Scythian had, more than a century
previously, employed his leisure hours in concocting
it, and, little dreaming of the future, bequeathed it
to his friend Terebinth; whether the latter, trying
to promulgate it, failed in his attempt, and bequeathed it to a rich widow, his sole follower, and
therefore selected by him as his heir; whether she,
being childless, purchased a slave named Manès,
whom she adopted, had educated, and to whom she
bequeathed the doctrine, already a century old, and
as yet unpublished to the world, mattered but little.
Whether conceived or inherited, the doctrine proceeds from Manès. He fanned its dying embers, and
launched it on the world in two different garbs.
First, under a heathen garb, and with marked failure.
Knowing that Christianity had made too much way
for any system ignoring it to succeed, Manès turned
to the Gospel, and adroitly mingling it with the
teachings of the east and west, moulded this renowned system, the most long-lived and most frequently condemned of all; which the emperors
attacked, but could not destroy; which reappeared
in the middle ages, menacing Christian Europe at the
moment when the Church had attained the zenith of
her power; then disappeared from view, but perhaps
still lives. For who can say that there are not secret
societies existing at the present day which ascend by
an unbroken chain as far back as Manès?

It is easy to assert that Augustine was caught in

the meshes of a foolish heresy, the least countenanced
and most unreasonable of all.* In point of fact this
is quite true, for what can be more ridiculous than to
suppose the existence of two eternal principles, the
one good, and the other evil; two gods, irrecon-
cilable enemies, hostile, and yet unable to conquer?
What more absurd than to admit the existence of
two souls in man, the one urging him to commit
good, the other evil? What can be more absurd and
immoral than this? It would not do to tell man
openly that he is urged on by a fatal necessity, lest
he should rejoice in feeling himself set free from all
responsibility and freedom of action, and startle the
world by the depth of his corruption. Undoubtedly
this was Manès' real doctrine, but he took care not to
present it in this light. Only truth is of such perfect
beauty that she needs no veils. Error always has
recourse to them, in order that she may not be seen
in her true light, borrowing them from the age in
which she takes her rise, and from the ideas and
passions of men. Knowing what was the condition
of the human intellect and of society in the fourth
century, it is not difficult to say whence arose the
incontestable charm of this heresy.

Christianity had just roused the human intellect,
which, weary of examining problems it could not
solve, had sunk into indifference, or found amuse-
ment in sophism. Strengthened and renewed by
this light, the mind eagerly turned to those questions which have so deep and lasting an interest for

* Tillemont, *Hist. Ecclés.*, vol. xiii., p. 18.

mankind at large: God; the soul; the fall of man; the struggle between good and evil; the world's future; the definitive triumph of truth. On all these points a host of strange, profound, and perilous systems had appeared from time to time during the three preceding centuries, in which systems were to be found the ancient oriental ideas regarding the struggle between good and evil; the Pythagorean doctrines touching the soul; those of Plato on the purification of the heart; in fine, all the traditions of the east and west united and harmonized, they said, in Jesus Christ. For each of these systems, and that of Manès in particular, the latest born, and fashioned more in accordance with the teaching of the Gospel, treated of Jesus Christ. The Messiah's advent, the Incarnation, redemption by the Cross, illumination by the Holy Ghost: all this, interpreted, it is true, after their own fashion, formed the basis and chief pivot of Manès' system.

It not only treated of those eternal questions, God and the soul, but of the temporal question too, the social condition of the world. Its sufferings at that epoch have rarely been equalled, and every doctrine that ignored its woes, or offered not a remedy, would have met with no response whatever. Therefore Manicheism announced the reform of the world; a complete amelioration in its laws, manners, and institutions; an immediate and complete regeneration by the speedy effusion of the Holy Ghost. Rather a mystic doctrine, we must avow, and one which would seduce but few at the present day; but which met with a ready welcome at an epoch when nothing more was to be hoped for from human interference, and when the world, discouraged, and seeing that the efforts made by the Christian emperors were not more availing than those of the pagan Cæsars, felt that God alone could raise it from its abyss.

Such was Manicheism. A system of philosophy; theology; religion; a form of worship; with the perspective of a social reform, complete and near at hand. Doubtless there was a want of logic in these inharmonious ideas; but does logic govern the world, or is it a favourite with her? Doubtless there was in this chaos much that was silly, but it was mingled with much that was sublime; lofty aspirations, with ignominious results! a divine but unattainable goal, consequently just what is needed to enchant the unreflecting, daring minds of youth. Show them a grand idea, a noble aim; and to attain it they will, without perceiving it, swallow the most monstrous absurdities.

To all these seductions, add the still greater charm of successive and mysterious initiations; for Manicheism was a secret society. The doctrine was propounded, not in its entirety, but partially and by slow degrees; so that a solution of every difficulty might be hoped for at some future day, when the revelation should be complete: it also favoured the concealment of the profound corruption of manners dishonouring the sect, by only raising the veil gradually.

But this was not the greatest snare. The right of

private judgment was conceded; there was no authority to which the intellect was compelled to bow. St. Augustine says: "The stern, dread authority of the Church was ridiculed and set aside." They believed only what they liked to believe. The right of private judgment was erected into a dogma full a thousand years before Luther's day.

How all-seductive must this have been to a youthful mind, weary of the yoke of authority, and glorying in human reason ;* thirsting after truth, but wishing to find it for himself;† ardently desiring the solution of the grandest problems, but never dreaming that their solution is found in Jesus Christ;‡ consumed by passions, and yet not sorry to find a doctrine that dispensed with repentance, by robbing him of remorse.§ These seductions ensnared Augustine, for he turned a deaf ear to the teaching of the Church, and fell a ready victim to their wiles. Without consulting his mother, he, unknown to her, publicly abjured the faith of his childhood, and had his name inscribed on the list of auditors, this being the first initiatory degree in admission to the sect.

Let us reflect a moment, to contemplate the change that had taken place in Augustine, before the completion of his twentieth year. One trembles at the sight, so rapid and so alarming is the growth of the passions! At the age of sixteen their voice makes itself heard; he does not stifle them, so they increase in strength, and at nineteen they have bound him

---

* *De Utilitate credendi*, cap. i. p. 35.   † *Confess.*, lib. III., cap. vi.
‡ *Ibid.*, cap. iv. .   § *Ibid.*, cap. vii. and viii.

in the chains of a guilty paternity, and plunged him into an ignominious depth, from which he will not emerge for fifteen years. As his heart grows corrupt, his intellect becomes obscured; the clouds thicken; faith is quenched. He seeks the truth, and no longer discerning it in the Church, because truth can only be discerned by the pure in heart, he casts himself headlong into a gross heresy, in whose meshes he will struggle for nine miserable years. He has not attained his twentieth year, and is already fettered by the ties of a guilty connexion, and ensnared by a false doctrine. "O eternal King! behold, such are the objects Augustine prefers to Thee, by which his noble soul is dazzled, his mind darkened, and his heart blinded!" would Bossuet here exclaim.*

The year 374 is assigned as the date of Augustine's admission into the ranks of the Manichean catechumens. We shall see later on why he never rose beyond those ranks, into which he brought the ardour, sincerity and zeal which marked his search for truth, and which were his safeguard and shield amid the different errors which he embraced. He made himself the apostle of Manicheism; promulgated it wherever he went; challenged the Catholics to conferences, which challenges they accepted, and in which conferences, unhappily for them, and more unhappily for him, success was on his side, for these triumphs inflated him still more and more, gradually leading him to incur the most fatal danger to which those

* *Oraison funèbre de la princesse Palatine.*

are exposed who wander in the mazes of false doctrine: the danger of self-will and obstinacy.*

As may be supposed, the majority of Augustine's victims consisted of his friends and fellow-students,† who were seen grouping themselves around him, bound to him by ties of the deepest affection, evoked by the infinite charm of his intellect and manner, and the ardour of his love. We have already made acquaintance with Romanien; later on we shall do so with each one of his friends: the chaste and gentle Alipius; the youthful and admirable Nebridius;‡ and Honoratius, the inmost depths of whose soul were stirred by the mere name of truth. How fervently were they loved by Augustine, and how glowing the terms in which he described the joy he felt in their society! " Sweet intercourse of friend with friend; to read pleasant books together; to jest and then be grave together; to dissent from one another sometimes, without ill-will, as a man would do from himself, and by this disagreeing in some few things, to season as it were and better relish our agreeing in many others; reciprocal instructions; regrets for the absent, joyous welcomes to those who returned. These and such like signs, proceeding from the heart and expressed by the eyes, lips, and acts of such as mutually love one another, were the fuel that melted souls and fused them into one."§ Such was Augus-

---

* August., *De duabus Animabus*, cap. ix.

† August., *Ad Prosperum et Hilarium*, lib. II., cap. xx.; *Confess.*, lib. IV., cap. i., and lib. III., cap. xii.

‡ *Confess.*, lib. VII., cap. vi.   § *Confess.*, lib. IV., cap. viii.

tine's heart. He loved much, and therefore was much beloved; his ascendancy over his friends was so great that the major part left Africa to follow him to Rome, Milan, Ostia, &c. When once he was known, it was impossible to live apart from him, therefore it is no wonder that his friends were seduced by his teaching. Nearly all succumbed to its pernicious influence: Alipius, Honoratius, Nebridius, and Romanien, too, whose death will so soon overwhelm Augustine with such profound sorrow.

None of Augustine's movements escaped Monica's watchful and anxious gaze. She had seen his faith perish with his virtue; and whatever hope she may have cherished in seeing love of truth and contempt for terrestrial things awakened within him by the perusal of the *Hortensius,* must have vanished when she beheld the disgust with which he closed the holy Scriptures, his proud self-confidence, and his disdain for the Church's authority. She watched the restless heavings of this sea of passion in her son's heart, as a mother who, standing on the shore, sees her son a prey to the angry billows, and who, hearing the rending sails and shivering anchors, knows shipwreck to be inevitable, and yet is powerless to avert it.

But when she heard of his apostacy, and the friends of Alipius, Romanien, and of that other young friend (all three natives of Tagaste,) came to her weeping, and told her of his zeal and obstinacy in heresy, who shall depict her astonishment and grief? St. Augustine seeks a simile whereby to make us comprehend their depth, and after using countless forms of speech to express the abundance of his mother's tears; after comparing them to overflowing rivers, and finding that simile too weak, finds no other grief wherewith to compare hers, than the grief of a mother at losing her only son. " For she looked on me as dead, by the faith and the spirit which she had from Thee; and therefore she bewailed me with deeper grief than mothers weep for the corporal death of their children."[*]

On learning this sad intelligence, St. Monica did more than weep. Tears might suffice, when Augustine's heart only was in fault, and conscience and faith still burnt brightly, encouraging Monica to hope; but now that, not content with offending God by his crimes, he denies Jesus Christ, and apostatizes from the Church, tears no longer suffice; the hour had come, when, in order to save her child, she must employ all the weapons with which God arms every mother.

The vacation was at hand, and Augustine was on the eve of returning to Tagaste. St. Monica resolved to learn the truth from his own lips, for she could not believe it possible that her son was indeed guilty, so she hoped against hope. But when there was no further room for doubt, and Augustine re-entered his paternal abode with the proud air of a sectarian, at the first allusion to his heresy, (maternal duty, how sternly terrible thou art!) St. Monica recoiled with horror, with indignation, I was about to say,

---

[*] *Confess.*, lib. III., cap. xi.

for she felt herself wounded in her holiest and dearest feelings. Her love for God, her attachment to the Church, her affection for her wandering son, the fear of losing him eternally, her detestation of heresy, all combined to urge her to one of the noblest and most energetic acts in the annals of Christianity. She drove Augustine from her house, declaring that she would neither allow him to remain beneath her roof nor sit at her table; and detesting the blasphemous doctrines he professed, full of that sublime wrath which invests a mother with such irresistible author- ity, she commanded him never again to set foot in her house. Such behests are not to be disobeyed; with bowed head Augustine quitted the maternal roof, and withdrew to Romanien's house.

It was a stern and cruel necessity that compelled Monica to act in this way, and unless aided at once by God, no mother could resist succumbing beneath the heavy burden of sorrow consequent on such a step. So was it with Monica; her whole being seemed shattered by the heavy blow, and no sooner had Augustine taken his departure, than Monica, who so loved him that she could not forego the happiness of seeing him, even for a single day, throwing herself on her knees, gave free course to her tears, and called on God for help.[*]

God heard her prayer, for soon after, probably during the night succeeding that sad day, our saint, exhausted by her grief, fell asleep for a brief moment, and dreamed as follows: " She saw herself standing

* *Confess.*, lib. III., cap. xi.

upon a certain rule of wood, and a beautiful young man coming towards her, cheerful and smiling upon her who was so sorrowful and spent with grief. He accosted her, enquiring the cause of her sorrow and tears, with intention to instruct her, and not learn from her. Monica having replied that she bewailed her son's loss, he bid her be easy, and pointing to the rule on which she was, added: 'Where you are, there is also your child;' upon which, looking, she perceived me standing by her, upon the same rule." He adds: "Whence was all this, but from Thy ears being open to the cry of her heart?"

Overcome by emotion, Monica ran to Romanien's house in search of her son, to whom she joyously related her dream. Augustine listened attentively, for he knew his mother's veracity too well to doubt her words, which, however, he tried to interpret to his own advantage. He told her that the meaning of the vision was this: that what he was, Monica would also be at some future day. "No, not so, for it was not said to me, Where he is, thou wilt be; but, Where you are, there will he be."* Full of hope, certain now that God would restore her son to her, when the measure of her tears was full, humbly accusing her own lack of self-sacrifice and fervour in prayer, she withdrew the prohibition that had cost her so dear, and reinstated Augustine in her own home.

This was about the year 374, during the September vacation. Soon after, Augustine, having attained his twentieth year, and completed his studies, left Car-

* *Confess.*, lib. III., cap. xi.

thage; and until the time arrived for his entering the legal profession, towards which his talents and tastes attracted him, he settled in Tagaste, where he opened a grammar school.* But alas! he returned not alone, and although Monica had withdrawn her prohibition, it was impossible for him, accompanied as he was, to return home, therefore he accepted Romanien's offer, and took up his residence in a house belonging to this generous friend, and in which he resided during the time of his stay at Tagaste. But he was constantly at his mother's house. He says: "My mother's affection for me was so great, that she could not endure to see me sad, nor pass a single day without seeing me." Also, notwithstanding his passions and obstinate heresy, Augustine was one of the most affectionate, attentive, and respectful of sons.

Both mother and son carefully avoided all discussion: the latter, from filial respect; the former, because this was her constant line of action, and also because, in Augustine's case, she relied more on the efficacy of her prayers than on controversy. "Whilst I lay wallowing in that mire of the deep, and in the darkness of error," writes St. Augustine, "that chaste, devout, and sober widow, (such as Thou lovest, O Lord!) more cheerful indeed in her hopes, yet no ways slacker in her sighs and tears, ceased not in all her prayers to bewail me in Thy sight. Her prayers were favourably received by Thee, although the hour was not yet come for me to emerge from the darkness in which I was involved."†

* Possidius, *Augustini Viti*, cap. i. † *Confess.*, lib. III., cap. xi.

But though Monica abstained from all controversy, partly from her lowly opinion of her own powers, and partly from a reluctance to wound Augustine's feelings unnecessarily, she looked about for those whose talents and authority might win them a ready hearing with her son, entreating them to enter into controversy with him, and show him the truth and beauty of the Catholic faith.

One day she heard of the arrival of a venerable, learned bishop, (whose name has not been handed down to us,) deeply versed in the Christian mysteries and in the holy Scriptures, and who in his early years had been a partisan of the Manicheans. Joy of joys for Monica! She hastens to find the holy man, fully convinced that her vision is on the eve of realization. She tells him the story of Augustine's wanderings, entreating him to save her child. But this venerable man, skilled in the knowledge of the human heart and the discerning of spirits, shook his head, replying that the time had not yet arrived; alleging that Augustine was as yet indocile, and puffed up with the novelty of his heresy. " Let him alone," said he, " only pray to our Lord much for him." Then, to console Monica, he related his own history, telling her how he himself, when a little one, was by his deceived mother given to the Manicheans, and when older, had not only read, but transcribed almost all their books, and in doing so had of himself found out, without any one disputing with or convincing him, how much that sect was to be abhorred, and had therefore forsaken it; adding, " so will it be with your son." But St. Monica, not being satisfied, but still importuning him with many tears that he would see Augustine and discourse with him, he said to her, " Go your way; it is impossible that the child of such tears should perish."[*]

These words seemed to Monica as an oracle from heaven, and sank into her inmost heart. They were indeed heaven-sent words, intended for her consolation, and for that of all Christian mothers similarly situated ; and, but for our readers' anxiety to learn the termination of this history, we would endeavour to indicate briefly how much light, comfort, and deep instruction are hidden in these simple, beautiful words, " It is impossible that the son of such tears should perish."

In our opinion the venerable bishop's words have a two-fold sense. First of all, these words had their birth in, and sprang from faith; from a clear insight into God's goodness, tenderness, mercy, and infinite love for man; from the impossibility of God's turning a deaf ear to any human being who suffers, weeps, and prays. If a human being can move his fellow-creature to sympathy, it is impossible but that the Creator will heed His children's cry. And if ever the day came when man should cease to pray, one voice would still be heard,—the voice of a mother bewailing her child ; and if ever the day came when God should swear never more to listen to human prayer, there are certain tears that will ever find a ready welcome with Him,—the tears shed by one who weeps over

---

[*] *Confess.*, lib. III., cap. xii.

the impending loss of her child's soul. How shall
God resist a prayer so sublime, pure, unwearied,
unselfish, affecting, and, if I may be allowed the
word, divine? Shall this cry move the hearts of
savage beasts to pity, and fail to move the heart of
God? If so, how could He be the great and good
Being in whom we hope, even when all else has failed
us? Ye mothers, whose sons have gone astray in
the paths of wickedness and folly, blame not heaven;
blame yourselves; strike your breasts; weep that
you know not how to weep; and rest assured that
your wandering sons will then be restored to you,
when the measure of tears demanded for your son's
ransom shall be full.

Such is the first meaning of those words, "Impossible that the son of such tears should perish."

They also have another, and, in our eyes, far more
beautiful signification, discernible by the moralist
and the man versed in the knowledge of the human
heart. "It is impossible that the son of so many
tears should perish," might be rendered thus, "It is
impossible that the child of such a mother should
perish." As if the aged prelate, seeing that weeping
mother, had said within himself, "Impossible that
the work of such a mother should perish. The conscience she has enlightened never can remain in
lasting darkness; some sparks of the sacred fire
enkindled within her own heart must have been
transmitted to his; a mother of such deep faith,
inspired with such a horror of sin, and loving God
with so pure and intense a love, must have created

depths within her son's soul safe from the reach of passion.

"Doubtless he may wander for an instant, seduced by the ardour of youth and the temptations peculiar to the age; but even should he forget the faith of his infancy, forget his mother's God, or apostatize from her faith, ah! let her not be discouraged; the fire is there, though hidden; the arrow is in the wound; beneath the scorching waves of passion there will ever remain, in a conscience moulded by a Christian mother, some one of her lessons, and some ineffaceable traces of the faith, as a beauteous vase of alabaster that has once held a precious perfume, returns its fragrance, happen what may."

Such was the meaning of those words. Monica went home, meditating on them; and as we sometimes see the last ray of light still the winds and clear the sky, so these simple words, uttered by aged lips, joined to the vision she had seen, began to appease her anxiety and revive her hope.

Moreover God added other signs, which Augustine has not thought fit to reveal to us; "precious pledges, which Monica treasured in her heart; a kind of promise signed by the hand of God, which she presented to Him incessantly in her prayers, to remind Him of His word."*

* *Confess.*, lib. V., cap. ix.

CHAPTER VII.

THE REMNANT OF THE SACRED FIRE.—ARRIVAL OF FAUSTUS.
—POWER OF A MOTHER'S TEARS.—AUGUSTINE ABJURES
MANICHEISM.

377—383.

If we study Augustine as he was at that time, we
shall see how accurate was the aged bishop's opinion.
His mind and heart had wandered from their allegiance, but were not hostile to God. A remnant of
the sacred fire was still smouldering within the inmost recesses of his conscience. Faith was no longer
there; but probity, honour, nobleness and delicacy of
sentiment, love of truth were: and even amid the
sway of passion there remained within his soul a
certain modesty which, as a fragrant balm, prevented
the corruption from being irremediable. These were
the *handles*, to use St. Francis de Sales' words, by
which God would one day seize and save him.*

Much is said of St. Augustine's irregularities, but
we must understand them aright, and not allow ourselves to be misled by the language he in his humility
made use of. Doubtless there was much amiss with
heart and will, but he had not descended, and never
did descend, to those degrading excesses from which

* *Traité de l'amour de Dieu,* part I.

there is rarely any return, and which prove the grave of honour, fidelity, and self-sacrifice, as well as of conscience too. Observing an inviolable fidelity to the mother of Adeodatus,* and devotedly attached to the latter, (born in the twentieth year of his father's age,) whom, after the manner of so many young men, it would have been extremely easy for him to disown; he, for their sakes, devoted himself to arduous labours, that marred his future and wearied his mind. "He retained," expressively says M. Villemain, "dignity of soul in the very midst of the passions with which he has so bitterly reproached himself."†

Though Augustine had wandered from the truth, his mind was as little depraved as was his heart. The heresy he had embraced and promulgated among his relations and friends had only been accepted and preached by him because he deemed it true. "O truth, O truth, how did I then sigh for thee from the inmost depths of my soul, when they were often repeating thy name to me in many ways, not by word of mouth only, but by their writings also. I hungered for thee, and such were the empty husks they offered wherewith to appease my longings."‡ And again, "O my God, (to Thee I now confess, who hadst pity on me when as yet I did not confess,) in striving to find the truth, it was Thee I sought, but I sought Thee afar off, whereas Thou wert more

* *Confess.*, lib. IV., cap. ii.

† *Tableau de l'Eloquence chrétienne au iv. siècle*, p. 378.

‡ *Confess.*, lib. III., cap. vi.

interior than what was most intimate in me, and higher than what was highest in me."*

This is what God discerned in Augustine's conscience. He clung to error, but loved and sought for truth alone.

True it is that pride had her dwelling in his soul. Conscious of his own genius, he, desiring to soar aloft on eagle-wing, and dazzle the world by the splendour of his intellect, thirsted for glory and for the victor's wreath, and the applause bestowed on the successful candidate for the prize in poetry. But nothing would induce him to attain his wish by dishonourable means. " I remember also, when I had undertaken to try upon the theatre for a prize in poetry, a certain soothsayer sending to me to know what I would give him that by his help I might overcome, I repulsed him full of horror."† He won the prize notwithstanding, and was publicly crowned in the theatre by the Proconsul Vindician, probably about the year 378.

The same rectitude and loftiness of sentiment were also discernible in the manner in which he fulfilled his duties as professor of grammar and of rhetoric. Deep was the degradation into which the divine art of speech had fallen. This, the noblest of all arts, demanding, if I may be allowed the expression, as much virtue as genius, had been shamelessly degraded by the sophists; some ridiculing it, others trafficking in it, and all influenced by mercenary motives. Such a spectacle was revolting to Augustine, whose aim it was to restore

* *Confess.*, lib. II., cap. **vi.**   † *Confess.*, lib. IV., cap. ii.

language to her pristine use, that she might be the pure organ of truth, virtue, justice, and right, all of which the world so often sets at nought and tramples underfoot; this was the noble office for which he desired to train the youths entrusted to his care.*

Such was Augustine at twenty-two; enslaved by error, fettered by the chains of a guilty love; an alien from the true faith, and rushing headlong to perdition; but still retaining some remains of those sentiments, which, even in his early years, had been instilled by his mother: elevation of mind, dignity, delicacy, devotedness, fidelity, in fine, all those virtues which, though they do not palliate his serious failings, plead in the culprit's favour, and often win his pardon. "Thou, O God, whilst I was staggering on my slippery way, didst behold some sparks of probity and honour amid the dense cloud enveloping my soul."†

St. Monica, who amid the profound grief awakened by the sight of her son's passions and errors, had so much need of hope, and who eagerly sought for the faintest promise of amelioration on the part of her child, now received fresh proofs that the sacred fire was not quenched in Augustine's heart. The unexpected death of one of his young friends awoke such a torrent of tears that to those cognizant with the human heart it was evident that Augustine's case was not hopeless. Where the passions reign supreme, the heart dies, and none is so callous to the pure, sweet, and delicate joys of friendship as he who

* *Confess.*, lib. IV., cap. ii.   † *Id.*, ibid.

has lavished his affections in the excesses of guilty love. "In those years when I first began to teach in my native town," says St. Augustine, "I had a friend whom similarity of age and studying together had much endeared to me. We were of one age and flourishing in the bloom of youth. From childhood we had grown up together: went to the same school, played together, though at that time he was not so great a friend as afterwards, nor indeed was he so later on, according to the rule of true friendship; for that only is true friendship that subsists between those whom Thou, O Lord, unitest by the charity shed abroad in our hearts by the Holy Ghost."[*]

After quoting the venerable prelate's words, the youthful Augustine adds: "But yet that amity was exceedingly sweet, formed by the eager pursuit of the same studies. For he also had renounced the true faith, of which he had but an imperfect knowledge, perverted by me, who had imbued his mind with those superstitious and pernicious fables, for which my mother was bewailing me. In his mind he was going astray with me, nor could my soul be anywhere easy without him."[†]

For more than a year this sweet union had subsisted, when his friend was seized by an illness which eventually proved fatal. Burning with fever, he lay for a long time unconscious, bathed in that mortal sweat which precedes and heralds death, so that his recovery being despaired of, he was baptized in that state; for he, as the majority of young men of that

---

[*] *Confess.*, lib. IV., cap. iv.   [†] Ibid.

day, was only a catechumen. Of this, Augustine was an indifferent spectator, persuaded that a little water sprinkled on his friend's body would be incapable of effacing the sentiments with which he had imbued his mind. "Therefore," he goes on to say, "as soon as I could speak with him, (which was as soon as he could speak, for I departed not from him, so great was our intimacy,) I was inclined to jest at what had occurred, expecting that he would do the same, now that he had recovered consciousness, and had been acquainted with the fact of his baptism. But he repelled me with horror, as if I had been his enemy, and with a wonderful and unexpected frankness, adjured me, in the name of our friendship, to speak no more to him in that manner."*

Augustine, astonished at these words, was silent, thinking it best to defer giving vent to his feelings until his friend had recovered strength and was in a fit condition to listen to his arguments. But it being God's will to rescue this young man from the impending danger, he, within a few days, and during Augustine's absence, was again seized with an attack of fever, which proved fatal.

We should never have known the depth of Augustine's overwhelming grief, and the tears he shed at his friend's death, had he not recounted them himself. "Sorrow for his loss filled my soul with gloom, investing everything with the hue of death. My own country became insupportable to me, and my father's house a wonderful misery. All those things in which

* *Confess.*, lib. IV., cap. iv.

we had taken pleasure together were now unendurable to me. I missed him continually; all was a void to me now that my friend was no longer there, and no one henceforth could say, as heretofore in his absence, Behold, he will soon return. Life became a burden to me, and tears were my only solace."*

In vain did his mother seek to comfort him, and his friends to alleviate his grief: no ray of light illumining his gloom, no heavenly succour at hand to alleviate his grief, he sank beneath its weight. " I was restless, sighed, wept, and was distracted, bereft of ease and counsel; for I carried about with me a soul all wounded and bleeding, impatient to be any longer carried by me, and where to lay it down to rest I knew not. I no longer took delight in pleasant groves, nor in plays and song, nor in fragrant odours and banquets, nor in sleep, books, and poems. I loathed everything, even the very light, and whatever was not my friend was insupportable to me, save sighs and tears, for in these I found some slight alleviation."†

The place where they had lived together became unendurable to Augustine, who felt indignant at seeing the routine of daily life proceeding as usual. He says: " I wondered that the rest of mortals could live, now he was departed whom I had loved as if he were never to die; and much wondered that I myself, who formed but part of him, could live when he was gone. Well does that poet express himself who terms his friends the half of his soul; for I felt that

* *Confess.*, lib. IV., cap. iv, † *Confess.*, lib. IV., cap. vii.

my soul and his were but one soul in two bodies; and therefore I loathed life because I was unwilling to live by halves."*

Fears now began to be entertained for Augustine's health. He was wasting away with grief, wept the live-long day, and was incapable of any exertion. Seeing that something must be done to divert his thoughts from his recent loss, Augustine's friends advised his leaving Tagaste and returning to Carthage. He consented, hoping that change of scene, the stir of a larger town, and the absorbing occupations awaiting him there, might prove some alleviation to his grief.†

This second separation was a fresh trial to St. Monica; for though she was doubtless content to see him leave Tagaste, for the sake of his health, she trembled at the thought of his return to Carthage, where he had lost both faith and purity, and where she feared the few remaining gleams of the sacred fire might be extinguished within his soul.

Fortunately, the school of grief is a grand one, and especially so for a noble soul. Augustine returned to Carthage, not converted, far from it; not even disenchanted nor roused from his illusions; for it appears that ambitious motives made him resolve on returning to that city. Yet he had learnt something of the vanity of this world. Job's complaint had risen to his lips, and he began that grand death-

---

* *Confess.*, lib. IV., cap. **vi.**

† Possidius, *Vita sancti Augustini*, cap. **i.**

chaunt which purifies the soul ere its first notes have died away.

It consists of two parts. The first is in the minor key. It has for its theme the transitoriness of terrestrial things, the unsatisfactoriness of worldly joys. This was Augustine's theme on setting out for Carthage. " O my God, what save grief can the soul find in this world, who seeks beauty and rest apart from Thee? Vain is the beauty of creatures. They have their rising and their setting. In their rising they begin, as it were, to be ; they grow up towards perfection, which, when they have attained, they fade away and perish, for all things fade and die. So that when they rise and tend towards their being, the more speedily they advance to be, the more haste they make not to be. Suffer not my soul to cleave to them, O Lord, for they flee away, leaving the soul wounded that clings to them......She would fain take her rest in the things she loves; but she cannot rest in them, for they never stand still, but haste away, are incorporeal, and cannot be retained, and no sooner do they appear than they begin to vanish."*

Such is the first part of this funeral hymn, which is beneficial to the soul who knows but this half, and regards the world in this sorrowful light. What must it be to him who soars still higher, and hymns that second part, in which sorrow is swallowed up in joy? Yes, all passes away, but only to return; all fades, but to re-flourish; all dies, but to spring to life and be transfigured anew. Thus did Augustine sing

* *Confess.*, lib. IV., cap. x.

with divine eloquence a few years subsequently, when, converted, baptized, and having attained the sublimest degree in divine love, he had found the secret of life :

"What knowest thou, O my soul? Only a few parts of the whole; thou knowest not the whole of which these are parts, and yet it delighteth thee. Ah! if thou wert capable to comprehend the whole, and hadst not been confined for thy punishment to the prospect only of some small part, thou wouldst have wished for a speedy passing away of all that which at present exists, that thou mightest behold the rest. When thou listenest to what is spoken, thou wouldst not have one syllable stand still, but desirest them to fly away that others may succeed, and so thou mayest hear the whole. So with the world, where things make up one whole, and where, if each individual part delight, the whole would delight far more, could it be perceived all together."*

Such is the grand outlook which comforts and sustains the soul amid this perpetual change. Happy he who gazes from this elevation, and watches this succession with joy, or at least with consolation. At the time of which we write Augustine had not attained this eminence. Only bitter mournings were on his lips. He essayed to raise his gaze heaven-wards, but heaven was empty. He found nought save a phantom powerless to console. What should he do? Drown himself in study in order to find

---

* *Confess.*, lib. IV., cap. xi.

distraction and oblivion? He resolved on this, and taking his pen in hand, composed his first work.

The selection of his subject reveals the upward tendency of Augustine's soul at that epoch, and a certain lull in his passions. He selected "The Beautiful" as the subject of his treatise. What do we love, if not the beautiful? What does the youth seek in his reveries? On what do the thoughts of the aged dwell in reverting to the past? What do we demand from nature, heaven, sea, lofty mountains, man, and art? After what does our whole being sigh? is it not for the beautiful? But in what does beauty consist? And then, with his souvenirs of Plato and Cicero, and all the beautiful ideas which were then beginning to fill his soul, he defined, described, and depicted the beautiful.

This book, which we should like to read, inasmuch as it would reveal to us the mind of Augustine, such as it was in the first bloom of youth, and would also, perhaps, afford us a clear insight into his heart at that time; (he was then commencing his twenty-fourth year,) he could therefore have had no more eager peruser than St. Monica; and we may readily suppose what St. Augustine tells us, that it afforded her some little joy and consolation. At least, it contained nothing that could wound her faith; nothing denoting the sectarian, occupied, as in preceding years, to destroy in others the faith which he had lost; who can say whether its beauty of style, elevation of thought, purity of sentiment, did not strengthen that maternal heart in the belief that such a soul could not remain for ever far from God, who alone was capable of satisfying all its longings? On this point we are reduced to conjecture only, for the work in question has not been transmitted to us; earnest of future eloquence, it has vanished from sight, even as the twilight that heralds the dawn of day, whose absence we regret not when the orb of day ascends the horizon.

To these poetical and artistic studies,—which Augustine reverted to so often, one might say incessantly, during the course of his life,—was united another study, more austere, but very beautiful too; that of mathematics, physics, and astromony, which studies he pursued with his usual ardour, applying his luminous intellect to the solution of their difficult problems; charmed by the relations which he began to discern as subsisting between numbers and art, harmony, music, and poetry also; relations these, which he was destined to develope at some future day, with such originality and depth; enlivening his studies and widening his intellectual horizon by the light of philosophy: thus ascending after the manner of noble minds, and with his own peculiar ease and perspicuity, from art, poetry, astronomy, physics, numbers, and all else, to God, whom he discerned at the basis, middle, and apex of all things. Strange fact, and one that was about to verify his mother's presentiments, for we remember that she incessantly urged him to these noble studies, persuaded that science would one day lead him back to God. And such indeed was the case, for his mathematical and physical researches awoke within his mind the first doubt as to the truth of Manicheism. It occurred thus.

With his doctrinal teachings respecting God and the soul, which, erroneous though they were, were yet not devoid of the charm of novelty as regarded his mode of explaining the eternal problems of human destiny, Manicheus had interwoven (for what reason is unknown,) a number of notions respecting astronomy, the equinoxes, solstices, and eclipses, which he asserted had been divinely revealed to him with his other doctrines, but which, having been extracted from ancient authors, and compiled by an unscientific person, were manifestly false in many respects, and this, recent discoveries and the most accurate observations on the part of Roman astronomers had fully proved. Augustine's surprise was overwhelming. "Who inspired this man to write about things of which he was ignorant? What confidence can I now have in him? If I can detect his errors in these matters within, how shall I trust him in those which are beyond my ken?"*

A more close examination awoke within him the most formidable objections to the Manichean doctrines. Moreover, the doubts as to the truth of this teaching, awakened by a certain Helpidius, who, during his recent stay in Carthage, had openly attacked Manicheism, and proved its falseness, not only from its own teachings, but from certain passages in the Old and New Testament, redoubled and threw

* *Confess.* lib. V. cap. v.

him into a state of profound anxiety. Five years previously he had relinquished the study of ancient philosophy, because it offered him but shifting sand on which he could erect nothing stable; and now, in the hour of his sorrow, when standing in need of some safe shelter for his wearied soul, Manicheism failed him likewise. Instead of affording him the strong, steady light he looked for, all was pale and flickering, and disquietude filled his soul.

For truth's sake, and also that we may rightly understand that complicated thing called a soul, we must add that the desire of light, certainty, and peace, experienced by Augustine, had its origin in the lower as well as the higher parts of his nature. In reality, Augustine found this heresy a convenient one, inasmuch as it left full scope to his passions, and therefore he naturally desired to remain in it. Feeling uneasy at these rising scruples, desiring to allay them, and fearing to fall a prey to his former anxieties, he resolved to consult the Manicheans. But it was in vain that he submitted his difficulties to the leading members of the sect, who had a reputation for wisdom; none could solve them. Eloquent and clever in refuting their adversaries, the arguments they brought forward in support of their own tenets were weak in the extreme. As skilled hunters lay their snares around a spring, and, in order to attract thither the thirsty birds, drain or cover all the other springs with foliage, the Manicheans thought that in destroying theories opposed to their own, they had done all that there was to do. This method may succeed with ordinary minds, but Augustine's was of too lofty a stamp, and too piercing a ken, not to discern the weakness that lay at the root of all this. His soul, thirsting for infinite truth, which alone could still its desires, finding nothing save vain conjectures, became a prey to restlessness and anxiety. Again and again he returned to the charge; plied the Manicheans anew with his questions, redoubled them; but all in vain.

In order to soothe him a little, and dispel his impatience, the Manicheans announced the speedy arrival of one of their bishops, named Faustus, a man of great learning, who, so they asserted, would dissipate his disquietude, and clear up his doubts. Augustine hailed these tidings with joy, for in reality all he desired was to be confirmed in those false doctrines, which left his passions full scope, and which, by lulling his anxieties, had afforded him several years of apparent, but pleasant calm, which he was unwilling to resign.

As we can readily imagine, Monica's vigilant eye discerned Augustine's restlessness, and rejoiced at it. Keenly alive to hope, as are all mothers, moreover, full of confidence, arising from her dream and the aged bishop's words, so soon as she beheld Augustine restless and agitated, she thought he was converted, and knelt at the altar with a heart in which confidence for a moment triumphed over anxiety. But so soon as she knew of Faustus' arrival, and heard of this dangerous man's powers of fascination, her fears returned. She redoubled her tears, and burying herself in the most profound solitude, multiplying her prayers and austerities, she waited with the anxiety of a mother who feels that her son's fate is about to be decided.

At last Faustus arrived. His fame had preceded him: he was said to be, not only an illustrious orator, but one of those grand and noble souls who give up all for the sake of the truths they preach. He had left father, mother, children, wife, and country, that he might devote himself wholly to the arduous labours of the apostolate. He cared not for gold and silver; was content with daily bread, taking no anxious care for the morrow; was poor, gentle, peaceful, pure, noble, and generous-hearted; and would gladly have laid down his life for the cause of truth.* So the report ran, for later on the fallacy of these assertions was discovered; but as, at the time to which we allude, the truth had not come to light, his two-fold reputation for eloquence and virtue attracted crowds of hearers.

Foremost among these was Augustine. He was enchanted. The intellectual keenness and vivacity of Faustus, the facility with which he expressed his thoughts, his modest and dignified countenance and manner, and the eloquence of his language, charmed Augustine. "I rejoiced with the many, and excelled them in my enthusiastic praise of him."† Later on, he heard St. Ambrose, whose limpid, harmonious eloquence could not efface that of Faustus. "I was delighted with the elegance of his discourse, which,

* *Confess.*, lib. V., cap. iii. and vii.   † *Confess.*, lib. V., cap. vi.

though more learned than that of Faustus, was not so pleasing and winning."*

As we see, the danger was great. Happily Monica was warned, and had recourse to prayer.

When a little recovered from the effects of this dazzling eloquence, Augustine began to reflect and examine, and the first thing that struck him was that Faustus taught nothing new. "When he came, I found him pleasant and agreeable in his discourse, and saying the same thing that others say, only with far more grace. But what relief was it to my thirst to have these beautiful, but empty cups set before me?" Though more brilliant, the arguments of Faustus were not more sound than those of the other Manicheans. He handled difficult questions with greater dexterity, but left them unsolved; and when Augustine, full of anxiety to have one of his doubtful problems solved, beheld it either adroitly avoided or unsatisfactorily answered, he could not repress a feeling of impatience and anger. He would have liked to interrupt him, in order to communicate to him his difficulties, and by conferring familiarly receive answers to his doubts. But then, as now, such interruptions not being allowed, he entreated his friends to obtain him an interview with Faustus.

This was easily arranged, and Augustine exposed his doubts, but on so doing quickly found his rising apprehensions fully verified. Faustus was no philosopher; he was a stranger to all the liberal sciences, excepting grammar, of which he had but an ordinary

* *Confess.*, lib. V., cap. xiii.

knowledge; he had read some of Cicero's orations, a few books of Seneca, some of the poets, the best written books of his own sect; and as he was naturally graceful of speech, by daily exercise of his talent he acquired the eloquence by which he charmed his hearers, and which was the sole charm of his discourses. Augustine was deeply dejected at the result of this first visit. He had so ardently looked and longed for peace, and now saw all that had ministered to his consolation for so long a time melt and fade away.

He made a second trial, and a few days later on had another interview with Faustus, consulting him no longer on philosophy, but science. The reader has not forgotten that the first cause of Augustine's perplexity was the discrepancy he remarked subsisting between the scientific and mathematical calculations of Manicheus and the observations of the most accurate Roman astronomers. The Manicheans could never clear up this difficulty for him, but always assured him that Faustus would do so when he arrived. In this hope Augustine visited Faustus. But the latter modestly excused himself from undertaking the task. "For he was not," says St. Augustine, "like those great talkers whom I had met before, who undertook to teach me, and yet said nothing to the purpose. He was modest and reserved, and though ignorant as regards divine things, was not ignorant of his own ignorance, nor did he blush to avow it to me."*

* *Confess.*, lib. V., cap vii.

8 M.

This behaviour increased Augustine's esteem for Faustus, at the same time that it dispelled his illusions. And since one whom the Manicheans exalted above all others, and whom they declared was a divine being sent to teach them the truth, had been unable to clear up his doubts, he felt convinced that they could never be dissipated.* "Thenceforth," he says, "all my pretensions of making further progress in that sect fell to the ground; not that I quite forsook them, but not finding anything better, I determined to remain where I was until I could discover something more worthy of my choice. Thus this Faustus, who was to many the snare of death, began unwittingly to set me free." †

Who sent this happy ending to a conference apparently so fraught with danger? With his usual promptness Augustine's grateful heart hastens to reply: "O my God, Thou didst not abandon me in that critical moment, because my mother offered Thee day and night for me the sacrifice of a bleeding heart by her incessant tears." ‡

As we proceed in this history, it is well to note the ever growing strength of language in which Augustine alludes to his mother's grief on his behalf. The sight of his early wanderings drew tears from her eyes; now she offers on his behalf a bleeding heart, wounded and broken by the greater peril to which her son is exposed.

After nine years' duration, thus ended the Manichean

* *De Utilitate credendi*, cap. viii.
† *Confess.*, lib. V. cap. vii.   ‡ Ibid.

crisis, that is, the second deadly peril Augustine
had encountered in his search after truth ; and notwithstanding the absence of written evidence, we
seem to discern clearly the admirable line of conduct
pursued by Monica during those nine terrible years.
At the outset she warned him of the fearful danger to
which he had exposed himself, by the holy zeal which
led her to chase him from her roof, and forbid his
reappearing in her presence.   During the whole time
of the crisis, she aided him by her never-ceasing tears,
daily counsels, warnings, by the conversation of
eminent men, theologians, and bishops ; by the acts
of humility, abnegation, and penance, which she
ceased not to offer up on his behalf ; then, after doing
all this when the danger is at its height, she shields
him more efficaciously than she has ever done before,
and saves him by virtue of a cry and prayer so deep
and poignant that Augustine compares it to the blood
poured from a wounded, suffering heart.   Precious
revelations, showing what a mother can do, and what
a mother should do !

Ere St. Monica could rejoice in the victory won by
her tears, she received a letter from Augustine which
awoke deep anxiety within her breast, and prepared
her for greater trials. Augustine was not yet converted, or rather, he was about to fall from one danger
into another more perilous still, from which his mother
would extricate him, but only by dint of increased
zeal, self-sacrifice, prayers, holy abnegation, and a
love for God, and for her son, which was now about to
attain its highest degree.

CHAPTER VIII.

AUGUSTINE'S DEPARTURE FOR ROME.—HIS ILLNESS.—THE
VALUE OF A MOTHER'S TEARS.—NEW CRISIS, MORE
TERRIBLE THAN THE PREVIOUS.—ABSOLUTE DOUBT.
MONICA HASTENS TO HER SON'S RESCUE.

83—385.

Augustine wrote, telling his mother that he had
decided on quitting Carthage and settling in Rome,
not only for the sake of the greater profits and honour
which were promised to him by the friends who had
for some long time persuaded him to take this step,
but chiefly, and in reality, because he was weary of the
disorderly and unruly Carthaginian students, and
hoped to meet with quieter, more attentive and
respectful scholars in Rome. *

Though the motive was good, St. Monica trembled
on reading her son's letter. Separation was painful
enough to one who had never left him, or at least
had remained near enough to hasten to him at the
advent of each new peril; but the thought of his
leaving for Rome was so unexpected that she shuddered at the very idea.

The Rome of that day was far different from the
Rome of later days. It was not yet transformed into

* *Confess.*, lib. V., cap. viii.

that beautiful land, full of holy pictures and quiet domes, whither we turn our steps in order to forget the world, and refresh our souls by the hallowed memories with which it abounds, and the sentiments it awakens. A Christian woman and saint, living at the close of the fourth century, regarded Rome as the persecutor of God's people; the spot whence were promulgated decrees which caused torrents of blood to flow, and doomed millions to a martyr's death; the land where paganism (chased from all other lands for upwards of fifty years) had taken refuge and still maintained its sway; the home of corrupt manners, immoral plays and dances. Jerome had all but succumbed while there, and the remembrance of that perilous Roman society tormented this grand athlete when in the desert, evoking those cries of repentance and alarm which still resound in Christian ears.

What then must St. Monica's anxiety have been! Had Augustine been pure of heart, pious, fervent, she would even then have trembled; how much more so now that faith was dead, his mind a prey to every wind of doctrine, and his soul consumed by passion! She soon resolved on the course to be pursued, for she was a woman of singularly prompt determination, and unswerving in carrying out her designs. She made up her mind that Augustine should not set out for Rome, or that if he did, she would go too, for she had resolved not to part from him in his then spiritual condition.

Augustine had not expected this. He wished to go

to Rome, but alone. He had outgrown that age when
a mother's presence is indispensable to happiness, nor
had he attained the second stage of life, when the
sight of advancing years, and the near approach of a
future that we dare not dwell upon make us cling more
closely to a mother's side, awakening within us a new
feeling, more akin to worship than to love. Augustine
was thirty, and at that age the heart is incapable
of such feelings as those to which we allude. It is
wanting in its early simplicity, and is still too ardent.
Augustine was young, free, enterprising, inexperienced, desirous of knowing more of the world;
therefore he viewed his mother as a hindrance, and
though he loved her tenderly, resolved to set out
alone.

He was not sufficiently quick in carrying out his
arrangements; for whilst preparing for his journey,
Monica suddenly appeared. She had hastened to
Carthage at the first tidings of his project, and resolving to prevent his departure, threw herself on his
neck, clasped him in her arms, and with floods of
tears conjured him not to go, unless he took her
with him. So grievously did she lament his departure that Augustine, not knowing how else to induce
her to leave him, as well as touched by the grief of
her he loved so deeply, promised not to leave Africa.*
But he still went on with his preparations secretly,
and when the time for embarking had arrived, asked
permission to accompany a friend, his intended
fellow-traveller, to the vessel, reiterating his promise

* *Confess.*, lib. V., cap. viii.

not to leave Africa, and saying that he would return as soon as he had seen his friend off. "Thus I told a lie to my mother, and to such a mother," exclaims St. Augustine, "but this sin Thou hast pardoned, with many others."*

Augustine hoped that by deceiving his mother in this fashion she would have remained in the town, and have allowed him to accompany his friend alone to the place of embarkation. But she would not quit his side, and went down with them to the shore.

Night came on. The stormy sea grew calm, but only slowly, still lashing the strand with its angry waves. A land breeze drove all the ships to shore, and the vessel in which Augustine and his friend were to sail was still at anchor, awaiting a favourable wind, in order to set sail and leave port, which they hoped to do the same evening.

Meanwhile, Augustine and his friend paced the shore, Monica remaining near them, to the embarrassment of them both. The hours sped away; day-light waned; the night was dark; and as the wind still remained in the same quarter, Augustine and his friend began to remark aloud, that it was evident they could not start that night; that it was necessary to seek repose; especially so for Monica, overwhelmed as she was with fatigue and emotion. By dint of entreaties, and renewed promises not to quit Africa, Augustine at last induced her to take a little rest.

On the shore, a short distance from their ship, was a little chapel (the ruins of which are to be seen at

* *Confess.,* lib. V., cap. viii.

the present day,) dedicated to St. Cyprian, the illustrious Bishop of Carthage. There St. Monica agreed to retire, for in her condition she felt the need of prayer more than sleep. In that spot she passed the night, praying and weeping.* "And what did she entreat of Thee, O my God!" exclaims St. Augustine, " but that Thou wouldst not permit me to sail away ? But Thou in the depth of Thy counsel, hearing the sum of her desires, didst not regard what she requested at that moment, in order that Thou mightest accomplish the main thing which she always requested of Thee."†

During the night the wind blew fair and swelled out the sails; the anchor was weighed, and ere the first ray of light illuminated the horizon, Augustine, seated on the poop, with his gaze riveted on the little chapel where his mother was praying, saw his native land fade fast away.

When morning dawned, St. Monica quitted the chapel, and finding the shore deserted and the vessel no longer there, became "mad with grief." ‡ She paced up and down the shore, making the sea resound with her cries. She blamed her son. She complained that God had despised her prayers,§ wished to find a vessel in which to sail after Augustine, and if need be, perish with him; then, carrying her thoughts to that stormier world on which he would shortly enter, she, no longer able to contain herself, fell into a state of deep and silent dejection. " For she loved me far more than ever mother loved her child, and she

* *Confess.*, lib. V., cap. viii.   † Ibid.   ‡ Ibid.   § Ibid.

did not know how much joy Thou wast preparing for her by taking me away, therefore she wept and lamented, seeking with sorrow what she had brought forth with sorrow." *

At last, worn out with weeping, crushed and exhausted, after having accused her son of deceit and cruelty, finding it impossible to follow him across the sea, she returned to Tagaste, "there to pour forth those floods of tears with which she daily watered the spot where she prayed for me." †

St. Augustine arrived in Rome in 383, in September probably, during the vacation. We should much like to know what were his impressions on beholding this great city, then in all her splendour. The barbarians had not yet ravaged her, neither had time done more than enhance her beauty by just tingeing her edifices with a hue of gold and bronze. Twenty years prior to the time of which we write, St. Jerome, a young Dalmatian, all but barbarian, had traversed it with vivid emotion; wandering incessantly from the Capitol to the Pantheon, from the Coliseum to the Mole of Adrian, then wending his steps to the Forum, quoting long extracts from Cicero, and even descending to the Catacombs, whither he went with his friends, having Virgil's lines upon his lips:

Luctus ubique, pavor et plurima mortis imago,

Was it so with Augustine? His soul was not less enthusiastic, but of finer mould, more tender, and of an exquisite delicacy. Those grand buildings, with

* *Confess.*, lib. V., cap. viii. † Ibid.

their beautiful background ; those aqueducts, temples, palaces, triumphal arches, proclaiming the power and greatness of its people ; that Campagna, studded with ruins and tombs, speaking more majestically still of the vanity of those who erected them, must have deeply moved Augustine. And if it be true that the sadder the heart the more congenial does it find this spot, the soil of which is composed of the ashes of the departed, Augustine must have been enchanted there.

And yet the year spent there was a painful one for Augustine. The last gleams of faith had disappeared, his hopes had vanished one by one, as autumn leaves.

On arriving in Rome he went to the house of a Manichean to whom he had an introduction, for though he doubted their doctrines, he still associated with those professing them. Whether he lived on more familiar terms with them, or whether, for he had made no mention of his doubts, they were less guarded than they would otherwise have been, the suspicions that dawned on him in Carthage were now fully verified. Most impure morals, scandalous orgies, and a corruption increasing in proportion to the degree of initiation and height of the dignity attained : these quite removed the veil from his eyes ; for this corruption was the result of the most secret teaching of the master, and was justified by him in his most confidential lessons. Augustine's honest heart revolted at this, and he swore that he henceforth would have nothing more to do with any disciple of Manicheus.

This was a grand step ; it seemed that there was

but one more thing to do : lift his suppliant gaze to the Catholic Church, and beg of her that truth which he had vainly sought elsewhere. Had he done so, he might have shortened the sad road he had to traverse ere attaining the truth.

The Church shone then with that beautiful light, slightly mingled with shade, which, for our trial, God only grants His Church in the days of her exile. In some of her members were to be discerned blemishes which cause the impious to smile, and the faithful to weep. But side by side with these shadows, what wonderful splendour !

At the helm of St. Peter's bark was St. Damasus, a holy and a great man. His secretary was the same Jerome whose enthusiasm and failings we have so lately alluded to, and who, changed by penitence, and transfigured by Divine Love, was now beginning to fill the whole Church with his eloquence. The year before Augustine went to Italy, the Pope, in order to solve certain questions which were then agitating men's minds, had convoked a General Council, to which the most illustrious bishops of antiquity hastened : St. Ambrose of Milan, St. Epiphanius of Cyprus, St. Valerian of Aquilea, Paulinus of Antioch, and a number of venerable men of eminent virtue. Therefore, on reaching Rome, Augustine beheld one of those striking proofs of unity, catholicity, and infallibility which God has only granted to His Church eighteen* times.

* Written previous to the Vatican Council, held under His Holiness Pope Pius IX.

From another point of view the Roman Church presented to Augustine's eyes a still more touching sight. Virginity and Charity, those two sisters born on the same day at the foot of Calvary's Cross, still traversed the world, hand in hand, scattering roses and lilies on their way. Even in Rome were to be seen the descendants of such men as Scipio, Gracchus, Camillus, and Marcellus, establishing hospitals, and the noble young maidens, their daughters, tending the sick, dressing their wounds, kissing their feet, thus compelling an astonished world to acknowledge that where such love existed, there was the truth.

And inasmuch as holy souls, whose ardent faith and piety lift them far above this sad world, ever aspire to find guides who will aid them to ascend to still loftier heights, such chosen souls as Paula, Fabiola, Eustochia, and Marcella, were seen grouped around St. Jerome, who expounded to them the Scriptures, irradiating their understandings with floods of light, which, as is ever the case, transformed itself into acts of self-devotion and self-sacrifice of every kind.*

Had Augustine deigned to look around at this sight, he would doubtless have been enchanted. But there are frames of mind when one is blind to all, and frames of feeling when one sees but comprehends not. So fully was Augustine persuaded that the Catholic

* Interesting details respecting the Church at this epoch will be found in a book published by my excellent friend M. l'abbé Lagrange, Vicar-General of Orleans. The title of the work is: *Histoire de Ste. Paule.*

Church held absurd doctrines respecting God and man, doctrines incompatible with reason and subversive of intellect, that he never dreamed of turning his eyes in that direction.* But being sincere, he had for a brief instant thought of consulting some learned member of the Roman Church, capable of explaining to him the true doctrine; but whether from a persuasion that such a step would be unavailing, or from a secret and intuitive dread of the true light and the sacrifices it would entail, he refrained from this step.†

Prejudiced against the Church, convinced by his own experience of the falseness of the Manichean doctrine, remembering that his philosophic researches had been unavailing, he began to doubt everything, and exclaiming bitterly that truth was but a dream, entered one of those schools of philosophers named Academicians, who taught that there was no such thing as absolute certainty.

Strange and miserable sight! Here we have the noblest intellect, the most piercing, lofty, and active mind, seeking for truth through many a long year, and after being tossed hither and thither as a rudderless bark at the mercy of every wind and wave, folding his wings, and giving up the search as hopeless! All around is doubt and uncertainty! no ray of light pierces the gloom, all is but mockery and delusion! Such was the pillow on which Augustine was hoping to rest his weary head, and close his tired eyes. But

* *Confess.*, lib. V., cap. x.   † *Confess.*, lib. V., cap. xi.

nunc, reges, intelligite! Now, O ye mighty intellects, understand; ye who seek for light, give ear!

Can any man find rest in such a state as this? I know not: all I know is that Augustine found none. He was too noble-minded, and though all was not right within, he was not depraved enough to love darkness. Neither the amusements of Rome, nor the intellectual pleasures he enjoyed there, nor the success which crowned his labours, could still the agitation of his soul. A deep sadness overwhelmed him, and as a sick man who, turn where he will, finds ease nowhere, he tossed uneasily on that pillow which could never afford him rest.

So great was his disquietude that a violent fever soon set in, and his life was in danger. "I was going down to the grave, laden with all the evils I had committed against Thee, myself, or my neighbours: many and terrible were they; besides the guilt of original sin, from which I have never been cleansed." Not one suppliant gaze did Augustine lift heavenwards. Twenty-two years before, when he was a little child beneath his mother's fostering wing, all thought of bodily pain was merged in anxiety for his soul. Now that he was grown to man's estate, a dweller in a mighty city, far from his mother's eye, he was about to die impenitent, unabsolved, without Christ and without God; or rather, he was about to die with sarcasm on his lips and impiety in his heart. "I did not so much as desire Thy baptism in that my great danger; and, fool as I was, I derided the prescriptions of Thy medicine. O my God, whither should I have gone, had I died at that time, but into that fire and torments which my deeds had deserved in the immutable order of Thy Providence?"*

Fortunately the fever abated, and in a short time Augustine was out of danger.

As was the wont of that lofty and reflecting mind, which ever strove to fathom the cause of all things, Augustine asked himself why God had delivered him from this peril, and what hand had, at the very moment when he was insulting God, even on the brink of the grave, turned aside the sword of avenging justice. Here, as elsewhere, he ascribes all to his mother. "She did not know I was ill; and though absent, was praying for me. No words of mine can sufficiently express her love for me, and with how much greater pain she travailed of me, to bring me forth to a spiritual life, than she had suffered before at my carnal birth." Then he adds these words, exceeding in eloquence all that the tongue or heart of man can utter: "Thou didst not permit me to die in the state in which I then was, for my death would have been such a wound to my mother's heart that I see not how she would have been cured, if such a sad death of mine had pierced the bowels of her love."†

It is said that a mother never recovers the loss of her child; her sufferings, physical and mental, are irremediable, her grief lasting and inconsolable. What then must be the pangs of a Christian mother who sees her child die guilt-stained and impenitent!

---

* *Confess.*, lib. V., cap. ix.   † *Ibid.*

That saintly heart, so tender that it cannot behold a crucifix or a tabernacle without a lively emotion of faith and love, what must not be its agony at beholding her own offspring, the better half of her own self, for ever separated from the Divine Presence! "No, no," says St. Augustine, "never would my mother have recovered from such a wound." "Moreover," he continued, "what would then become of her many prayers, so fervent, ardent, and unremitting! Or couldst Thou, O God of mercy, despise the contrite and humble heart of so chaste and sober a widow, giving frequent alms, ever devoted to Thy saints, never omitting for one day the oblation at Thy altar! Couldst Thou despise and reject her tears, with which she did not beg of Thee gold or silver, or any fading, perishable good, but the salvation of her son's soul! No, certainly not, O Lord! Therefore didst Thou hear her, and accomplish her request, according to the immutable order of Thy love." *

Augustine, as we have already stated, soon recovered from his illness, and resumed his studies and lessons in Rome. But though health returned, he was still a stranger to faith and happiness; or rather, cherishing universal doubt, persuaded that there is nothing certain in this world, resolved to give himself no further trouble as to doctrinal questions, he grew more and more dejected than he had ever done before.

External troubles now arose. Augustine had opened a free school in Rome, but in spite of his

* *Confess.*, lib. V., cap. ix.

great talent, saw himself surrounded by only a few not over-zealous disciples; this, in addition to the want of delicacy and principle evinced by many, wounded his sensitive spirit, and finally disgusted him with his position.*

He had lost faith in God, he now began to lose faith in men. What a torment for such a heart and mind as Augustine's! At that very time, just as he was about to give way to discouragement, he heard that the chair of rhetoric in Milan was vacant. Such a position as that was exactly in harmony with his tastes. The professor was appointed and paid by the town, and therefore not at the mercy of thoughtless, inconsiderate pupils; the position was an honourable one, and independent, and the emolument considerable. Moreover, the chair of rhetoric in Milan was a noted one, inasmuch as the emperors, by residing in that city, had made it the second capital of the world. Having applied for, and obtained the professor's help, after a public trial of his ability, in which he successfully distinguished himself in the presence of Symmachus, prefect of Rome, Augustine started hastily for Milan, somewhat consoled by the honour conferred on him, envisaging the future less gloomily, but more uncertain than ever as to the truth, he resolved to banish the subject from his thoughts, and consecrate his rare genius wholly to the study of rhetoric.†

Whether or no Augustine's recent letters revealed the sadness of his soul, or Monica's heart responded

---

* *Confess.*, lib. V., cap. xii.　　† *Confess.*, lib. V., cap. xiii.

13　　　　　　　　　　　　　　　　　B. M.

to the secret grief that was consuming her son, she resolved to rejoin him. The journey was long and painful. She had to traverse the Mediterranean, leave home and country, break up old habits, and, as she was poor, she possibly had to sell her little all, in order to provide for the expenses of the way. But what sacrifices can arrest a mother, and such a mother as St. Monica!

She embarked in 385, probably at the very port where she had been deserted by her son a year before; and if time permitted, we may be sure that she repaired once more to the little chapel of S. Cyprian, where she had passed so sad a vigil, entreating that she might not only have the joy of beholding her son once more, but the greater happiness of converting and consoling him.

It seemed at first as if God intended to withhold from her the joy of seeing her son; for scarcely had the shores of Africa faded from her vision, than a horrible tempest arose, lashing the waves in its fury, and threatening to destroy the shivering vessel. The very sailors trembled; St. Monica alone was calm. How was it possible for her to perish until she had seen her son? God would not allow her to die before she had converted her son! of this, her Christian and maternal heart was assured. Therefore she stood erect on the prow of the vessel, calm and composed, reassuring the sailors, and declaring in soul-penetrating accents, that the tempest would soon be over, and the port reached in safety. And indeed such was the case; the winds fell, the clouds dispersed, revealing the radiant Italian shores.[*]

Monica instantly hastened to Rome, impatient to embrace her son, and judge for herself as to his spiritual condition. Imagine her grief at finding Augustine no longer there. He had already left for Milan.

It is probable that Monica started for Italy just as Augustine had despatched his letter to her, announcing his departure from Rome, for we are quite sure Augustine was far too affectionate and respectful a son to have left his mother in ignorance as to his movements; indeed it is highly probable that the mournful tone of Augustine's recent letters, in which he announced the closing of his school and his intention of leaving Rome for Milan, so deeply impressed St. Monica, that she suddenly resolved to set out. Augustine, leaving for Milan sooner than he at first expected, wrote a hasty letter acquainting his mother with the fact, never suspecting that she intended to rejoin him, much less, that she was already on her way.

However great St. Monica's disappointment at not finding her son, she did not hesitate for a single instant. Milan is two hundred leagues from Rome, and the road thither traverses the Apennines; but she had already made a voyage of four hundred leagues across the angry billows, so she started at once, full of her usual ardour, and sustained by the firm belief

[*] *Confess.*, lib. VI., cap. i.

that she would again behold her son and effect his conversion.

This indomitable faith, existing in every maternal heart where Divine Love reigns paramount, was augmented by God in St. Monica's case, so that she might surmount every obstacle, for her presence was indispensable to her son. He was on the eve of the grand crisis which precedes the revival of faith, and was to purchase this happiness by an agony far greater than any he had as yet experienced. At such a moment Monica's presence was imperative; her help indispensable.

Besides this, God had resolved to comfort His servant after so many a year of anguish, disquietude, and tears, therefore He leads her to Milan just at the moment in which Augustine was about to emerge from darkness to light. She had been present at the agony, it was therefore meet she should be present at the resurrection and the glory.

CHAPTER IX.

LAST CRISIS.—DOUBT IS AT ITS LOWEST EBB.—ST. MONICA APPEALS TO ST. AMBROSE FOR AID.—TO ENSURE HER SON'S SALVATION, SHE REDOUBLES HER FERVOUR.

384—386.

Augustine had reached Milan, and entered on the duties of his profession, in the dangerous frame of mind to which we have alluded in the preceding chapter; he had sought for the truth, but his efforts had been unavailing; he had not ceased to love it, but despairing of finding it, he persuaded himself that they were the wisest who believed nothing. Last abyss this, deeper and darker than all others, and wholly unsuited to a mind such as his, but which would hold him captive for two years, and from which he would finally emerge a Christian. And well that it was so, for had it been otherwise he would have been irretrievably lost. Therefore, because of the imminence of the danger, God sent St. Monica to guide him to the light.

And yet, however indispensable her presence at that critical moment, she was not all-sufficient. Maternal hearts are all purity, tenderness, and strength; but, dare I say it? not strong enough nor pure enough to light their children back to God. Such a task as this demands a soul that has received, in virtue of a higher consecration, mightier life-giving powers than hers. That which the mother has begun by tears, the priest must complete by virtue of the authority and Blood of Christ; and the lower the abyss, the more carefully chosen are the Christian mother and the priest who must co-operate in this sublime rescue. Hence the reason why, after allotting St. Monica to Augustine, God prepared for him St. Ambrose too.

The saintly bishop seemed exactly suited to Augustine's needs, and able to understand this restless, sad, and ardent young man, for whom there was as much to be hoped as feared. His early years had been spent in the world, amid study and business; this was the first similitude between Augustine and himself. Then he studied rhetoric, and when quite young had attained considerable eminence at the bar; this was their second point of union. Moreover, though the child of a Christian mother, he remained a catechumen beyond his thirtieth year, even as was the case with Augustine; but he was guiltless of Augustine's doubts, irregularities, and heresies. This very fact probably drew them nearer to each other, for he who has always enjoyed serenity, light, and peace, compassionates and sympathizes more readily with the restless, storm-tossed soul. Therefore we see that (with the exception of Augustine's irregularities,) up to their thirtieth year there had been a strange degree of similarity in their lives. Then an unforeseen event suddenly changed the career of Ambrose. The episcopal see of Milan was vacant. There were two contending parties, whose animosity seemed likely to end in bloodshed. Ambrose, at that time Prefect of Milan, entered the church in order to appease the tumult, and addressed the people with much eloquence, when a child's voice was heard exclaiming: "Ambrose is bishop! Ambrose is bishop!" The voice of innocence seemed the voice of heaven, and was hailed with loud acclamations; both parties mutually agreed to install Ambrose in the vacant see.

Ambrose, then a simple catechumen, received Holy Baptism, and after a week spent in solitude, prayers, and tears, was first ordained priest, and immediately after was consecrated bishop, on the 7th December,

374. As a flower that needed but one more ray of sunshine to exhale its full perfume, so was it with Ambrose when consecrated bishop. All the treasures of his beautiful soul became apparent. He was both bishop and statesman, a watchful guardian of souls and yet deeply interested in the social condition of his flock, traversing the world in the interests of peace and honour, and devoting hours to the conversion of sinners, whose hearts he melted by his tears; penning daring letters to kings, and composing hymns of exquisite purity and tenderness for those who had dedicated themselves to God; a man of world-wide sympathy, replete with courage and virtue; in fine, a bishop in the true sense of the word, and as such, duly appreciated by his contemporaries.

As time passed on, he continued to advance in holiness, thus preparing himself for the, as yet, unknown part God had destined him to play, and for which end alone he had, perchance, been endowed with such noble qualities.

The act to which we allude, and which won him such immortal renown, is known to all; who but has heard of that admirable scene, when Ambrose, at the vestibule of his cathedral, forbade the blood-stained Emperor Theodosius to advance a single step farther? The emperor was worthy of the bishop; and their noble conduct on this occasion will ever remain graven in the memory of posterity.

However powerful the words of St. Ambrose on that day, he uttered others that redounded still more to the glory of God. Let us cross the threshold of the holy bishop's dwelling, following the steps of the young man who precedes us, and listen to the words about to fall from the lips of St. Ambrose. Those words made Augustine a saint, and gave the Church her greatest doctor.

One of Augustine's first acts on arriving at Milan was to call on St. Ambrose, his official position rendering this duty incumbent on him, but he was also drawn thither by a higher motive. It has been said by one, " that the first visits paid by a young man to those who have preceded him in the journey of life are of great moment, specially so when glory seems to stand sentinel at the threshold !"* Much more is this the case when sanctity is there also.

Augustine writes: " Having arrived in Milan I went to Ambrose the bishop, known to the whole world as one of the most excellent men and Thy devout servant, O my God. Blind as I was, Thy Hand conducted me to him that he might open my eyes and lead me to Thee. That venerable man received me with fatherly affection, and with a charity worthy of a bishop assured me that he was rejoiced to welcome me to Milan. I began to love him, not at first as a doctor of truth, which I had no hope of meeting with in Thy Church, but as a man who was kind to me."†

The reception accorded to the young Augustine by the holy and illustrious Ambrose; the serenity of the one and the agitation of the other; the one

* Le P. Lacordaire. *Notice sur Frédéric Ozanam.*
† *Confess.*, lib. V., cap. xiii.

star about to set in radiance, and the other star, greater still, not yet emerged from the surrounding shadows, form one of those touching and solemn scenes we would fain see depicted by a master-hand.

After this private interview, Augustine wished to hear Ambrose in public. The saintly bishop preached to his people every Sunday, explaining the Holy Scriptures simply and eloquently, shunning controversy, substituting clever and ingenious allegories for erudition, thus shedding light on the most obscure passages of holy writ. Nothing was so congenial to Augustine's sick and wounded spirit as this sweet, elegant, harmonious, and noble language. He thoroughly enjoyed listening, very intent on the words, never suspecting the deep wounds such gentle words were capable of inflicting.

But scarcely had he listened, when he felt his despair augment. He recognized the fallacy of the Manichean teachings, and assuming (without caring to examine as to the ground of his assumptions) that the truth was not to be found in the Catholic Church, he despaired more than ever of finding it. What was to be done? Despise all doctrines, interest himself only in temporal matters, devote his energies to the study of rhetoric, the only thing in which he had any faith. "Such was my state," he says; "despair of finding the truth had plunged me into the lowest abyss; I clung to forms of speech, taking no note of, and despising the subject matter; only this vain care now remained in me, who despaired of finding my way to Thee."*

* *Confess.*, lib. IV., cap. xiv.

That is, Augustine was on the eve of becoming a Sophist, a dealer in fine words, a seeker of antitheses, an arranger of phrases. Therefore, not only heart and conscience, but genius too, were at stake.

St. Monica arrived just at this time, and it is easy to divine what must have been the meeting between such a mother and such a son. Never is family affection so justly appreciated as in the hours of sadness. Thus was it with Augustine and Monica; their souls met in a long embrace; their tears mingled.

As soon as they could find words, Augustine, in order to console his mother, whose enquiring, anxious gaze had doubtless been riveted on her son, hastened to tell her that he was no longer a Manichean. He hoped to see her thrill with joy, but was disappointed; she appeared neither surprised nor happy. Why should she be surprised that Augustine could not cast anchor on such shifting sand as the Manichean doctrine was? this was no more than she had expected. She was not happy, for it did not suffice her that her son had renounced Manicheism; she had hoped better things from his tears. She desired to see him a devout, pious, fervent Christian; less than this would not suffice her, and this she was sure of obtaining.

She therefore told Augustine that she desired to see him a faithful Catholic; then, mingling a mother's intuition with a saint's firm assurance, she told him many times, full of confidence, that before she died her wish would be fulfilled. Augustine shook his head, and replied with a mournful smile, for, doubting and despairing of finding the truth, he had resolved, as we have already stated, to trouble himself no further about doctrinal questions.

This it was which inspired St. Monica with hope; she knew her son too well to believe such an empty void would content him, or that aught short of faith and love would satisfy such a heart as his. Therefore, seeing him tossed on a sea of doubt, with no plank wherewith to escape the shipwreck, she knew this was the commencement of the grand crisis, and that after an instant of the most terrible danger, he would traverse it safely. Consoled, but trembling still, she resolved to lose not a single moment, but redoubled her prayers, sacrifices, pious and saintly labours, in order to obtain from God the abridgment of that dread moment, and the hastening of his conversion.*

Therefore, her first thought, after embracing her son, was to hasten to St. Ambrose; for knowing how instrumental he had been in bringing St. Augustine to this doubtful, wavering state of mind, she was impatient to thank him, also to know what he thought of Augustine, to confide to him her doubts, fears, presentiments, hopes, and to conjure him, even more fervently than the aged bishop whom she had met at Tagaste, to interest himself in her son, and soon make him a Christian.

Ambrose welcomed St. Monica with glad emotion, nor did he weary of contemplating that face on which divine love and maternal affection had left so deep an

---

* *Confess.*, lib. VI., cap. i.

impress; it never faded from his memory, nor did he ever see Augustine without congratulating him on possessing such a motl er.[*]

St. Monica, on her si'e, was moved to tears at sight of him whom she looked on as the destined instrument of her son's conversion, and who had already impressed him so deeply. The piety, gentleness, attainments, and modesty of the holy bishop, both charmed her and augmented her hopes. She opened her heart to him, and from the very first held him in that loving esteem which every mother feels for the heaven-sent guide who guards, protects, and rescues her children, or effects their conversion.[†]

We cannot doubt that she chose him as her own spiritual guide during her sojourn in Milan. What better choice could she make, than entrust the guidance of her soul to him whom she felt convinced was destined by God to convert her son? Who so fitted as Ambrose to direct her in her present needs? Who could better understand her case, and aid her in her efforts to become more watchful, humble, and devoted, so that by living ever nearer to God, she might hasten the moment of her son's conversion?

Also we must remember that, though still young, St. Monica had but two more years to live; years these, the most beautiful of her whole life, in which, (as is the case with all the saints) her soul matured rapidly and brought forth its most perfect fruit. Divine Providence had decreed that these closing years of life should be spent in the vicinity, and

---

[*] *Confess.*, lib. **VI.**, cap. ii.   [†] *Confess.*, lib. **VI.**, cap. i.

under the guidance of the most celebrated director of that epoch. Such is often God's plan. When a soul has flourished in solitude, and is on the eve of unfolding its bloom, He suddenly transplants and places it under the care of a wise director, whom He has secretly prepared for this task, and whose it is to perfect the wondrous work.

Now that she had made acquaintance with St. Ambrose, Monica endeavoured to deepen the intimacy between the saintly bishop and her son. She frequently made the latter accompany her in her visits, and would often find excuses to send Augustine on messages to Ambrose, ostensibly for advice on some matter relative to herself, but in reality to afford her son another opportunity of conversing with this renowned bishop.

For example, one day being in doubt as to whether she should fast on Saturday, for such was the custom in Tagaste and Rome, though not in Milan, instead of herself consulting St. Ambrose, as she could easily have done, she, with a pious mother's ready ingenuity, preferred despatching Augustine, to whom this reply, since then so celebrated, was given : " Follow the custom of the Church wheresoever you may happen to be. If in Rome, fast with the Church of Rome; but when in Milan, do not fast when the Church of Milan does not fast."

In the following we have a proof how love for Augustine was mingled with veneration and obedient, tender, and deep respect for St. Ambrose. When in Africa, she had been accustomed, in accordance with the custom prevalent in the Church there, to bring bread, wine, and cakes, to the tombs of the martyrs, which, after being offered as oblations, were distributed amongst the poor, and the rest eaten. As we have already stated, this custom, to the minds of the early Christians, seemed a kind of participation in the merits of the saint in whose memory it was observed. The first time she was about to perform this devotion in the cathedral of Milan, with her usual little basket of offerings, she was stopped by the porter of the church, who told her that the archbishop, fearing the abuses already allied to this custom, in itself so beautiful and sublime, had forbidden it. As Monica was ignorant of this, she may have been pained and surprised at the porter's conduct, but not a shadow of regret was visible on her countenance. St. Augustine says, " She most willingly submitted, and instead of a basket full of the fruits of the earth, she henceforth learned to carry to the memory of the martyrs a heart full of more purified vows, to give what she could to the poor, and these fruits of the earth she replaced by the communion of the Lord's Body."* Such was her obedience. " But," St. Augustine gently adds, "it seems to me that my mother would perhaps not have so easily yielded, had this custom been prohibited by any other for whom she did not entertain so much regard as she did for St. Ambrose, whom, for the sake of my salvation she loved very much ; as he also loved her for her most religious conversation, assi-

* *Confess.,* lib. VI., cap. ii.

duous frequentation of the church, and her zeal in
good works, so that he would often break forth in her
praise, congratulating me on having such a mother,
not knowing," he humbly adds, " what a son she had
in me."*

Moreover, at the very moment when such a holy
friendship sprang up between St. Ambrose and
Monica, God was so arranging events as to awake
also within Augustine's heart a noble and enthusiastic
affection for the holy bishop. Ambrose had arrived
at one of those momentous epochs when a truly great
soul shines forth in sublime light, and when the raging
storms of persecution and calumny do but the better
reveal its magnanimity and grandeur. The Empress Justinia, who some years before injudiciously
brought in her train a few courtiers appertaining to
the Arians, and who, more wrongly still, allowed
herself to be governed by this turbulent minority, had
at Easter, in the year 385, requested St. Ambrose,
in the name of her son Valentinian, then only a child,
to cede to the Arians in her court one of the churches
belonging to the Catholics, either the Portian Basilica
(outside the city walls) or the new Basilica, in which
St. Ambrose ordinarily officiated, and which was the
metropolitan church also. The saint refused to accede
to this request, and with noble courage replied that
he would never surrender the church. This refusal
and message made him incur the hatred of a woman
whose power was unbounded, and who was capable of
anything. A band of soldiers were sent to take

* *Confess.*, lib. VI., cap. ii.

forcible possession of the Portian Basilica, and they even surrounded the church, in which St. Ambrose then was. But as the people took the bishop's part, the soldiers, not daring to enter the church, withdrew to the other basilica, followed by an angry and indignant crowd. During many days a species of civil war raged in Milan.

During these events, Ambrose did not quit the church, passing his time either praying and weeping before the holy altar, entreating God that no blood might be shed in his behalf, or in the pulpit, expounding the Scriptures, appeasing the populace, enforcing clemency, obedience to the laws, at the same time that he eloquently and energetically discoursed on the freedom belonging to the faithful and to the Church, which is their country, their refuge, and their mother.

To the counts and tribunes who summoned him to cede the basilica, saying that it was the emperor's by right, for that he was master of all, Ambrose replied: "If the prince asked me for what is my own, my lands or my money, I would not refuse him, although all I possess belongs to the poor; but he has no right to that which belongs to God. Let him take my patrimony, if it be that which he desires, or if he desire my life, I cheerfully surrender myself to his will. Imprison, or slay me, I will offer no resistance, nor flee to the altar for sanctuary; rather would I lay down my life to spare it from pollution."

On the chamberlain Caligonus saying to him: "If thou despisest Valentinian's commands, I will behead thee;" Ambrose replied, with even more noble intrepidity: "God grant thou mayest fulfil thy threat; I shall die as a bishop, and thou wilt act as a eunuch."

When the imperial guard, seeing the growing anger of the people, and fearing an insurrection, entreated him to appease the populace, he replied: "It behoves me not to arouse their passions; but when once they are roused, none but God can calm them." On their exclaiming that he was a tyrant, and abused his influence with the people in order to endanger Valentinian's throne, he rejoined, smiling: "Oh! oh! Maximian does not accuse me of acting tyrannically to Valentinian, for he complains that I barred his own progress when he wished to invade Italy." And, in truth, it was Ambrose who hasted to plead, and won the cause of the infant orphan Valentinian, when Maximian, coveting the empire of the latter, had crossed the Alps. "Moreover," continued Ambrose, "if I am a tyrant, why delay putting me to death? I have no arms save courage. I am ready to die, but God forbid I should surrender the heritage of Jesus Christ, the heritage of my predecessors, the heritage of St. Denis, who died an exile for the faith, the heritage of Myrocles and of all the holy ishops my fathers. I render to Cæsar that which is Cæsar's, and to God that which is God's." And in order to show his readiness to obey, he left his door open night and day, remaining in his accustomed room, ready to go into exile or to prison, as the order might be.

Alarmed at such noble and courageous behaviour,

Justinia desisted for awhile, but soon wove a new and subtle web in which she hoped to entrap Ambrose. An Arian doctor suddenly assumed the title of Bishop of Milan; and Ambrose, having refused to appear before the tribunal appointed by the empress to judge between Ambrose and his competitor, the saintly bishop was declared an intruder, condemned to exile, and soldiers were sent to take forcible possession of him, and conduct him beyond the Italian frontier. The saint took refuge in his cathedral, as on the former occasion; and it was a truly edifying scene to behold this venerable old man, in whom were personified all the rights of conscience, standing in the sanctuary of his own church, invincible, though disarmed, and the wrath of the most supreme terrestrial power fall powerless at the threshold of the sacred edifice. The people also remained in the church; they crowded round their bishop, and when night came, they would not go, but remained there, armed and menacing.*

This species of siege continued during eight or nine days, about Easter time, in the year 386; this was the occasion when, in order to fill up those weary hours, St. Ambrose introduced into the church of Milan the eastern mode of singing the psalms, since adopted throughout the west. And in order to vary and give life to the singing, he added some hymns composed

* The churches of that day were surrounded by many external buildings, such as porticoes, chambers, halls, gardens; this accounts for the populace being able to remain there night and day. There were also places where people could take their meals and pass the night.

by him for the occasion, which hymns so charmed the
people, that St. Ambrose's enemies declared that he
had bewitched them with magic songs.* The majority
of these hymns are still in existence,† and never
should we dream that they had been composed amid
the din of arms and the clamours of an excited populace, by one who knew not when morning dawned
whether evening would see him on the road to exile
or within the walls of a prison. Nothing can be more
sweet, refreshing, elevating, and pure, than these
hymns. Here, for instance, is the morning hymn:

> "O Thou, the Father's image blest!
>   Who callest forth the morning's ray;
> O Thou eternal Light of light
>   And inexhaustive Fount of day!

> True Sun! upon our souls arise,
>   Shining in beauty evermore;
> And through each sense the quickening beam
>   Of Thy Eternal Spirit pour.

---

* Ambros., *Opusc. de Spiritu sancto, in Epist.* xxxi.

† The following are the hymns assigned (with most certainty) to St.
Ambrose: *Æterne rerum Conditor. Deus creator omnium. Jam surget
hora tertia. Veni, Redemptor gentium. Illuminans Altissimus. Fit
porta Christi pervia. Orabo mente Dominum. Somno refectis artubus.
O lux beata Trinitas. Consors Paterni luminis. Æterna Christi
munera.* (See dom Ceillier, *Histoire des auteurs ecclésiastiques:* St.
Ambroise.) Besides these eleven hymns, the Blessed Thommasi, in his
Hymnal, adds fifty-two others, particularly: *Jesu, nostra Redemptio.
Conditor alme siderum. Rerum Creator optime. Splendor Paternæ
gloriæ. Immense cœli Conditor. Cœli Deus sanctissime. Nox atra
rerum contigit. Magnæ Deus potentiæ. Tu Trinitatis Unitas. Æter-
na cœli gloria. Plasmator hominis Deus. Summe Deus clementiæ.
Lux ecce surgit aurea, etc. etc.*

Rule Thou our inmost thoughts; let no
    Impurity our hearts defile ;
Grant us a sober heart and mind ;
    Grant us a spirit free from guile.

Still ever, pure as noon's first ray,
    May modesty our steps attend ;
Our faith be fervent as the noon ;
    Upon our soul no night descend."*

And this charming commencement of another morning-hymn.

" The star that heralds in the morn
    Is fading in the skies ;
The darkness melts : O Thou the Light !
    Once more in us arise."

The following is an evening hymn. When we reflect what poetry was at that time, and note how beautiful are the strains which fall from the lips of this aged man, we shall understand somewhat of the charm which pervaded the whole being of this saintly prelate.

" Our limbs with tranquil sleep refreshed,
    Lightly from bed we spring ;
Father Supreme ! to us be nigh,
    While in Thy praise we sing.

above and the two following translations are taken from wall's " Hymns and Poems," second edition.

Thy love be first in every heart,
    Thy name on every tongue ;
Whatever we this day may do,
    May it in Thee be done.

Cut off in us whatever root
    Of sin or shame there be ;
So evermore from bosoms pure
    Be rendered praise to Thee."

We never find a single allusion to the troubled state of the city. If so, but a single word such as the following :

" Before Thy eyes we lay our woes and fears,
    And all our secret crimes with grief declare ;
And with our prayers we mingle bitter tears,
    Oh ! may Thy mercy pity us and spare !"

Or again,

" Oh ! may a holy, joyous zeal
    For ever guide our feet,
And may thy faithful people feel
    A peace profound and sweet !"*

The author of such harmonious strains must indeed have been endowed with much strength of mind and self-possession to have composed them amid the din of a popular tumult. These hymns were

---

* For the English rendering of these stanzas the translator of " *The History of St. Monica*" is indebted to the Rev. Father Matthew Russeil, S.J., of St. Francis Xavier's, Dublin.

welcomed most enthusiastically, the people sung them night and day, and so charmed were they that they asked to die with their bishop. From time to time Ambrose stopped the singing, and ascending the pulpit, with deep emotion and gratitude he thanked and encouraged his flock, in words whose eloquence far exceeded aught that he had uttered before.

These events transpired in the years 385 and 386, that is, during the time that Augustine was teaching in Milan. Such a sight must have deeply impressed him, for though a stranger to the true faith, he was keenly alive to eloquence, poetry, honour, magnanimity, the rights of conscience, and liberty. How must he not have gazed in admiration at this aged man, nobly risking his life rather than fail in duty; invincible, though unarmed; and rewarded, as is ever the case, by the applause of those whose praise is worth having! "My mother," says he, "bearing her part in the solicitudes and watchings, lived in prayer, and I, though cold as yet with regard to the heat of Thy Spirit, was stirred up, nevertheless, by the concern and trouble of the whole city."* Augustine was moved to enthusiasm by the sight of the holy bishop's moral greatness. "As for Ambrose, I looked upon him as a man happy, according to the world, in being so honoured, only his celibacy seemed to me painful. But what hope he entertained in his soul, and what conflicts he sustained with the temptations besetting his lofty position, what comfort he felt in his adversities, and what savoury joys he

* *Confess.*, lib IX. cap. vii

tasted in feeding on the bread of life; these I knew nothing of."

As for St. Monica, she, beholding her spiritual father, to whom she looked for her son's salvation, transformed into a hero and a saint, thrilled with a joy no words can express. She was a zealous attendant on his preaching, hanging on his lips and bearing her part in the woe and anguish of the Church. She lived for God alone; and beneath the watchful guidance of this saintly prelate, edified by his hymns and fervour, and surrounded by such holy influences, she rapidly advanced towards perfection. Faith, love, fervent hope, peace, and trust in God, filled her soul with their divine fragrance, and it was easy to see that the crowning hour was near at hand.*

CHAPTER X.

GOD BEGINS TO GRANT ST. MONICA'S REQUESTS.—DAWN OF LIGHT IN AUGUSTINE'S SOUL.—WISDOM OF THE PLAN ADOPTED BY ST. AMBROSE AND FOLLOWED BY ST. MONICA. —THE TEMPEST.

385.

As we have already seen, St. Monica did not rest content with taking Augustine with her during her visits to St. Ambrose; she was still more zealous

* *Confess.,* lib. VI., cap. i. and ii.; lib. VII., cap. vii.

in making him accompany her to the holy bishop's sermons; she had no difficulty in doing so, inasmuch as Augustine was a great admirer of his eloquence, and even before his mother's arrival, often went to hear him. In Milan the pulpit is still to be seen whence the saintly bishop addressed his flock, and which, during the years 385 and 386, he never entered without having as his near auditors St. Monica and that son who was "the object of so many tears."

Unfortunately, in attending St. Ambrose's discourses, Augustine came not with those dispositions which are indispensable for the right reception of the Divine Word. He came as a judge, not as a disciple. "I diligently heard him when he preached to the people, not with a right intention, but only to make trial of his eloquence, whether it were answerable to the fame thereof, or whether it were greater or less than was reported. For hours I would listen, delighted with the eloquence of his discourse, intent upon his words, though despising the things of which he treated."*

Such was the frame of mind in which Augustine listened, and yet, in spite of this, the divine light penetrated into his soul, gently and almost imperceptibly. "But whilst I cared not to learn what he said, but only how he said it, there came into my soul, together with the words which I valued, the things which I slighted, for I could not separate them. And whilst I opened my heart to the eloquence of his

* *Confess.*, lib. IV., cap. xiii.

sayings, there stole into my soul the truth of what he said, though but by gentle degrees."*

So gently, gradually, and almost imperceptibly, did the day-spring arise in Augustine's soul. "First it began to seem to me that the things he said might be defended, and that the Catholic Faith, for which I had before supposed nothing could be said in answer to the objections of the Manicheans and others, might be plausibly maintained."† This was the first ray of light, which he thus characterizes: "I took great delight in listening to St. Ambrose, and though I was not prepared to accept his doctrines as true, they did not seem to me inconsistent with truth."‡ And again: "Thenceforth I was convinced that whatever my uncertainty as to the truth of her doctrines, the Catholic Church was guiltless of the charges that had been brought against her. I was in a state of perplexity and confusion, and rejoiced secretly that the Catholic Church, in which, when a child, I had learnt the name of Christ, held no such foolish doctrines."§

Thus did Augustine's opinions gradually undergo a transformation. Each day he was surprised to find that the Church did not hold the doctrines with which she was charged. Certain passages of Scripture, which formerly appeared irrational, now seemed capable of a rational, and even sublime and beautiful interpretation. Certain dogmas that had roused his ridicule or his aversion were not held by the Church; she taught the

---

* *Confess.*, lib. V., cap. xiv. † *Confess.*, lib. V., cap. xix.
‡ *Confess.*, lib. V., cap. xiv. § *Confess.*, lib. VI., cap. iv.

very contrary of that with which she had been charged. Many objections advanced against her he now discerned to be totally unfounded, and his honest soul blushed that he had so maligned the Church. "I was ashamed to find that for so many years I had been barking, not at that which was indeed the Catholic Faith, but at the fictions of my carnal imagination; for I was so rash and wicked as to be more ready to impose falsehoods upon them, than by inquiry of them to be informed of the truth."*

Soon, a far brighter ray illumined his mind. In listening to St. Ambrose, Augustine began to examine the method pursued by Catholics in regard to the truth, and was much impressed thereby. The Catholics insist that men should believe what is not demonstrated; faith, acknowledging that there is much absolutely incomprehensible to the human intellect, yields a reverential assent, conscious of the finiteness of human reason.

Such a mode of procedure struck Augustine as far more modest and truthful than that of the heretics, "who," he says, "prated only of liberty, evidence, reason, the right of scrutinizing and testing everything, and then, a host of things which could never be demonstrated were by them imposed to be believed."†

Not only did the Catholic method seem to him more modest and straightforward, but however distasteful to the natural man such a course of procedure might be, it soon appeared to him to have truth

* *Confess.*, lib. VI., cap. iii.   † *Confess.*, lib. VI., cap. v.

on its side, and to be marvellously in harmony with our nature. Let us listen to him, and observe the gradual dispersion of the darkness that environed him. "I began to note how many things I believed which I never saw, nor was present when they occurred, as well in history and in the accounts of places and cities where I had never been, as in many things which I believed on the words of my friends, or of physicians, or of other men, where, if I was to suspend my belief, an end must be put to all human commerce. I am the son of Patricius and Monica; this I firmly believe, and yet I cannot know it save by believing those from whom I heard it."*

Therefore, if faith is indispensable in all the relations of life, social and otherwise, why should it not be so in the life of the soul? If every human being born into this world is taught by his parents, his country, and his age, why should he not be taught by his God? And if God has indeed instructed man, is not man bound to listen, believe, trust, and ground his religion on the same basis as that on which family affection, friendship, and all the noblest and holiest sentiments are grounded, whose very life is faith, trust, and confidence?

Such was St. Augustine's mode of reasoning, and, did we not know his tender, loving heart, we should deem we heard his mother's voice; for such is the light in which religion appears to a Christian woman. She does not attempt to fathom or discuss these obscure, ineffable, mysterious, august, and important

Confess., lib. VI., cap. v.

first principles; she feels they are true. These clear and profound intuitions have their source in the heart, and not in the intellect.

This principle, whether discovered by himself or received from others, having been accepted by Augustine, was submitted to the investigation of his logical intellect, and the result was a flood of light.

Admitted that God has indeed spoken to man, what should be the character of His word? Totally different to that of man. Man is insignificant, finite, subject to the limits of time and space; and such is his language, too. God, on the contrary, is infinite, eternal, independent of time and space, omniscient; such must be the characteristics of His word. Thereupon Augustine opened the sacred Scriptures, which the Catholic Church holds within her hands, and which she holds to be the true word of God, as it has resounded from age to age. He was surprised to find they resembled nothing that he had met with, wide though his studies had been; words ancient as the world; universal as space; breathing truth and virtue; unchangeable and indestructible, though constantly attacked; rich in fecundity; of the highest moral beauty; in fine, words such as could have proceeded from none other than an eternal, omnipresent, omniscient, holy being, even God Himself.

What most struck him was its wonderful adaptability to the needs of the human heart, and this was to him a proof of the divinity of its Author. "Its authority appeared to me so much the more venerable and worthy of credence, in that, though easy of comprehension, it yet preserved the dignity of secrecy beneath the veil of its simplicity. So simple, clear, and humble in its style, that all can understand it, and yet exercising the best attention of the loftiest intellect. With open bosom receiving all, yet containing profound depths for the piercing eye of genius."

This additional characteristic began to reveal to his delighted gaze the incomparable beauty and universality of the Catholic Church, illumining with the same light those of high degree and low degree, the learned and unlearned, the lofty genius and the man of lowly mind; so different from the schools of philosophy, false religions, and sectarians, which have ever been local, cramped, and narrow, as the minds which gave them birth; some of them being intended for the lofty intellect, and therefore unadapted to the lowly intelligence; others intended for the many, and despised by the chosen few; but all falling short of their aim, inasmuch as the marks of Catholicity were not to be found therein. " Such were my thoughts, and Thou wast with me; I sighed to Thee, and Thou didst hear me; I was tossed by the waves, and Thou didst steer my course; I walked in the broad way of the world, and Thou didst not forsake me."*

These new views delighted, but did not convert Augustine. Although he discerned that the Catholic faith was able to refute its adversaries' objections, and to the studious eye bore the impress of moral

* *Confess.*, lib. VI., cap. vi.

beauty, he did not therefore conclude that it was the true faith, but simply that its teaching was beautiful, rational, even sublime; professed by mighty intellects; believed in by those whose honesty and sincerity he could not doubt, such as St. Monica and Ambrose, and consequently worthy of careful study and respectful treatment. The following sentence graphically depicts his state of mind at that time, a state far from peculiar to himself alone. "The Catholic faith seemed to me not conquered, neither was it as yet victorious."*

From that day he ceased to rail against the faith; his contempt for her ceased, and he was one step nearer the light. "Therefore, wholly renouncing all other teachings, I resolved to continue a catechumen in the Catholic Church, into which my mother had introduced me, till some light should arise, to which I might steer my course."†

It would have been easy for Augustine to find this light had he but sought some confidant. But like a sick man who, having fallen into the hands of an unskilful physician, fears even to trust a skilful one, so he hesitated to communicate his doubts, and ask for healing.

There was but one who could have taken the initiative, and that was St. Ambrose, who, strange to say, appeared as indifferent as if he were ignorant of the doubts and anxieties of one bound to him by the tie of mutual affection. "Ambrose knew nothing of my doubts, nor the depth of my danger. For I could

* *Confess.* lib. V., cap. xiv.   † Ibid.

not confer with him as I wished to do, by reason of the number of people who came to him for advice and help; and the time that he was not with them was either taken up in the necessary refreshment of the body by daily food, or of his soul by reading."*

It appears wholly incomprehensible that Ambrose could indeed be in ignorance of the doubts and anxieties of one with whom he had such frequent relations, and who, in virtue of his public office and reputation for eloquence, was so well known in Milan. Besides, was not St. Monica living in the same town, and frequently seeing St. Ambrose? What other topic could have occupied the mind and tongue of this inconsolable mother, save the doubts and disquietudes of him whom she loved so dearly? And how could such a learned, zealous bishop, whose word carried such weight, refrain from endeavouring to win Augustine to God? Augustine says he was too busy. But could any work be more noble, more pleasing to God, or more worthy of a bishop, than that of removing the honest difficulties of one who, when converted, might prove so great an ornament and so firm a defender of the Catholic Church?

And yet St. Ambrose not only refrained from seeking an opportunity for doing so, but when an opportunity presented itself, refrained from taking advantage of it. We must here quote a page from Augustine, in which, as on the golden background of a beautiful miniature, we see the fine countenance of St. Ambrose, full of the serenity and repose of faith,

* *Confess.*, lib. VI., cap. iii.

and at his side, the youthful Augustine, restless and agitated, observing him in admiring silence, but not daring to interrogate him. "Often when I went to see him, (for no one was refused entrance, nor was it the custom to give notice of any one's coming,) I have seen him reading to himself, and never otherwise; and I have sat down, and after a long silence, (for who could find in his heart to disturb one so intent?) I have gone away, presuming that in the brief moments which he had for the repairing of his mind, free from the noise of other men's business, he was loath to be disturbed; and that perhaps this was the reason why he did not read aloud, lest his auditor, being attentive to the reading, might possibly desire the exposition of some obscure passage, and by this means his time might be abridged and he himself hindered in his reading. Or, perhaps, he read in silence from a wish to spare his voice, which was easily weakened. But whatever his motive was, the intention of such a man was certainly good."*

These last words show us Augustine's veneration for St. Ambrose, consequently, the ease with which this saintly bishop might have gained his confidence, or solved his doubts. But Ambrose appeared blind to this fact. "Thus, I had no opportunity of consulting this holy oracle, save when the audience could be but brief, whereas my perplexities required one perfectly disengaged, to whom I might impart them all, and I could never find him so much at leisure."†

Evidently there is a mystery here. When St.

---

* *Confess.*, lib. VI., cap. iii.   † Ibid.

Monica entreated the aged African bishop to enter into controversy with her son, the saint replied: " Of what avail will that be?" And on her persisting in her request, his rejoinder was: "Continue thy prayers, for it is impossible that the son of such tears should perish." St. Ambrose pursued the same plan. He knew of Augustine's doubts; but would not enter into controversy with him. Who has ever been converted by controversy? Augustine was proud of his reason and mighty intellect. Being a keen logician, a difficulty non-solved, or which he imagined to be so, or an argument which he considered unrefuted, would but have confirmed his doubts and strengthened his conviction that truth was not to be found in the bosom of the Catholic Church, any more than in the sects and schools of philosophy, the hollowness of whose teaching he had discovered.

Besides, if convinced, would his heart have yielded assent? Plato says that where goodness is, there is light, and that the soul can only soar upwards on the wings of virtue. This St. Ambrose knew even better than did Plato; also he was aware of what was amiss with Augustine's heart. She who for fourteen years had come between Augustine and his God, had also followed him to Milan, where their guilty connection was a matter of notoriety. Under such circumstances, what would be the use of argument? Was it not far better to pray and entreat God to effect this conquest and render St. Monica's tears irresistible.

Such was St. Ambrose's plan. Therefore, while remaining on friendly terms with Augustine he pretended to ignore his doubts, studiously avoiding discussions which might only prove unavailing. He did not refuse to gather the delicious fruit, but only left it to ripen.

Monica, although impatient to see her son a Christian, knowing the motives by which St. Ambrose was guided, resolved to leave all to his wise direction, and continued to pray and weep in silence at the foot of the holy altar. "Like that mother who, weeping, followed her son's bier, and at sight of whose tears Jesus Christ gave her back her child, so," says St. Augustine: "did my mother bewail me, carrying me forth on the bier of her thoughts, that Thou mighest be pleased to say to the son of the widow: 'Young man, I say unto thee arise.'"[*]

The event justified the wisdom of the plan laid down by St. Ambrose and pursued by St. Monica. The more others abstained from arguing with Augustine, the more he argued with himself. Like a sick man, who, turn as he will, finds no ease, so was it with Augustine. The voice of conscience rose louder and louder as the flood of St. Monica's tears deepened, and soon the storm raged in all its fury. He himself has graphically described this struggle; in an admirable dialogue, in which passion and conscience speak alternately, we catch some glimpses of the storm which now began to agitate his soul.[†]

---

[*] *Confess.*, lib. VI., cap. i.

[†] *Confess.*, lib. VI., cap. xi.

PASSION.

"O academicians," exclaimed Augustine, when passion held her sway, "ye have excelled all the philosophies, for ye have taught us that nothing can be certainly known for the regulating of life."

CONSCIENCE.

"Nay, but let us not despair, but seek with greater diligence. Why be discouraged? For it is no slight matter that many passages of holy writ no longer seem absurd to me, but appear to me capable of rational interpretation. Here, then, let us remain, on the threshold of the Church, where my mother placed me as a child; and there let us confidently await the dawn of faith."

PASSION.

"But when or where shall we seek truth? Ambrose has no leisure to listen to my doubts, nor have I leisure to read. Moreover, had I leisure, where should I procure the proper books, or who would lend them me?"

CONSCIENCE.

"Nay, but let us make time, and devote certain hours of the day to the salvation of our soul. Great hope appears. The Catholic Faith does not teach that which we thought, and unjustly laid to her charge.

If we know this much, why not seek for further en-
lightenment? The morning is set apart for our
scholars; but what do we with the remainder of our
day? Why not devote it to this important study?"

PASSION.

"When, then, must we wait upon our influential
friends? When prepare the lessons for which we are
paid? When rest our wearied, anxious mind?"

CONSCIENCE.

"Let all these vain empty things perish! let us
devote ourselves wholly to the inquiry after truth.
This life is full of misery, death is uncertain; if it
should come upon us unawares in what state should
we go hence? Where learn what we have neglected?
And how escape the punishment due to such neglect?"

PASSION.

"But what if death put an end to all?"

CONSCIENCE.

"This then, must also be examined into. But no,
such a thought is criminal. It is no vain empty matter, that the authority of the Christian Faith should
have attained this glorious eminence over all the
world. Never would God have wrought such great
and wondrous things for us, if the death of the body
were to put an end to the life of the soul. Why

do we delay renouncing the hopes of this world to give ourselves up wholly to seek after God and true beatitude?"

PASSION.

"But stay a little; worldly joys are sweet and pleasant; we must not part with them too hastily, for it would be disgraceful, after once renouncing, to return to them again. I am on the eve of obtaining an honourable post which will afford me ease and competence. I have powerful friends, and may reasonably hope for a presidentship. Then I may marry a wife with some fortune, who will therefore be no burden to me, and so shall I be happy! Many illustrious men worthy of imitation have been married and yet have devoted themselves to the pursuit of wisdom."*

"Thus," adds Augustine, "as I was tossed hither and thither by contrary winds, time ran on, and I remained irresolute."†

Such was the commencement of the conflict between Augustine and his conscience, a conflict destined to last more than a year, and which was accompanied by such strange vicissitudes; a conflict which Augustine often tried to end by seeking to stifle the voice of conscience, but which conflict Monica awoke again and again, knowing that in it lay his last hope of safety, and which did indeed terminate in victory, but by a dearly bought one, as regards both the mother and he son. This wondrous conflict with self reveals the

---

* *Confess.*, lib. VI., cap. xi.   † Ibid.

greatness of the man. To yearn after truth, ardently
desire it, to shrink from the sacrifice it involves and
yet make the sacrifice, though it cost many a bitter
tear is, as Seneca has so grandly said, worthy of a
god. *Ecce par Deo spectaculum: vir cum adversis
compositus.* And St. Paul, soaring still higher, after
having depicted man as hesitating between good and
evil, and drawn in different directions by his conflicting passions, exclaimed: *Spectaculum facti sumus
Deo, et angelis, et hominibus.*

And yet, grand as the sight is, there is one grander
still; the power that a mother possesses of rousing
such storms as these in her children's breast, whether
in virtue of the divine aspirations implanted in the
days of infancy, which aspirations no terrestrial passion can quench; or in virtue of her prayers, which,
when passion seems to have extinguished all, are
capable of reviving the dying spark, and, as we shall
see farther on, of kindling so sublime a flame.

CHAPTER XI.

THE REAL IMPEDIMENT.—ENERGY AND DELICACY WITH
WHICH ST. MONICA STRIVES TO REMOVE IT.—THE SUN
OF FAITH ARISES IN AUGUSTINE'S SOUL.

386.

Had Augustine's heart been pure, the flame of faith
and of divine love would have been readily kindled;
but, as we already know, he was entangled in the

meshes of a guilty liaison of more than fifteen years
duration. His ardent, early wish had been realized;
and if the prospect of a long and perilous voyage of
six hundred leagues had failed to retain Monica in
Africa, so was it with the mother of Adeodatus; she
had rejoined Augustine in Rome, accompanied him
to Milan, where they lived together, in the company
of Adeodatus, who was growing up, and who not
only formed an additional link, but gladdened them
by his precocious genius. How escape from such a
position? and yet, until those bonds were severed,
what possibility was there of arriving at the faith, or
participating in the sacraments of baptism, penance,
and the Holy Eucharist, in which the full and perfect
Christian life consists? Such was the constant
subject of Monica's reflections. She clearly observed
that the arena of the conflict was changing, that from
the intellect it was removing to the heart. That
between God and himself it was no longer a question
of light, but of virtue, was very evident; and this it
was which alarmed St. Monica; for, knowing Augustine's heart, and how deep and faithful was his
attachment to the mother of Adeodatus, persuaded
that he would never separate from her, Monica asked
herself in alarm, by what means she could remove
this obstacle, the most formidable of all.

At that time, the best and dearest of Augustine's
friends, a young man, named Alipius, with whom
we shall soon become more intimately acquainted,
was with him in Milan. Their acquaintance had
commenced in Africa, they had met in Rome, and

Alipius, finding himself unable to live without Augustine, had rejoined him in Milan. He had been seduced by Augustine into the paths of false doctrine, in which he was still straying, but was naturally strongly inclined to virtue, and though for a brief instant he had wandered therefrom, his return was prompt, and marked by remorse and detestation of his own transgression; since then he had led a life of perfect chastity. He incessantly urged Augustine to do the same, enthusiastically vaunting the joys of that austere, sublime, wholly spiritual life, whose sacrifices were wholly compensated by a peace, liberty, and strength, to be found nowhere save in the contemplation of virtue. Unhappily, such counsels met with no response in Augustine, to whom life would have been a worthless burden, if unshared by her to whom for fifteen years he had been united in the bonds of a guilty union. "I thought I could not live if deprived of her affection; not knowing the strength with which God endows the chaste soul, I felt incapable of a single life. But Thou wouldst indeed have given me this strength, had I with hearty sighs knocked at Thy ears, and with a sound faith cast my care upon Thee."*

But, alas! he scarcely bestowed a thought on this. "Being delighted with pestiferous pleasure, I drew my chain still after me, being afraid to be loosed from it; rejecting all that could be said in praise of virtue, as the hand that would unchain me from the bondage I loved."†

* *Confess.*, lib. VI., cap. ii.   † *Confess.*, lib. VI., cap. xii.

It is evident that in such a case as this there was but one remedy that could effect a cure. Since Augustine felt himself incapable of the austere solitude involved in a life of chastity, he should have sought the divine benediction in marriage. This was ever present to Monica's mind, and was the subject of her earnest prayers; fully persuaded that with the holy and legitimate affections of married life Augustine's mental difficulties would vanish entirely, she entreated God with all the fervour of which her heart was capable.

The simplest plan would have been for Augustine to have married the mother of Adeodatus. But, although we are ignorant of the reason, such a course was impossible; for, knowing as we do how painful it was to Augustine to sever the tie that bound him, it is evident that the laws, customs, or circumstances unknown to us, placed insurmountable obstacles in the way of such an union. Equally unable to marry the mother of Adeodatus, or tear himself away from her, Augustine was in a state of great mental anxiety; for beneath all this hesitation, disquietude and delay, was the still deeper, more important, and touching question of his own eternal salvation. Who more deeply feels and knows all this than does a mother? And yet, there was not a moment to lose, for since the guilty tie could not be transfigured, it must be broken; and the sole way to render such a wound supportable to Augustine, was to afford him the prospect of some noble union wholly worthy of himself.

St. Monica probably had recourse to St. Ambrose to aid her with his influence in this difficult undertaking. " She prayed with redoubled ardour ; she importuned Thee with loud cries, that Thou wouldst be pleased to reveal to her what course to pursue in such a difficult and urgent matter."* To conclude ; after much diligent effort and prayer she had the happiness of meeting with a young girl pertaining to a Christian family, in whom seemed reunited all the qualities a saint could desire in one to whom she was about to entrust a soul such as Augustine's then was. She urged the matter on the attention of Augustine, who, overwhelmed, and feeling that he must resign himself to the sacrifice, daring neither to acquiesce nor refuse, allowed his mother to do as she liked. Therefore, St. Monica, on her son's behalf, demanded the hand of the young maiden : her request was complied with ; but as the young girl had not yet attained a marriageable age, it was agreed that the union should be deferred for two years. It is also probable that such a delay seemed desirable to both families, in order to afford Augustine time to reform.

However this may be, it was impossible under these circumstances for Augustine to remain in a position as false as it was indelicate, therefore the separation was insisted on, and accomplished.

St. Augustine alludes to it in words as brief as they are expressive ! " I allowed her to be removed who had hitherto shared my existence; and my heart, which had cleaved to her, being now torn away, as it

* *Confess.*, lib. VI., cap. xiii.

were, from her, was wounded and bled."* Farther on, he adds, "This wound would not heal, and for a long time caused me acute pain."†

As for the mother of Adeodatus, it is easy to imagine her tears and groans, although history is silent on the point. What we are glad to learn is, that after disputing with God the possession of Augustine's heart for the space of fifteen years, she, yielding at last to divine grace, and seeing all earthly love give way, turned heavenwards, seeking refuge in a convent, and spending the remainder of her days in entreating the divine pardon for having enslaved such a heart, and so long retarded the triumph which this great genius would afford the Church. "She was better than I was," says St. Augustine, "inasmuch as she manifested a courage and a generosity which I had not the strength to imitate."‡

St. Monica thanked God from her inmost soul, and began to envisage the future with more hopefulness than before. Had she not the right to believe that the storm of passion in Augustine's soul would now subside, and that after the consummation of such a sacrifice, nothing would henceforth be capable of arresting him in the way of truth and virtue?

And there was indeed at this epoch a ray of peace illumining Augustine's soul, as the heavens are illumined a brief instant, until the returning clouds herald the approach of another storm. The bonds were burst, the sacrifice accomplished. As a vessel freed from its load, even so Augustine's soul regained

---

* *Confess.,* lib. VI., cap. **xv.**　　† Ibid.　　‡ Ibid.

its natural elevation. His mother was at his side, radiant with happiness; his friends were enthusiastic in their philosophic researches; and each day brought from Africa one or other of Augustine's compatriots, rejoicing to behold again their youthful master, or their old friend. Romanianus for instance, whom some interminable law-suits had drawn to Milan, and who, ever faithful to the son of Patricius and Monica, placed, with the same delicacy as heretofore, his large fortune at Augustine's service; Alipius, whose acquaintance we have already made, and who, having subsequently taken up his abode with Augustine, was destined to prove so sweet a consolation and so tender a friend; Nebridius, who had left Carthage, and his father's vast domain, home, and mother also, for the sake of prosecuting his philosophical studies. Younger than Augustine, but, like him, tossed hither and thither, seeking and not finding the truth, groaning beneath the burden of his doubts, Nebridius, whose intellect was so deep and keen, was specially dear to Augustine's heart. Seven or eight others, chiefly from Africa, grouped themselves around Augustine, pursuing the same studies; addicted to literature, they propounded the most sublime questions on God and the soul; indulged in many a dream, among others in the following charming one. "Many of us friends," says St. Augustine, "weary of the troubles and vexations of life, had almost resolved to withdraw from the world, and live in quiet. Our plan was, that each should bring in what he had to the common stock, where, by sincerity of friendship, one should not claim this, and the other that; but the whole should belong to every one, and everything to all. There were about ten of us that were ready to join this society, amongst whom some were very rich, especially Romanianus, my fellow-townsman and familiar friend from my childhood, who was the most in earnest in this matter, and having much larger means than any of the rest, had the most power to promote it. It was agreed that two of us yearly, like magistrates, should take the management of affairs, and the rest, being quiet and without trouble, should devote themselves to the pursuit of wisdom."*

Such was Augustine's dream; and not only his, but that of all great souls, even from the times of the ancients downwards; it was the dream of Plato, Socrates, Pythagoras, Cicero; of all, who, at some time or other, either from natural elevation of character, or disenchantment as regards the world, have desired to withdraw into solitude for the sake of attaining true wisdom. It now seemed as if this noble dream, the realization of which had so often been vainly essayed, was now about to be realized at last. The friends were there, the master also, and funds were not lacking. "But," says Augustine, " when we began to consider what we should do as regards our wives, for many of us were married, the whole design, so well conceived, fell in pieces in our hands, was broken and thrown away, and we returned again to the sighs and groans of our miserable life."†

* *Confess.*, lib. VI., cap. xiv. † Ibid.

Indeed, two things were essential to the realization of this dream. The gates of this beauteous republic of noble souls, bound by mutual ties, freed from mundane cares, and at liberty to soar more readily heavenwards, must be guarded by chastity, and its walls be cemented by divine love. Wait for a few years, and we shall see Augustine return to this noble dream. The same friends will range themselves around him. The youthful master will be their law-giver, and his rule will be world-wide, and be the admiration of posterity. And when, in the course of ages, St. Dominic, St. Gaëtan, St. Francis of Sales, wish, in their turn, to form kindred associations, whither pure, free, and generous souls will enter, forsaking all else in order to devote themselves wholly to God, it is to St. Augustine they will turn for their plan, their constitutions and their rules.

But, alas! how fragile the human heart, how impe-rious its passions! To the sun of faith, now begin-ning to illumine his soul, Augustine, in separating from the mother of Adeodatus, offered the sacrifice which cost his tender heart the most acute suffering; he had been rewarded by the dawn of light and peace within his soul, and yet, incredible though it seem, he enchained himself anew. He had not the courage to wait two years for the youthful maiden, his mother's choice, who, in the retirement and solitude of a Christian life, was reserving for him her first affections. A slave to sensuality, unable to plead affection as the cause, the new chain with which he fettered himself was the most ignominious of all, inasmuch as love was absent; and the ingratitude and indelicacy of such conduct, following, as it did, immediately on his separation, stamped it with the brand of a triple disgrace. " Unhappy I, impatient of delay, a slave of passion, procured me another, though no wife, to sustain and keep up, by the continuance of custom, that disease of my soul, till the time of my marriage arrived. Neither was the wound of mine healed, that was caused by separation from my former companion, but after the most acute pains it had caused me, it became corrupt, and though the pain was deadened, it became a desperate sore." *

In perusing this, we can do nought, save veil our face and blush. See what human nature is without divine aid ! The loftiest and most piercing intellect lies grovelling in the dust. The noblest, most tender, delicate, and feeling heart, pursues the most vicious courses, and by some mysterious reaction, as the mind had corrupted the heart, so now the heart corrupts the mind: miserable and vicious circle, which would be interminable, did not God interfere a second time, to save Augustine from destruction.

Scarcely had he submitted to this fresh yoke, when all his passions re-awoke. That which is vilest and lowest in the human soul remounted to the surface, inspiring him with thoughts of which, hitherto, we have seen no trace. From the sublime heights, I say not of his dawning faith, but from the sublime heights of Plato, he fell into the ignominious depths

---

* *Confess.*, lib. VI., cap. xv.

of Epicurus, and we hear him panting for materialism in its grossest form. " I often discoursed with my friends Alipius and Nebridius, and declared that Epicurus above all men with me would carry away the prize. I said : Supposing us to be immortal, and that we might live in the perpetual enjoyment of sensual pleasures, without any fear of ever losing them, would not this be enough to render us happy ?"* So low had this noble, lofty, heaven-aspiring intellect fallen, that it was content with the grossest materialism, so that it were but eternal! " Nor was there anything that restrained me from sinking still deeper into the pit of carnal pleasures, but the fear of death and of Thy judgment to come, which, in all the variety of my opinions, never wholly departed from my breast."†

Ah! at these last words we breathe once more. Augustine's conscience was still alive, St. Monica's work had proved indestructible. Powerful indeed are the teachings of a Christian mother, since they proved capable of shielding Augustine amid the deadly peril encompassing his soul.

Moreover, because the relapse was more ignomini-ous, and heart, mind, and senses had fallen so low, Augustine's disquietude and dejection were deeper than before. " Woe to the audacious soul, that, after departing from God, vainly hopes to find something better. She turns and re-turns herself on back and sides, but in vain : all is hard, and Thou alone her rest."‡ And again : " What torments I then endured

* *Confess.*, lib. VI., cap. xvi.　　† Ibid.　　‡ Ibid.

Thou only knowest, and no human being ; for what could I have said, or how could my tongue have expressed the whole tumult of my soul, to the ears of even my most intimate friends ? But all my groanings were heard by Thee."* " Alas !" he goes on to say, "I sought for rest, but found none ; or if, thinking I had found some place of repose, I said to myself : It is well with me, here will I stay ; Thou with secret goads didst stir me up that I might be uneasy, and my soul restored to health by the secret touch of Thy healing Hand."†

That such was indeed the case, could be gathered from his increasing dejection, the utter impossibility of finding peace, and, let us add for Augustine's honour, from the courage he manifested. The first liaison had lasted for fifteen years : this last was only of a few months' duration. Probably St. Monica again intervened ; wept as she had never done before ; urged her son more vehemently ; counselled him more tenderly and lovingly ; vividly depicted to him the indelicacy and criminality of his behaviour, as regarded the pious young maiden whose hand he had demanded, and who already lived for him ; also as regarded Adeodatus, who was growing up in angelic purity, and who might perhaps be ruined by the sight of such deplorable weakness ; and especially as regarded God, whose most precious graces he was despising, and whose anger he would at last draw down upon himself. Augustine yielded, and, weary of seeking happiness where no happiness was to be found, broke

* *Confess.*, lib. VII., cap. vii.   † *Confess.*, lib. VII., cap. viii.

this last chain, and promised his mother that he would endeavour to await his now less distant marriage-day.

God, who had recompensed Augustine's first sacrifice by a ray of peace and light, had prepared a similar, but more precious reward, for this his second sacrifice. Hardly had he severed his bonds, when the remaining clouds vanished from his mind, and the full light of faith broke in on his delighted soul.

As our readers are already aware, the dawn had appeared long before. As after a storm on a warm summer evening the stars are sometimes seen gradually rising and shining through the vanishing clouds, so for some time past, in the stormy atmosphere of Augustine's soul, the grand verities of the faith had arisen one by one. He had conquered his doubt, or rather, had never been able to eradicate from his conscience his mother's teachings on the existence of God, on providence, on the soul's immortality, on the difference between good and evil, and on the last judgment. Amid all the varying doubts that had beset him, and amid all his wanderings in the paths of error, he understood how impossible it was for man to arrive at the truth by his own efforts, the need there was of divine teaching, the characteristics of such teaching, and its existence in the Catholic Church which he was beginning to view with growing admiration. Such were the stars which illumined his soul; their light still somewhat veiled, yet vivid and singularly gentle.

But, beautiful though they were, this radiancy was

not sufficient to render Augustine a Christian, for the most brilliant and most gentle star, the one that irradiates all with the light of truth, our Lord Jesus Christ, had not yet arisen within his soul. Not that Augustine had forgotten Him entirely, (too often and too lovingly had he drunk that adorable Name in from his mother's lips ever to forget it;) but amid so many bad books, pernicious teachings, and evil passions, which darken the soul, this divine face had almost vanished from his sight. He no longer comprehended the Incarnation, Redemption, nor the Divinity of Christ;—what do I say? the very existence of the Word and the Spirituality of God had become a problem. Therefore it behoved that the darkness should be dissipated, but who was the apostle chosen by God to effect this revelation none would ever divine.

In the days of antiquity, when Greece was in the height of her splendour, there lived a young man of incredible genius, and eloquence that has never been surpassed. The disciple of Socrates, whom he immortalized by lending him his own wings; the master of Aristotle, whose power he would have tripled could he but have imparted to him something of his own ardour; at the first glance he threw on creation he understood it to be only an image, a symbol, a shadow, and in his philosophic teaching started with this principle, that behind the visible world is the invisible one, which is not only the type of, but the key to the former. His second gaze revealed something still more beautiful. Ascending from man to God, and discerning with singular clearness the link uniting the two, he saw that man proceeds from and returns to God; but that during this short interval he is not separated from God, to whom he remains united and dependent, rooted as it were in Him, as Plato sublimely says; and that, however sad his lot may be, there is in the human heart a power sufficient to enable man to reascend the heaven whence he has descended; that this power is the consciousness man has of the divine existence, and his need of and aspirations towards God; this he termed the sense of the divine, which, together with the sense of the invisible, forms the two bases of his philosophy, or rather, of all philosophy worthy of man. After which, deeply moved by this insight, and desiring to know more, he traversed the world, visited its sanctuaries, consulted its priests versed in tradition, caused himself to be initiated in the mysteries, fathomed the creeds and restored them to their original integrity; and fortified in this manner, resuming his flight, he soared so high that the Fathers of the Church are undecided what name to give him, some regarding him as the most exalted type of human genius, others designating him a pagan Moses, a God-inspired prophet, an evangelic forerunner sent to the nations sitting in the shadow of death, all with one accord saluting this gentle and wondrous stranger as Plato the divine.

As yet Augustine, not being versed in Greek, had read nothing of Plato's works save what he had gathered from Cicero. Now, at the very moment when he was struggling with the latest objections with which the Manicheans had filled his mind, and trying to realize God as a pure Spirit, for till then he had pictured Him as a corporeal entity, one of his friends brought him a translation of Plato, just published by the famous Roman orator, Victorinus. Augustine took the book, and scarcely had he opened it, when there fell from his eyes the veil woven by heresy, which had prevented his comprehending the spirituality of God and the existence of His Word. Doubtless this was not yet the Gospel, but a kind of human preface, so beautiful that it dazzled Augustine. "At that time there fell into my hands a book, to use an expression of one of the ancients, all redolent with the most exquisite perfumes of Araby; scarcely was I conscious of the same, when, so soon as a few drops of it fell upon the tiny flame lately kindled in my heart, it was suddenly all aglow with a fire impossible for you, Romanianus, to comprehend, or for me to describe. Honours, worldly grandeur, glory, the charms and attractions of this terrestrial life, all paled before the flood of light which now began to inundate my soul."*

But we must allow him to relate these happy discoveries, still mingled with shades which will demand another hand to dissipate them, so that we may learn from his lips how certain souls are prepared to receive Christianity.

"In these books I read, not indeed in the same words, but with a striking identity of meaning, and

* *Contra Acad., lib. II., No. 5.*

that confirmed with a great variety of reasons, that, 'In the beginning was the Word, and the Word was with God, and the Word was God. The same was in the beginning with God. All things were made by Him, and without Him was not anything made that was made. In Him was life, and the life was the light of men. And the light shineth in the darkness, and the darkness did not comprehend it.' And that the soul of man, though it bear witness of the light, yet is not itself the light; but the Word of God is 'the true light, that enlighteneth every man coming into the world; that the world was made by Him, and the world knew Him not.' This I read in those books." That is, as we remark, the sublime opening of St. John's Gospel: *In principio erat Verbum.* "But, that He came to His own, and that to them who received Him He gave power to become the sons of God: this I read not there."

"Again, I read there that God the Word was born not of flesh, nor of blood, nor of the will of man, neither of the will of the flesh, but of God. But that this Word was made flesh and dwelt among us, I did not read there."

"Also, I discovered in those books, and that frequently repeated, and expressed in divers ways, that the Son 'is in the form of the Father, and thinks it not robbery to be equal with God, because He is of the same nature with Him.' But that He debased Himself, taking on Him the form of a servant, being made in the likeness of men, and humbled Himself, becoming obedient, even to the death of the Cross: this I found not in those writings."

"That Thy only begotten Son, begotten before all times, remains unchangeably co-eternal with Thee; and that, in order that they may be happy, souls must receive of His fulness; and that, to be wise, they must participate in His self-subsisting Wisdom: this I found there. But, that in due time He died for the wicked; that Thou, my God, didst not spare Thy only begotten Son, but gavest Him up for us all, is not to be found there. For Thou hast hidden these things from the wise, and hast revealed them to the little ones, that Thou mightest comfort them that mourn and are heavy-laden, and lead in the paths of righteousness those who are meek and humble of heart."*

That is to say, Augustine, in reading Plato's works, though he found not the infinite love and humiliations of the Word recorded there, found His glory, His eternal genesis, His radiance illumining all souls, of whom He is the true light. He was beside himself with joy, experiencing somewhat of the same happiness which he felt in his twentieth year, when reading Cicero's *Hortensius*, but in a higher degree, inasmuch as his soul was more freed from sensuality, and Plato soars higher, and carries souls with him in his upward flight more readily than Cicero does. "I entered within myself," he says, into those secret recesses of his soul, into which he had not dared to penetrate at the age of nineteen, "and at once saw

* *Confess.*, lib. VII., cap. ix.

the light: not this common light which is visible to all flesh, nor any greater light of the same kind, only clearer and brighter, but a light wholly different. Who knoweth the truth, knoweth this light," he exclaims, "and he who knoweth this light, knoweth eternity. It is discernible to one eye alone, for it is charity that knoweth it."*

" O eternal truth !" he cries, overwhelmed by this new light. " O true charity ! O lovely eternity ! Thou art my God ; for Thee I sigh day and night."

" But, alas !" he resumes humbly, " when I strove to know Thee, I became conscious of two things : that there was much to be seen, and that I was as yet incapable of seeing. So clearly did I perceive these two things that I thrilled with desire and fear, and found that I was at so vast a distance from Thee in those lower regions where my sins had plunged me, that discouragement would have seized me, had I not heard Thy voice saying to me: 'Courage, I am the food of the strong: grow thou up, and thou shalt feed upon Me. But I shall not be converted into thee, like thy corporal food ; but thou shalt be changed into Me.' "

A little later on, a prey to new anxiety, he heard the same voice saying with singular authority: " I am that I am." " I heard this not in my mind, but heart," says St. Augustine. " All my doubts vanished, and I could rather have doubted my own existence, than question a truth so patent to the eyes of the soul."†

---

* *Confess.*, lib. VII., cap. x. † Ibid.

Here we have a striking example of the mode in which the truth is born within the soul. After prolonged search, study, controversy with self and with others, suddenly, on the morrow of a sacrifice, without any human intervention, every obstacle melts, the clouds vanish, and truth dawns on the soul : the conscious enjoyment of light and peace testify 'to its presence. We marvel that any doubt could ever enter our soul, so clear is everything now. And when this light and peace have been preceded by thick darkness, protracted and cruel doubts, the rapture which follows is unending.

But, this first illumination, though very vivid, was insufficient, inasmuch, if I may be allowed the expression, it illumined but one half of the divine countenance of our Lord Jesus Christ. In perusing Plato's works, Augustine had glimpses of the spirituality of the Divine Entity, and of the existence of His Word; but, as we have already said, knew nothing of the love or the humiliation of the Word Incarnate. He now soared high enough to comprehend that God was invisible, glorious, far above all created beings; and even amid the dazzling radiance of the divinity perceived something of the divine nature : a kind of reflected light, brilliant as that whence it had its origin ; grand intuitions doubtless ; so grand, that we ask if human intellect could ever attain to such a height, and whether Plato's words are not the faithful echo of ancient traditions. But, a God who became poor, and who, for man's salvation, so humbled Himself as to assume our human nature ; a

God who so loved man as to suffer and die for him, neither Plato, Socrates, Cicero, nor Vigil ever dreamt of. Only the heart that is capable of effecting this could conceive it. Therefore, one greater and even holier than Plato was needed to reveal such astounding mysteries to Augustine's heart and mind.

Invisibly guided by the merciful Hand that had led him back from his prolonged wanderings, Augustine opened St. Paul's Epistles; but he did so tremblingly, as if, after so much disquietude and opposition, he had a presentiment of the sacrifices this perusal would entail. "I felt myself constrained," he says, "to turn my eyes towards that holy religion which had been so profoundly imprinted on my memory whilst I was a child; but I hesitated and wavered, although I felt the force of its attraction. At last, in a state of restless uncertainty, willing and not willing, it was with a feverish and trembling hand I seized St. Paul's Epistles."*

In those pages God awaited Augustine. "The greatest of doctors," said Fléchier, "must needs be the conquest of the greatest of apostles." Moreover, St. Paul is the theologian of the Word Incarnate, and would bear that name, save for St. John. Only, strange to say, he who leant on the Saviour's breast in the intimacy and affection of earthly love, has made the sublimity of the Word his theme; whilst he, who, on the journey to Damascus, and later on, was, according to his own strong expression, bowed down by the weight of glory, has made the divine humili-

---

* *Contra Acad.*, lib. II., No. 5.

ations his theme. A persecutor of Christ ere becoming His apostle, a worker of evil ere a worker of good, St. Paul has illumined the abysses of the Fall, the Incarnation, and the Redemption, with a light so intense as at first to dazzle the eye; and so powerful are his faith and language that the unprepared mind is bewildered thereby. But when, by dint of re-perusal, we gradually become accustomed to his abrupt and unmeasured periods, we are overwhelmed with admiration. St. Paul is excelled neither by David, Isaias, nor even by St. John; and, as none has felt more deeply the magnitude of the fall of man, since it was Paul the persecutor, and Paul the hater, whom God cast headlong to the ground, none has excelled him in magnificence of language, when he describes the need there was that man's redemption should be purchased by the humiliations, sufferings, and death of a God.

At the first lines Augustine was struck with admiration. He, but lately so deeply affected by the Platonic writings, experienced emotions wholly new. "Oh! didst thou but know," he wrote to Romanianus, "what light suddenly broke in on me. Not only would I have liked to show it thee, who hast so long desired this sight; but to that cruel enemy of thine, who has so long hunted thee from tribunal to tribunal, seeking thy goods. And certainly, did he see it as I see it, he would renounce all: gardens, houses, banquets, all that entices him now, and as a faithful gentle lover would fly enraptured towards this beauty."

This was only Augustine's first glimpse; the second was a deeper one.

He beheld the veil withdrawing from a grand mystery, which as yet he did not understand, and of which Plato was wholly ignorant; hence his inability to teach him the path of virtue, which the Manicheans had vainly essayed to solve by the existence of the two principles, and which St. Paul alone revealed to him in dazzling brightness. He saw that man was no longer in the state in which God had formed him; that he had been created holy, innocent, replete with light and intelligence, made to behold the Divine Majesty, and already beholding it; but that man, overwhelmed by his weight of glory, became guilty of presumption, desired to be supreme, and independent of God; that he has been forsaken, blinded, chased far from God, and so great is his corruption that sin abides within him; that in him there dwells a miserable, odious creature, hostile to truth, incapable of virtue, prone to evil; "the man of sin," as says St. Paul, "the old man," as he elsewhere terms it: strange expressions, full of profound sadness and sublime hope, for they denote that there is in man a new creature also. This Augustine soon learnt in proceeding with his reading. In the same pages he saw that to conquer man, this odious mixture of pride, concupiscence, and disobedience, the Word was made flesh, and lived a life of humility, obedience, and sacrifice; abasing Himself so low that he might heal man, and raise him to God. The whole mystery of the Incarnation and the Redemption unveiled itself before his eyes, and overwhelmed him with admiration. He was conscious of having surmounted every obstacle; that he had soared beyond the regions of human thought; touched that sublime point where man vanishes and God appears; and, overcome with astonishment and emotion, he threw himself on his knees. "Ah!" he exclaimed, "how wide the difference between the works of the philosophers and those of God's ambassadors! All that is good in the former is to be found in the latter, besides the knowledge of Thy grace, O my God, so that he who knows Thee, may not only cease his self-glorying, but may be healed, strengthened, and attain to Thee."

"Moreover, what do these great philosophers know of this law of sin incarnate in our members, which struggles with the law of the mind, making us slaves to sin? What know they of the grace of Jesus Christ, that innocent Victim, whose blood has effaced the decree of our condemnation? On these points all their books are silent."

"There we neither learn the secret of Christian piety, nor the tears of penitence, nor the sacrifice of a humble and contrite heart, much less the grace flowing from the precious Chalice which contains the price of our redemption."

"We seek there in vain for these canticles: 'O my soul, submit thyself to thy God; for He is thy God, thy Saviour, and thy Protector. Leaning on Him, what hast thou to fear?' Nor this sweet invitation: 'Come unto Me, all ye that are weary and heavy-laden, and I will refresh you.' These wise ones knew not that the Incarnate Word is meek and lowly of heart. Divine mysteries, which Thou, my God, hast hidden from the wise and prudent, but revealed to the humble and little ones."*

Such were the truths which penetrated into Augustine's soul whilst reading him who calls himself " the least of the apostles," and the sight of such wonders overwhelmed him with admiration. "Oh !" exclaimed he in closing the book, " it is one thing to see afar off from the summit of a wild rock the city of peace, without being able to attain it, do what you may ; and another, to find the way, and be possessed of a guide who will lead you thither, and defend you from those who would arrest you in your course."†

That is to say, the last shades were vanishing from Augustine's mind ; the ice was melting from his heart ; with light, love was reviving also ; and, seeing the shores of his father-land, that had so long been veiled in mist, unroll before his charmed gaze, it was easy to foresee that soon he would tread its soil, in all the triumphant joy of penitence.

* *Confess.*, lib. VII., cap. **xxi.**   ‡ Ibid.

CHAPTER XII.

ST. MONICA'S ANXIETY IS AUGMENTED ON BEHOLDING
AUGUSTINE SHRINK NOT FROM THE TRUTH, BUT FROM
THE PRACTICE OF VIRTUE.—HIS PEERLESS MOTHER'S
TEARS ARE TRANSFORMED INTO TEARS OF JOY.—AUGUS-
TINE'S CONVERSION.

386.

Behold Augustine in possession of that blessed
light for which he had sighed so long, and which his
mother had entreated for him with so many tears.
He had pierced every veil, and now, having reached
God and His Divine Son, our Lord Jesus Christ, who
died for love of us, there seemed but one thing to be
done, to arise, run to his mother, and say: Weep no
more, your son has become a Christian.

But Augustine had not yet arrived at that degree.
The vivid ray had pierced, but not dissipated the
clouds. Augustine's mind was still obscured by a
multitude of false, incorrect, and crude ideas, which
he had imbibed from the Manichean writings, and of
which he found it no easy matter to free himself:
these last shades vanished but slowly.

Had he but had courage to kneel, strike his breast,
and prepare himself for the Sacraments of Penance
and the Holy Eucharist, these shades would have

been dispelled; for in the grand search after truth there comes a moment when an act of humility and abandonment to the will of God are requisite for further light. We must be ready to sacrifice all, would we see this lingering darkness disappear. God grants His favours at this price.

Augustine had a vague consciousness of this, but was alarmed. Before he knelt, he wished to see more clearly; meanwhile, he multiplies his studies, readings, mental efforts, in order to increase the light he already had.

St. Monica, an anxious, but happy witness of this slow recovery, would have liked to hasten its progress. How often, at the foot of the altar, in her prayers and in her communions, did she entreat God to perfect His work, and take even forcible possession of her child's heart! Many a time did she pour out her rising hopes into the heart of the saintly Ambrose, learning from him to act towards Augustine with the same tenderness, patience, and gentleness, with which we tend a sick friend whom we fondly love. How often, confident of her son's progress, must she have urged him, saying: "Make your decision; you believe, why do you not act?"

Why did he not act? Alas! he humbly tells us why: two wings were wanting, without which none can attain virtue, nor yet remain for any length of time in possession of the light: humility, the wing of the mind; purity, that of the heart.

"I was assured of all the truths of faith; but was yet too weak to enjoy them, for I was eaten up by pride, vanity, and conceit. Though full of my misery, I wished to pass for learned, and instead of bewailing my crimes, was puffed up with vain science."* And inasmuch as he was not yet sufficiently humble, he could not fully apprehend our Lord Jesus Christ. "For I did not then as yet apprehend my most humble Master, our Lord Jesus Christ, neither did I comprehend the deep mysteries of His weakness. For Thy Word, the Eternal Truth, which soars far above the loftiest works of Thy Creation, raiseth up to Himself those that are subject to Him; and in these lower regions He has made to Himself an humble abode, so that He may bring down the loftiness of those whom He would have as His subjects, so that beholding at their feet the Divinity made weak, by taking upon Himself the vestment of our flesh, they, being wearied, might cast themselves down on Him, that so He arising might raise them up also."†

Behold the first wing which Augustine needed in order to soar to God by Jesus Christ. But this was not all; for, though he had severed the most sensual and guilty ties, there was still many a secret wound in the depths of his heart. Listen to his own words, more humble than before. "I now began to love Thee, O my God, and was filled with delight; but I did not stand still to enjoy Thee, but was one while strongly attracted to Thee by Thy beauty, and then presently hurried away from Thee by my own weight, and I fell down, groaning amongst those things below

* *Confess.*, lib. VII., cap. xx.
† *Confess.*, lib. VII., cap. xviii.

Thee, even by the weight of my own sinful habits and passions. But I did not wholly forget Thee, nor doubt that Thou wert He to whom I should cling, though as yet I was not in that state in which I could adhere to Thee, for the corruption of the flesh weighed down my soul, and the earthly dwelling pressed down the mind that was desirous of soaring aloft."[*]

But although Augustine did not as yet possess the divine wings of humility and purity, strong as they are light, with which we soar and descend at ease, he began to rise upwards in the light. Often he took his flight through created things, mounting step by step, and ladder by ladder, from the world of bodies to the world of souls, from soul to angel, from angel to God; he pierced every veil, and arrived at that Being, the faintest ray of whose splendour fills us with trembling. "But, alas!" he says, "I could not fix my eye, and falling to earth by reason of my weakness, I carried nothing away with me, but a memory enamoured of Thee, and regret that I could not enjoy at my leisure those meats whose fragrance I had discerned."[†]

This ray of glory, the darkness that succeeds the loving memories, the vanishing fragrance, the regrets: such is life! Thus in the early days of conversion does God sustain the soul, raising her a little above that world of which she must still remain a denizen, and sending fragrant breezes and sweet foretastes of heaven to strengthen her in her contempt of earth, and her longings for the celestial country.

[*] *Confess.*, lib. VII., cap. xvii.   [†] Ibid.

Nevertheless, with this increasing light the voice of Augustine's conscience grew louder and louder, giving him no rest. Soon he discerned the murmur of these words, which would henceforth resound in his inmost heart, and burst forth with a voice of thunder. " Hitherto thou hast pleaded thy uncertainty as to the truth as thy excuse for not fulfilling thy duty. Now all is clear, the truth shines before thy eyes. Why dost thou still hesitate?" "I heard," says St. Augustine; "but I heeded not; I refused to advance, though not able to make any excuse. My pretexts were now exhausted and confuted, and there remained only a dumb fear and apprehension, dreading to be restrained from that desperate course which I had hitherto pursued."*

Indeed, for a long time Augustine had not had the courage to believe; now he believed, but had not the courage to act. At first the obscurities of the Faith were an impediment; now, it was the practice of virtue that alarmed him. "I had found that good pearl which was to be bought by selling all that I had; and this I demurred to do."†

Agitated, undecided, urged by his mother, tormented by his conscience, Augustine at last resolved to consult a holy priest, named Simplicianus, whose beautiful life he had long admired.

He was one of those venerable old men, such as are often to be met with in the Catholic Church, who, having passed their youth in chastity and their mature years in a chastity, if possible, more perfect

---

* *Confess.*, lib. VIII., cap. vii.   † *Confess.*, lib. VIII., cap. i.

still, are blessed by God with a green old age, and present to our reverential gaze a venerable picture of peace and virtue. The passionate heart of youth delights to approach and calm itself in their soothing influence.

Therefore Augustine went to confide to Simplicianus the troubles of his life, and the secret weaknesses which now made him shrink, not from light, but virtue.

The good old man received him with a sweet smile, heard his recital of his wanderings without any expression of surprise, congratulated him on having studied such elevating writings as those of Socrates and Plato, instead of the debasing works of the atheist and the materialist. Simplicianus, as all aged priests, knew much of the human heart. Not only was he intimately acquainted with St. Ambrose, whose early years he had directed, and to whom he had administered holy baptism, but also with a large number of philosophers, poets, Roman orators, particularly with Victorinus, the translator of Plato's works, which Augustine was then studying. Also, as all other men of advanced age, Simplicianus loved to relate stories, and being skilled in the science of the human heart, knew how adroitly to conceal a lesson beneath the veil of fiction.

Seeing then this young man of such a great mind and noble character, already illumined by grace, but hesitating to follow its leadings, he skilfully turned to good account the name just uttered by Augustine, and after saying that he had formerly known this eloquent man in Rome, and wishing indirectly to point out to Augustine the path of courage and Christian honour, he related his history almost in the following terms.

As Augustine, so Victorinus had won distinction as an orator. As professor of rhetoric he had seen, not only the youth of Rome, but multitudes of senators crowding round his chair; he had translated, explained, and enriched the finest writings of ancient philosophy with luminous commentaries, and, on account of his eloquence, had obtained the rare honour of having his statue erected in the Roman Forum. When he had exhausted all the highest productions of the human intellect, he turned to the Holy Scriptures, read them attentively, then said to Simplicianus, not publicly, but secretly as to a friend, "Know that I am now a Christian." "I will not believe it," replied Simplicianus, "till I see you in the Church of Christ." On this Victorinus jested, saying: "Do the walls, then, make people Christians?" The fact was that he was afraid of offending his friends, lest those lofty cedars of Libanus, which the Lord had not yet broken in pieces, might maliciously fall on, and crush him.

Still he went on reading, and by much prayer and deep meditation gained fresh strength and courage. Soon, a day came when he feared more being denied by Christ, than mocked and despised by his friends; and fearing to betray the truth, he went to Simplicianus, saying: "Let us go to the church; I will be made a Christian." Rome was filled with astonishment, and the Church with joy.

When the time came to make profession of his faith in the presence of all the faithful, it was suggested to Victorinus that he should recite it in private, as was allowed in the case of those who, through timidity, shrank from doing so publicly. But this he refused to do, and courageously ascended the ambo. As soon as he appeared, every one that knew him repeated his name to his next neighbour, and in the joyful mouths of all was heard, with a low sound, "Victorinus! Victorinus!" As quickly were they silent again that they might hear him speak. He then made profession of the faith with wonderful confidence, and all present were so delighted at his courage that they were desirous to take him into their hearts: there they placed him by the hands of love and joy.

Since then, continued Simplicianus, laying a greater stress on each of his words, since then this illustrious old man gloried in becoming a child in the school of Jesus Christ, humbly allowing himself to be fed at the breasts of the Church, joyously bending that illustrious head to the yoke and reproach of the cross. Julian the Apostate, having, soon after this, forbidden Christians the profession of letters, he closed his eloquent lips, and crowned his life by the most beautiful and painful of sacrifices.*

This well chosen example, so perfectly suited to Augustine's position, moved him to his inmost depths. He went away, filled with enthusiasm, and reproaching himself for weakness and cowardice, re-

* Confess., lib. VIII., cap. ii.

turned home (where his mother had been praying for him) resolved to bring matters at once to a crisis, and do as Victorinus had done. " O my God," he exclaimed, in a species of transport, "come to mine aid! Act, O Lord; stir us up and call us back; kindle and rejoice our hearts; breathe forth Thy fragrance and become sweet to us; let us love and run after Thee." *

But, alas! the chain which Augustine had dragged for so many years was heavier than he at first imagined. He needed but to raise his hand to learn the difficulty of breaking fetters such as those. He did not refuse, and yet had not the courage to break them. " This course of corruption and of evil habits formed a chain which kept me close shackled in cruel slavery. I did indeed desire to serve God with noble and chaste love, and to enjoy Him alone; but this new will was not yet strong enough to overcome the other, which had been strengthened by the long force of habit. Thus there were two wills of mine: the one old, the other new; the one carnal, the other spiritual; and these two strove together with one another and divided my soul." †

Meanwhile, he strove to soothe his conscience, and when it told him that he must indeed come to a decision, he knew not what to reply, as the sluggard who exclaims: " Presently, by and by, stay a little;" but this "presently" did not come presently, and this "stay a little" was extended to a long time. ‡

* *Confess.*, lib. VIII., cap. iv.
† *Confess.*, lib. VIII., cap. v.   ‡ Ibid.

It is easy to imagine that this visit to the priest Simplicianus afforded hope to St. Monica. Such a step, at such a moment, seemed equivalent to a conversion. For she doubted not but that the saintly old man would induce her son to make the last painful effort, and rejoice in so doing. Therefore, on seeing Augustine still hesitating after this interview, she was seized with profound dejection. Her sole consolation was to see him suffer incessantly; to note his agitation increase, his assiduous presence at church, and that all the leisure remaining after the preparation of his lectures was employed in the eager perusal of St. Paul's writings.*

Just then, an old friend of Augustine's, named Pontitianus, came to see him. They were both from Africa, where they had known one another in former days. Only, that whilst Augustine had wandered on the sad road of error and oblivion of God, Pontitianus had remained a fervent Christian, living in Milan, where he held one of the highest military posts at the Imperial Court. St. Monica had rejoiced to meet him in Italy, and introduce to the society of Augustine, Alipius, and Nebridius, a soul so steadfast as to resist all the temptations besetting him as a courtier and a soldier.

Whilst engaged in conversation with Augustine and Alipius, Pontitianus, observing a book lying on a billiard table, opened it mechanically, as one is apt to do when talking; he expected that it was a copy of one of Cicero's or Quintilian's works, but finding it

* *Confess.*, lib. VIII., cap. vi.

contained St. Paul's Epistles, was not a little sur
prised, and smiling, looked at Augustine, who admitted that for some time he had studied the Holy
Scriptures with the greatest attention and delight.
Then the conversation took a decidedly Christian
tone.

Pontitianus had been a great traveller; he knew
Gaul, Spain, Italy, Africa, Egypt, and knew them in
their Christian character; that is, he had everywhere
studied the wonders wrought by the true faith.

Of all these wonders, at that epoch none was more
striking than the growth of virginity, charity, and
the religious life, to be met with in the Egyptian
desert and the Thebaïd. On the banks of the Nile,
in the interior of Egypt, the secret home of the
abominable practices of antiquity, had appeared bands
of virgins, living angelic lives, who, beneath that
ardent sky, and in that enervating climate, served
God with the purest love and most divine energy.
There were to be found all those who had been driven
from the world by contempt for its vanities, horror
of its corruptions, cowardice, and baseness, and who
desired to give their life in sacrifice; spotless virgins;
mothers, inconsolable for the loss of their children;
doctors and philosophers, trained in the ancient wisdom
of the Alexandrian schools, and thirsting for silence
and humility; soldiers who had traversed the world,
without finding God there; confessors of the faith,
and martyrs for the truth's sake, who, having escaped,
bleeding, from their beds of torture, came to revive
their courage in the refreshing streams of prayer

and penance. Their number was immense. There were more than five thousand on Mount Nitrius alone. A little farther on, at about half-a-day's march, in the interior of the desert, in a spot named Cella, were two thousand more. Moreover, there were about ten thousand under the goverment of St. Serapion, and almost as many under that of Macarius. St. Pacomius, who was just dead, had left seven thousand in the solitudes of Tabennus, and at the annual meeting of his congregation general, the monasteries following the rule had sent as many as fifty thousand. The cities were inundated by them. At Ancyra there were ten thousand virgins, and in the year 356, a traveller found in the city of Oxyrinka twenty thousand virgins dedicated to God.

These wonders, so long unknown, were beginning to astonish the world and fill Christian hearts with enthusiasm. St. Athanasius had just written the wonderful life of St. Anthony, the giant of the desert, and soon the lives of the most celebrated patriarchs of the Thebaïd, the Pauls, Hilarions, Pacomi, and Macarii, then being written by men, (also marvels themselves), by St. Jerome, St. Epiphanius, and St. Ephrem, would be given to the world.

Augustine knew nothing of all this. Like so many others, who, though the Catholic Church be in their midst, note her not, he had lived thirty years in Africa, close to Alexandria, without once hearing of St. Anthony, nor of the hermits, nor of the virgins, nor of any of those admirable works by which the Church was manifesting herself to be the true spouse of Jesus

Christ. He had not even perceived that in Milan, under his very eyes, were a number of virgins living in angelic purity, for whom Ambrose had written his three books, " *On Virgins*," and was then composing his beautiful " *Treatise on Virginity*." Therefore he listened eagerly with great admiration to the recitals of Pontitianus. " We were astonished," he says, " to hear of these miracles, so well attested, and of such recent occurrence (almost in our own day), wrought in the true faith and the Catholic Church ; indeed we were all surprised, we to hear such marvels, and he to find that they were unknown to us."*

But if these wonders had escaped Augustine's notice, they had none the less rejoiced the Church and proved her divinity, by showing what powerful spirit animated her; for as formerly the blood of the martyrs was the seed of the Church, so now it was virginity and the perfume from the desert which gave birth to apostles, doctors, and heroes.

Noting his friend's attentive silence, Pontitianus related how once when the court was at Treves, and the emperor one afternoon was attending the sports of the circus, he and three of his friends went out walking among the gardens near the city walls, and on their way two of them entered a cottage where some of those servants of God dwelt, poor in spirit, of whom is the kingdom of heaven; and in a cell there they found a manuscript containing the life of St. Anthony, which one of them commenced reading, and so admired, and was inflamed by it, that he was

* *Confess.*, lib. VIII., cap. vi.

seized with a desire to quit the world, and embrace
the same kind of life. Then, suddenly filled with holy
love and sober shame, angry with himself, he looked
at his friend, saying: "Tell me, I pray thee, whither
do our aspirations tend? What do we seek? For
whom do we fight? For what do we hope? To be
friends and favourites of the emperor? And then,
how fickle is fortune! What perils await us!
Whereas, if I wish to become the friend and favourite
of God, I may become so at once, and for ever." He
said this, and labouring in travail of a new life, his
heart was agitated, the waves thereof rolled to and
fro, but at last he gained the victory, and, wholly
God's, said to his friend: "All is over, I have bidden
a final adieu to worldly hopes, and am fully bent on
serving God, and to begin from this very hour." His
friend applauded his determination; both of them resolving on quitting the world, they left all, to erect
the tower that led to God.

"By this time," adds Pontitianus, "my friends
and I, ignorant of what had transpired, sought them
out, and having found them, minded them of returning
home, as the day was far spent. I then learnt what
had happened, as also their determination to dedicate
themselves to God's service. They entreated us that
if we would not follow their example, we would refrain from opposing them, therefore we withdrew,
bewailing ourselves, but piously congratulating them
and recommending ourselves to their prayers, and so
returned to the palace with a heart weighed down to
earth, while they with a heart raised heavenwards

remained in the cottage. Both of them were betrothed, but they to whom they were affianced, on hearing these things, also consecrated their virginity to God."[*]

Pontitianus, being carried away with his subject, had not perceived the effect produced on Augustine, who, so long as Pontitianus discoursed of the miracles of innocence, purity, austerity, and courage, to be witnessed in the desert, silently applauded, but whose conscience began to cry aloud, on hearing of the two officers quitting the world, in reply to these ardent words : " What do we ? Whither tend our aspirations ? Is it to be friends and favourites of the emperor ? What will this avail us ? Why not become friends of God ?" He says : " Whilst Ponti·tianus was speaking I was overwhelmed with remorse and confusion at the sight of my ugliness, deformity, spots, stains, and ulcers. The more I admired the beauty of the chaste lives just depicted, the greater became my self-abhorrence. So many years, more than twelve, squandered since I had been stirred up, in the nineteenth year of my age, upon reading Cicero's *Hortensius,* to the study of wisdom, and yet I still delayed to sacrifice worldly felicity to the pursuit of that happiness, the very search after which was to be preferred to the finding of treasures, kingdoms, and the voluptuous enjoyments of the world. Long ago I pleaded darkness as my excuse, but now that light had dawned, conscience exclaimed : ' What doest thou now that thou art excuseless, that all is

[*] *Confess.,* lib. VIII., cap. vi.

certain ?' Though oppressed by the vanity of earthly things, many a less ardent and anxious seeker for truth has outstripped thee in the heavenward race."* "Thus was I inwardly corroded," adds St. Augustine, "and extremely confounded with a horrible shame, my countenance sharing in the trouble of my soul, whilst Pontitianus was relating these things."†

At last Pontitianus left them, and Augustine, no longer able to restrain the anguish of his soul, retired to a garden, whither Alipius followed him. As for St. Monica, she, either present at the above-named interview, or warned by Alipius, or perhaps by God Himself, of what had occurred, now that the grand moment had arrived, withdrew to her chamber, and, falling on her knees, with the ardour of her maternal and saintly heart entreated help for her dear child in the hour of this, his last conflict with his God.‡

When alone with Alipius, Augustine, regarding him with emotion, cried out, "What is this we suffer? Hast thou not heard ? The unlearned take heaven by force, and we, with all our learning, cowardly and

---

* *Confess.*, lib. VIII., cap. vii.   † Ibid.

‡ This tradition is found in almost all the Augustinian Liturgies, and in the majority of the works composed in honour of their Father, by the different orders following the Rule of St. Augustine. The Rev. Father Louis of the Angels, Augustinian hermit, mentions this as a fact, (*Della Vita e Laudi del S. D. August.*, lib. II., cap. v.,) and the Rev. Father Archangelo of the Presentation, barefooted Carmelite, mentions it in several passages in his multitudinous and learned works on St. Augustine. (*Comment. in Confess. edit. Florent.*, 1757, *op. et studio Fr. Archangeli a Præsentatione, Carmel. excalceati.)*

heartless, see how we still wallow in flesh and blood. Are we ashamed to follow them? or rather, ought we not to be more ashamed that we have not courage to do the like?"*

Having said this, the agitation of his mind hurried him away from his friend ere the latter had time to reply. Alipius gazed at him in speechless surprise, for he spoke not as usual, and forehead, cheeks, eyes, colour, tone of voice, revealed the state of his mind even more clearly than the words he uttered.

Near the house was a little garden. "Thither," says Augustine, "this tumult of my breast carried me, where none might interrupt the hot conflict in which I was engaged with myself. Thither I withdrew with Alipius, for the presence of so dear a friend did not destroy my privacy. We sat down as far as possible from the house. I groaned in spirit, angry at myself with a most violent indignation, because I had not yet submitted myself to Thy will, O my God, nor yet entered into league with Thee, towards whom all the powers of my soul urged me, bidding me take courage. I suffered and was tormented by my bitter self-accusations, struggling with my fetters until I had snapped their last feeble link, saying to myself, 'Courage, courage; let us not delay.' And my heart was inclined to obey; I was on the point of acting, and yet acted not, and the nearer the crisis approached when my whole being would be transformed, the greater became my alarm.†

* *Confess.*, lib. VIII., cap. viii.
† *Confess.*, lib. VIII., cap. x. and xi.

"And those trifles of trifles, and vanities of vanities, my old friends, pulled me by the garment of flesh, softly whispering, 'Wilt thou, then, forsake us? and from this moment shall we no more be with thee for ever? and thou be no longer allowed to do this or that for ever?' And what things they suggested to me under what I call this or that, do Thou in Thy mercy efface from my soul. What filth, what infamy did they suggest!*

"But they no longer boldly confronted me as heretofore, but with timid mutterings behind me, pulling me by my garment to oblige me to look back at them. And the violence of evil custom said to me, 'Canst thou live without such things as these?' But this was now said very faintly, for in the direction whither I tremblingly turned my eyes I beheld the chaste dignity of continence, serene and modestly cheerful, kindly enticing me to come forward and to fear nothing, and stretching forth her loving hands to receive and embrace me, full of beautiful examples of boys and girls, a multitude of young men and maidens, persons of all ages, grave widows and virgins who had attained old age. And in all these continency herself was not barren, but a fruitful mother of children, that is, of chaste delights from Thee, O Lord, her heavenly bridegroom. She seems to laugh at me with a kind of derision by way of alluring me on, as if she had said, 'And art not thou able to do what these youths and maidens do? or are these able in themselves, and not in the Lord their

* *Confess.*, lib. VIII., cap. xi.

God ? Thou leanest upon thyself, and therefore thou dost not stand. Throw thyself upon Him: fear not, He will not withdraw Himself to let thee fall.'*

" And I was exceedingly ashamed that I should still hear the whisper of those vanities, and hang in suspense; and Alipius, who kept close by me, waited in silence for the issue of this strange commotion.

" But when deep consideration had heaped together all my misery before the view of my heart, there arose in me a mighty storm, bringing with it a very great shower of tears, which, that I might more freely pour it forth with proper words, I arose and withdrew from Alipius, conceiving solitude to be more fit for the business of weeping, and I removed to that distance where even his presence might not be burdensome to me. Something of this, I know not what, Alipius perceived from my words, in which the sound of my voice discovered that I was big with tears. I threw myself down under a certain fig-tree, and there gave free scope to my tears, floods of which broke from my eyes. And if not in these same words, yet to this purpose, I said unto Thee, ' And Thou, O Lord, how long, how long wilt Thou be angry to the end ? Remember not my past iniquities.' For I perceived myself to be held by them, and sobbing, I added, ' How long, how long? to-morrow and to-morrow ! Why not now ? Why not this very hour end my shame ?'†

" And behold, whilst speaking thus, and weeping with bitter contrition, I heard a voice from a neigh-

* *Confess.*, lib. VIII., cap. xi.　　† *Confess.*, lib. VIII., cap. xii.
18　　　　　　　　　　　　　　　　　　　s m.

houring house, as of a boy or a girl, I know not which, saying in a singing voice: 'Take up and read, take up and read.'*

"And presently, my countenance being altered, I began considering intently whether in any kind of play children were wont to sing such words, but I could not call to mind ever having heard the like. Then, the course of my tears being suppressed, feeling certain that it was nothing less than a divine admonition that I should open St. Paul's Epistles, I ran to the spot where Alipius was sitting and where I had laid down the book. I caught it up, opened it, and read in silence the words on which I first cast my eyes: 'Not in revellings and drunkenness, not in chamberings and impurities, not in contention and envy; but put ye on the Lord Jesus Christ, and make not provision for the flesh in its concupiscences.' I would not read further, nor was there need. For with the end of this sentence a light as of confidence and security had streamed into my heart, dissipating all its former obscurities.†

"Then, putting my finger or some other mark in the place, I shut the book, and with a countenance that was now tranquil and serene related all to Alipius, who in the following manner discovered to me what was going on in his mind, which I did not know. He asked to see what I had read. I showed it to him; he looked on farther than I had read, and discerned these words: 'him that is weak in the faith take unto you;' which he applied to himself, and

* *Confess.*, lib. VIII., cap. xii.   † Ibid.

strengthened by this admonition, without any hesitation he joined himself to me in this good resolution, which was very agreeable to his virtuous inclinations and manners, and we both hastened to my mother."*

Thus, after seventeen years resistance, Augustine surrendered, won by Monica's tears; and it is worthy of remark that this conquest, the most affecting of any in the history of the Church and of the human heart, was due to a revelation of purity and innocence; so true is it that it is easier to find the truth than return to the path of virtue.

The Church has deemed this conversion so great a miracle of grace, that it is the only one, save that of St. Paul, which she commemorates, and by a delicate attention has fixed the 5th of May, the day following St. Monica's feast, for its celebration. The closing words in the office for St. Monica's day mingle with the opening hymns which hail St. Augustine's conversion; the same solemnity re-unites and honours the mingled tears of the mother and the son.

After his conversion, Augustine's first thought was to run to St. Monica. He throws himself in her arms; bathes her with his tears. Mother and son are clasped in that close and silent embrace, the sole language that deep emotion allows.† Augustine was exultant, and in the new light illumining his soul he at last knew the value of his mother's tears. Unable to speak, he clasped her to his heart, by his silence telling her that which he never wearied of repeating

---

* *Confess.*, lib. VIII., cap. xii.   † *Confess.*, lib. IX., cap. 1.

to his last day. "Yes, Lord, if I am Thy servant, it is because I am the son of Thy handmaid." And again: "To my mother, to her prayers and merits, I owe all that I am."* And elsewhere: "If I love truth above all else, and for its sake would lay down my life, for this I am indebted to my mother, whose prayers God could not withstand."† Again: "My mother's constant tears obtained my conversion."‡ This is the key-note of his writings, and this feeling he intended to express by that long and mute embrace.

St. Monica's joy was boundless; she watered Augustine with her tears, and gazed at him with blissful rapture. All she had entreated was to see him a good Christian and a faithful husband: were this but granted she would have died happy. But now, as Augustine's emotion began to allow him to speak, unexpected wonders dawned upon her gaze. Not content with being a Christian only, he yearned after continence and solitude, desiring to quit the world and all its vanities in order to love God alone. Each word filled her with joy. Who knows but that God also granted her a presentiment of that which would come to pass; and, after her twenty years of anguish, gladdened her with a vision of her Augustine crowned with the doctor's crown, and the aureola of sanctity ? §

O blissful moment ! when a mother finds again the

---

* *De Beat. Vit.*, in fine Praefat.   † *De Ordine*, lib. II., cap. **xx.**
‡ *De Dono Perseverantiae*, cap. xx., No. 53.
§ *Confess.*, lib. VIII., cap. xii.

child whom she thought dead. But more happy, surely, that in which a Christian mother beholds faith, purity, courage, and virtue, spring to life in her son's soul: and, afflicted as every Christian must be at the Church's woes, foresees that this new-born son will become the Church's luminary, glory, and avenger!

At Milan they still show the little chamber where St. Monica prayed, and the garden where these touching scenes were enacted. Long will they be shown: when the ruthless hand of time has destroyed the last stone of that house, the spot will still be visited with affectionate emotion. The beauty of this young man, in whom shone all the lights of genius, and all the affections of the heart; his failings, and amid all these his glorious sorrows, which ensure him the sympathy of all hearts, innocent or guilty; his prolonged resistance to grace; his cries and struggles, like those of a wounded eagle that will not yield; and in face of all this resistance, the patience of God, who furnishes him so tenderly with the light he needs, and who, victorious at last, whilst leaving him a free agent, raises him from the abyss of doubt and of passion to the loftiest heights of truth, purity, and divine love; and above all else, in order to complete the picture, that incomparable mother's tears, constraining God to come to her son's rescue; all these are things which will ever remain graven on the minds of men, and which, to the final consummation of all things, will lead them, impressed and purified, to the scenes where these transactions occurred.

CHAPTER XIII.

CASSIACUM.—ST. MONICA TAKES AUGUSTINE INTO THE COUNTRY TO PREPARE HIM FOR HOLY BAPTISM.—SHE IS PRESENT AT PHILOSOPHICAL CONFERENCES.—THE MOTHER OF THE CHRISTIAN PLATO.

SEPTEMBER, 386—JANUARY, 387.

" O my God, I am Thy servant, because I am the son of Thy handmaid. Thou hast broken my bonds asunder; to Thee will I offer the sacrifice of praise. Let my heart and tongue praise Thee, and let all my bones say, ' Lord, who is like unto Thee?' Let them say this, and do Thou reply to my soul, ' I am thy salvation.' O Christ! O Jesus! Thou art my helper and my Redeemer."*

With this new sentiment of admiration and gratitude, which filled Augustine's heart on the morrow of his conversion, was mingled another as profound and calm. Augustine felt himself a new creature; that which had charmed him yesterday now inspired him with aversion only. " What joy was mine in detaching myself from those vain amusements. Thou didst expel them, who art the true and sovereign sweetness; Thou didst banish them, and didst come Thyself in their stead; Thou transcendent sweetness,

* *Confess.*, lib. IX., cap. i.

light, and majesty. Now was my mind free from the cares that beset those who pursue honours, earthly riches, and sensual delights; and my infant tongue began to address itself to Thee, my light, my riches, and my salvation." *

With a glad heart did St. Monica listen to these first heartfelt effusions. Equalling him in ardour, for she was so happy, she joined with heart and voice in singing those hymns with which the Church was now being enriched, and having attained the height of grace and sanctity, full of experience in divine things, she guided him tenderly in that sublime path, which, though new to him, was so well known to his mother.

In order to enjoy the happiness of his new-born religious feelings, and that he might have leisure for repentance and gratitude, Augustine would fain have been alone with his mother, in some solitude far from the haunts of men, where he might devote himself wholly to contemplation, thanksgiving, and praise. Unfortunately he was overwhelmed with work, having to lecture many times a week, speak in public, and give numerous lessons in rhetoric, the preparation of which made serious demands on his time. He was perplexed what to do. His first thought was to send in his resignation, and publicly announce that he had so done. But it was near the close of August; the vacation commenced on the 16th September, and as there would be only twenty days to wait, he questioned within himself whether it might not be better

---

* *Confess.*, lib. IX., cap. i.

to wait patiently, and withdraw quietly and unob-
trusively. Not that he feared their judgment. " For
Thou hadst pierced my heart with the arrows of Thy
love, and Thy words, O my God, were fixed in my inward parts; and the examples of Thy servants, whom
Thou hadst brought from darkness to light, and
from death to life, enkindled within me such ardour,
that any wind of opposition that could blow from a
deceitful tongue, instead of extinguishing, would but
have increased it." But though he feared nothing
from their criticisms, was there nothing to be dreaded
from their praise and their commendation ? For by
taking this step publicly, he would elicit universal
attention, and perhaps be the object of many en-
comiums.

These reasons appeared decisive; therefore, partly
from prudence, and partly from modesty, Augustine
resolved, cost what it might, to await the arrival of
the vacation.*

Even with such precautions as these it was no easy
matter to carry out his intention. For two years
Augustine had taught in Milan with extraordinary
success. His genius, eloquence, and affections, all of
the first order, were even heightened by his failings,
forming, as they did, an additional link between him
and the ardent spirits who always throng round him
who can inspire words with life. Unfortunately, he
had not only expended energy, but health, too, on
his youthful hearers. His lungs began to fail, and
his weak chest, unequal to any loud or lengthened

* *Confess.*, lib. II., cap. ii.

discourse, plainly testified that this young man, whose zeal exceeded his strength, could not long pursue his professional career.

When this sad fact first dawned on Augustine's mind he wept, but now that he yearned for contemplation and solitude, in which to meditate on divine love, he gladly hailed this excuse, and rejoiced that he could allege health as the plea for the retirement he so ardently desired.

There might have been another obstacle, for Augustine was poor, and for his own and his mother's support he had no other resource than his talent and his public lessons. Happily, Romanianus, ever generous and delicate, was in Milan, and had already often spontaneously offered to procure Augustine the solitude and leisure so necessary for the man of genius. " Thou, O noble friend," thus Augustine wrote to him some months later on, " who hadst already watched over the cradle and nest of my early studies, and later on aided my first daring flight, again didst come to my aid. Yes, if in the repose I now enjoy I rejoice to be free from so many hindering cares, if I breathe, and enjoy my liberty and leisure to devote myself wholly to the contemplation of truth, to thee do I owe this happiness; for no sooner had I disclosed to thee the trouble and agitation of my mind, and that no life would be congenial to me save that which would leave me leisure for the pursuit of wisdom, which leisure I could not hope to enjoy, inasmuch as I had to support my mother and my son, so deeply did you feel for me, that you not only promised me liberty, but promised also to share it with me."*

Relieved from this anxiety, thanks to Romanianus, and able now to see the end of his busy labours, Augustine completed his course of lectures. But these remaining twenty days seemed to him an age. His heart was no longer in his work, and his sole consolation, when he returned home in the evening, wearied and exhausted with the labours of the day, was to close his door, and in company with none save his mother, to discourse with her on the wonders God had wrought in him.

As soon as the vacation had commenced, Augustine accompanied St. Monica to the country. She was as impatient as he was to withdraw into solitude, and aid in the completion of the important work which was going on in his soul. A friend and colleague of Augustine's, named Verecundus, whom Augustine had made his confidant, had placed his country house at Augustine's service. Monica accepted the offer, and about the 16th or 17th of September, 386, installed herself there with her son.

The site of the house is not accurately known, but we have an exact description of it, and well know the landscape surrounding it.

It was one of those large and pleasant country houses, such as the Romans, towards the decline of the empire, loved so much,—spacious halls, vaulted porticoes, baths, a library, terraces adjoining, shady trees, no want of space, air, and light, in fine, all

* *Contra Acad.,* lib. II., cap. ii.

that can be desired by him who seeks for repose and enjoyment. At the foot of the house extended a lawn on which the eye loved to rest, and which, bordered as it was by lofty trees, formed an agreeable promenade, and afforded shade for conversation or reading. One end of this lawn was broken up by the rocky bed of a torrent, dry during part of the year, but which, when swollen by the winter snows and autumn rains, broke the stillness of the valley by the monotonous sound of its waters. From the windows and from the terraces adjoining the house the eye rested on a tranquil landscape, vast enough to give free scope to the gaze of the spectator, and bounded in the distance by lofty mountains, which seemed to lead the mind heavenward. These mountains belonged to the Alps and the Apennines; they formed an immense circle, in which were seen meadows, vineyards, orchards, little hills covered by lofty trees, and blue lakes glittering in the sun; something of the verdure of a Swiss landscape with the warmer tones of an Italian sky. The house had been built on an eminence in order that it might enjoy the grandeur and serenity of this pleasing picture.*

The summer was nearing its close. The cool rays of the autumn sun fell upon the landscape. The leaves had not yet begun to fall, but were already beginning to be tinged with those brilliant hues of red and gold which render the country so beautiful

---

* This description has been carefully taken from the different works composed by Augustine at Cassiacum.

in September. It was the moment when nature seems to be graver and almost to wear a hue of sadness, as if preparing for death. There are some moods in which the soul is keenly alive to the charm of such a scene.

At such a moment, and to such a serene and retired spot, did the happy Monica introduce Augustine; thither they went to hide their joy, and to prepare their souls for the great day of holy baptism.

A few young men had joined them. Ties of kindred, sympathy, similarity of rank, tastes, calling, anxiety, and passion, had drawn them around Augustine. And with him, all of them beheld the joyous dawn of the same faith arise from amid the same shades.

The chief of these were, first, Augustine's son, Adeodatus, or the gift of God. He was just emerging from boyhood, and gave promise of one day equalling his father, whose genius he shared. " We brought with us," writes St. Augustine, "the boy Adeodatus, carnally born of my sin; but Thou hast endowed him well. Though barely fifteen years of age, he surpassed in knowledge many grave and learned men ; each day revealed fresh tokens of his wisdom, so that I was astonished at his genius."* Happily he was not only talented, but extraordinarily pious and chaste. He it was who, on the question being asked, " In whom does God dwell?" replied, " In the chaste of heart." And on Augustine wishing to know if by that he meant the fleeing all that is

* *Confess.*, lib , IX., cap. vi.

opposed to the beautiful virtue of chastity, replied, " O no ; there is no soul truly chaste but she who has her gaze ever fixed on God, and who clings to none save Him." As yet he had not received holy baptism, but was preparing to receive that sacrament with an ardour so great that St. Monica was compelled to restrain it. On seeing this precocious genius and virginal purity, the beholder wondered what would be the future rôle assigned him by God in the day when the heart and mind of Adeodatus should be fully developed. That day never came. An angelic childhood, a pure youth, baptism received with the dispositions of a saint, and followed by an early death, such was the brief but holy life allotted to this child. " I think of him with joy," writes St. Augustine, after the death of Alipius, " not a cloud obscures his memory."*

The second was Navigius, Augustine's brother, and St. Monica's second son. Already baptized for some long time, pious, timid, feeble in health, almost always ill, and possessing none of Augustine's genius, but much of his mother's contemplative piety, his life was one of silence and prayer.

The third was Alipius, with whom our readers are already acquainted. Not bound to Augustine by ties of blood, but by those of the most intimate friendship, his heart's brother, so the saint beautifully designated him. A prey to the same disquietude and errors, but not to the same passions, light had dawned on his soul simultaneously with that of St.

* *Confess.*, lib. IX., cap. vii.

Augustine, from whom he could not bring himself to part. Together they prepared for holy baptism, both of them destined to become bishops, and consecrated to the Church, if not with the same genius, at least the same heart.

Augustine had brought two other youths with him, not exactly friends, for they were too young for this, but pupils whom he loved with paternal affection, and whose education he directed with the most tender solicitude. They were Licentius and Trigetius.

Trigetius was twenty years of age, fond of study, of exalted mind, and loving all that appeared great, noble, or tender. At first he thought of being a soldier, but, revolted by the brutality and vulgarity he met with in the military profession, resumed his literary pursuits, devoting himself especially to the study of history with an ardour unusual in one so young.* His vivacity and gaiety charmed Augustine, who with joy watched him prepare himself to receive holy baptism.

Licentius caused him more anxiety, for he was one of those fiery natures nothing can repress or satisfy. An ardent lover of poetry, paling at the recital of a noble deed, and composing verses even when at table. He sang Sophocles' choruses with extraordinary depth of expression; wept at reading Virgil; but cared little for philosophical and less for religious questions.

All this filled Augustine with the deeper disquietude, inasmuch as this brilliant youth was the

* *Contra Acad.*, lib. I., p. 424; *De Ordine*, lib. I., p. 533.

son of Romanianus, by whom he had been entrusted to Augustine when quite young. "Therefore," says Paulinus, "Augustine felt the tenderest love for him, and strove to be to him father, mother, and nurse." From the care he lavished on him we feel that he thus desired to repay the debt of gratitude he owed the father, ready to impose any sacrifice on himself so that he might make Licentius a distinguished man and a Christian. The first was an easy task, the second a more difficult one.

Such, with the addition of two of Augustine's cousins, Lastidianus and Rusticus, of whom we know nothing, was the youthful circle accompanying St. Monica and St. Augustine on their arrival at Cassiacum.

Two other friends of Augustine were wanting in this circle, and, alas! would ever be wanting there,— Nebridius and Verecundus.

Nebridius, of whom we have already spoken, had left all, father, mother, and country, to follow Augustine, and profit by his youthful master's instructions. An earnest inquirer after the truth, for which he sighed, but whose mind was obscured with errors regarding our Lord Jesus Christ; gentle, modest, shunning the world and all publicity, seeking solitude in order to devote himself more wholly to the grand questions occupying his mind, advancing towards the light by the same path as Augustine, his place was already awaiting him at Cassiacum. None felt his absence so deeply as did Augustine. But though absent in body, he was present in spirit; he wrote incessantly to Augustine, ever propounding some fresh question respecting the highest truths, for the solution of which he was so impatient that Augustine was compelled to entreat him to grant him a short respite. He was preparing to receive holy baptism with his friends, and from the font, whence he issued inflamed with apostolic ardour, dying shortly after, full of faith and piety, he passed, says Augustine, to Abraham's bosom. " Whatever it is that is meant by that bosom, there lives Nebridius, my gentle friend. For where else could such a soul be? He is in the abode of the blessed, concerning which abode he asked so many questions of me, a poor inexperienced mortal. No more he lays his ear to my mouth, but approaches his lips to Thee, O Fountain of life, and there drinks to his fill with a thirst ever new, happy for ever. And yet I cannot think that he is so inebriated therewith as to forget me, since Thou, the Fountain at which he drinketh, art pleased to be mindful of us."*

As for Verecundus, he it was who had lent his villa to St. Monica. Gentle, estimable, noble-minded, and married to a pious wife, he hesitated, why, we know not, to become a Christian. He died a little while after, but having received baptism, and adored with his last breath that God whom he was worthy to know. " Thus wast Thou pleased to have com-passion, not on him only, but on us," writes St. Augustine, " whose grief would have been insupport-able had we been unable to think of such a friend as

among the number of Thine elect. Yes, my God,
Thou wilt reward Verecundus for his hospitality at
Cassiacum, (where, retired from the world, we repose
in Thee,) with the eternal freshness and pleasantness
of Thy paradise."*

Such was Cassiacum. The locality, the peaceful
retirement, the season, the band of friends, and surroundings so thoroughly consonant with Augustine's
dispositions, tastes, and aspirations, none but a
mother could have selected such a cradle for her
son's new birth. St. Monica's maternal heart had
chosen a fitting spot, which she was about to illumine with the faith, sublimity, tenderness, and heroic
ardour of her saintly heart.

Moreover, her love for Augustine led her to extend the same affection to his friends, those youthful
souls, so agitated, restless, and so beautiful, in whom,
with a saint's deep instinct, she discerned the Christian, the future priests, perhaps bishops, doctors, and
apostles of the Church. "Therefore," St. Augustine
thus admirably expresses himself, "she took as much
care of us all as if she had been the mother of us all,
and served us as if she had been the daughter of us
all."† But her respect did not prevent her giving
each of them the direction they needed, which they
expected at her hands, and for which her age, sanctity, and parental character so pre-eminently fitted
her. She warned gently, remonstrated with gravity,
and with a single word or look raised their souls
heavenwards, employing her whole mind, genius,

* *Confess.*, lib. IX., cap. iii.   † *Confess.*, lib. IX., cap. ix.

heart, faith, all the ardour of her zeal, the ingenuity of her love, to second the divine action in their hearts. She was the apostle of this little band.

Before leaving Milan her first care had been to acquaint the holy bishop Ambrose with the wonderful change that had just taken place in Augustine, also to ask his advice as to the manner in which the latter should prepare himself to receive holy baptism. Besides solitude and prayer, Ambrose had recommended the holy Scriptures, and especially the prophecies of Isaias, as a fitting subject for meditation, doubtless thinking that the incomparable grandeur of his imagery would powerfully impress Augustine's heart and imagination; moreover, of all the prophets, Isaias is he who has spoken most clearly of the conversion of the nations to Jesus Christ, and who throughout his inspired page has uttered the most beautiful words respecting the preparation of the heart and the advent of the Messiah. Only, whilst the prophet addressed the nations in words such as these: " Be ye converted, O ye people, make straight your paths," he heard others which carried him away, as they will ever carry away all others into the depths of the eternal mysteries. Augustine began the perusal of these prophecies, but arrested on the very threshold by difficulties which he desired to fathom, feeling that if he went on reading would degenerate into study, he closed their pages, and in their stead opened the Psalms, probably at his mother's suggestion, and there learnt that which he needed,—how to pray and weep.

David's is pre-eminently the voice of prayer, and specially of penitent prayer. It is as if God had created him in order that every sorrow, danger, movement of penitence, and grief, of which man is capable, might find its parallel in him; and that he might furnish us with songs and tears for every situation in life. He is born in a hut, dies on a throne; tends sheep in Bethlehem's vales, and commands on the battle-field; he is the recipient of all glory, as of all happiness; excels in poetry, religion, and friendship: then we see him betrayed, persecuted, defeated, chased into exile, obliged to flee from his own son, who ignominiously perishes before his very eyes, whilst he is powerless to save him; the sport of good and evil fortune, which dispute possession of him and bear him successively to the extremes of all human things. Even this is but the most insignificant part of his life. Blessed by God from his cradle, he passes through a saintly childhood and youth, to a still more saintly middle age, flooded with a light exceeding that bestowed on the prophets, and hailing the Messiah with the most ardent and fervent love; then all at once he sinks from these sublime heights into the sins of adultery, perfidy, and homicide. But even in the depths of that abyss he neither despairs of the beauty of his soul, nor yet of the divine goodness; he raises his tearful eyes to the divine purity, and on the wings of penance soars higher than he had ever soared before. But his tears never cease, and grief, gratitude, and divine love mingled their voices with his harp, giving us strains unsurpassed even by the gospel, and which to the end of time will awaken an echo in every human breast. How then could Augustine fail to find that balm of which his soul stood in such need? There is a resemblance in circumstances, as in individuals. Therefore, hardly had he opened the psalms, than the pent up feelings of his heart broke through their barriers. "What cries did I send up to Thee, my God, when I, a novice in Thy pure love, read those psalms of David, those canticles animated by such humble and fervent faith! What affectionate words did I utter to Thee, and how much was I inflamed by them with love of Thee, and burned with a desire of reciting them, if I could, all the world over, to abate the swelling pride of mankind. By turns I shuddered with fear, was inflamed by hope, and thrilled with joy at Thy compassion, O my Father! And all these things issued forth by my eyes, and by my voice, when Thy loving Spirit, turning to us, says: 'Ye sons of men, how long will ye be dull of heart? Why do you love vanity, and seek after lying?' For had I not loved vanity and sought a lie? Therefore I listened, and was filled with emotion at the remembrance that I was one of these.

"Then I read: *Be angry, and sin not.* And how was I moved thereby, O my God, I whom Thou hadst taught, O my God, to be angry with myself on account of my past sins, that for the time to come, I might sin no more? For there it was, in the secret of my soul where I felt compunction, and where I had sacrificed to Thee, slaying my old life;

and there it was that Thou, my God, hadst begun to grow sweet unto me, and hadst given gladness to my heart, inundating me with joy, and each word I read pierced my soul and made me cry out.

"And the following verse, oh! how I watered it with my tears: *In peace, in the self-same I will sleep, and I will rest.* O happy words! *In Him alone will I rest and take my sleep.* Yes, my God, Thou art that self-same indeed, who changest not. In Thee is rest and oblivion of all labours. This it is whereon Thou hast established my hope.

"I read this, and was all on fire, and would fain have opened the ears of those that were dead, one of whom I had been, as pestilent as any of them, when bitter and blind I barked against Thy holy word, all radiant with heaven's own light and sweet as honey. I pined away with grief by reason of the enemies of those divine books. O my God, how shall I express all I felt at that happy time?"*

Whilst Augustine was thus engrossed, and was rejoicing in the ardour of his new-born faith, so great were Monica's gladness and admiration that she never quitted his side. She pointed out the psalms most suited to his needs, and read them with him. "Alipius," says St. Augustine, "read with me, as also did my mother, who could not tear herself from me." She even explained them, for she had advanced higher than he had in the science of divine love, and a mother once more, she gladly unfolded to him that world of light on which he had so newly entered, and

* *Confess.*, lib. IX., cap. iv.

in which he still proceeded with such uncertain steps. "For I was as yet but a novice in Thy love," he goes on to say, "and my friend Alipius was also a novice and simple catechumen like myself; but it was far otherwise with my mother, who, though a woman, had a man's strong faith, the serene light of age, a mother's tenderness, and a Christian's piety."*

Occupied though he was with preparing his son for the reception of holy baptism, he did not forget his philosophical studies. After giving the morning to reading the psalms and meditating thereon, either alone or with his mother and Alipius, towards noon he joined his young friends. If the day was fine and clear, they seated themselves under a tree on the greensward.† But if the weather was rainy or cold they betook themselves to a bath-room, the warm atmosphere of which was soothing to Augustine's weak chest. ‡ There they passed many a long hour in grave and pleasant converse on philosophical and literary topics. Sometimes they read half a book o Virgil, whose writings were ever such favourites with Augustine;§ at other times they selected one of Cicero's treatises, particular the *Hortensius*, which he held in grateful admiration.‖ But most often they discussed the sublimest philosophical questions, such as happiness, and in what it consists *(de Beata*

---

* *Confess.*, lib. IX., cap. iv.

† "Nous sortîmes, dit saint Augustin ; le jour était si doux et si pur, qu'il semblait fait, en vérité, pour épurer et éclairer nos âmes."

‡ *Contra Acad.*, lib. III., cap. iv.

§ *Ibid.*, p. 432.   ‖ *Ibid.*

Vita); the divine impress of order, *(de Ordine)*; the soul's need of truth, the inability of philosophy to wholly satisfy this want *(Contra Manichæos)*; God and the soul: subjects which the saint was then studying with all the ardour of his brilliant genius.

Augustine has been styled the Christian Plato. He was so at Cassiacum, but later on he will shine forth as bishop, controversialist, and doctor. He will wield his pen against the Donatists and Pelagians; will soar on eagle wings to the heights of Christian dogma; but at the time to which we allude, he was too young and being a layman he dared not touch the ark, therefore he contented himself with approaching those sublime questions of God and the soul, of which Plato had caught faint glimpses, but which Augustine saw in full light. Plato and Augustine are brothers, but of unequal age. The first, in the sweet and poetic spring time of life's morning has more flowers than fruit. His mind is full of dreams rather than realities. A sublime ideal is before him, which, though it fills him with enthusiastic transports, he never attains. He seeks the road, sees and describes it, but cannot enter there, and dies without realizing the promise of his spring. The second, after many a painful struggle and years of courageous labour, resolutely enters on the path indicated by his predecessor. It had been said by Plato: "That in order to enjoy the beatific vision, the heart must be purified, healed, and freed from all those fetters with which the love of riches and pleasure bind us to earth." Also he said: "Philosophy teaches us how to die. What will fit us to see God? Purity and death." This great art Augustine studied, he practised it at Cassiacum, and light, like a river that has burst through its dikes, flooded his mighty intellect. What with Plato was but hope and conjecture, Augustine really beheld. That which is an indistinct, but sublime presentiment in the rich imagination of the philosopher, is defined and clear to the luminous mind of the saint, from whose lips it wells forth in accents undreamed of by Plato. He who desires to know Augustine in those early days when first he tried his wings, should study the conversations and conferences held at Cassiacum. They partake of the early bloom of youth, a freshness that never returns; a sweet light such as heralds the approach of day, freshness of ideas and sentiment, quiet enthusiasm, and gentle gaiety. His genius, hitherto imprisoned, had recovered its strength on happy wing, soaring upwards to the true, the beautiful, and the good.

But during these intellectual transports, St. Monica clung to Augustine as assiduously as in the hours of his penitent and heart-felt effusions. Only, that whereas during the latter it was she who would not desert Augustine, during the former it was Augustine who would not allow her to absent herself from him. He desired her to be present at all the conferences held with his young friends; and on her modestly excusing herself, smilingly reminding him that a woman had never yet been seen seated amid a circle of men, he replied: "Even if true, what does that signify? Is not philosophy the love of truth? And you, my mother, do you not love truth? Why then should you not take your place with us? Did you but love truth with ordinary affection, it would be my duty to welcome you and listen. How much more, seeing that your love for truth exceeds that you bear me; and what that love is, I know full well! Nothing can wean you from the love of truth; neither fear, sorrow, nor even death itself! Is not this the very essence of philosophy? Wherefore, then, should I hesitate to avow myself your disciple?" * Overwhelmed by this eulogium, uttered as it was in the presence of all, Monica could scarcely find words strong enough · to assure Augustine with modest gentleness that never before had he been guilty of such a breach of the truth. †

But not only because she loved truth more than aught else, and was resolved to die for it, did Augustine desire his mother to be present at their conferences; he also wished for her presence because of her keen and penetrating intellect, which, according to Augustine, verged on genius. Not a question, however elevated and sublime, that Monica did not seize with promptitude and singular facility. For instance, one day Augustine was conversing with his young friends on numbers, particularly as regarded their connection with geometry and music. At the most knotty part of his subject he stopped abruptly, and looking at his mother, addressed her in the following beautiful language: "Though others dread

* *De Ordine*, lib. I., cap. xi. n. 32.
† *De Ordine*, lib. I., cap. xi. n. 33.

these abstruse points and intricate questions, they do not alarm you, mother, whose genius strikes me more and more each day, and whose soul, either from your age, or your wonderful virtue, soars so far above the frivolous realm of sense. All these questions will appear as easy to you as they will seem difficult to grovelling and terrestrial minds.*

"If I asserted that you would be able to express your feelings and thoughts perfectly, I should err," said he, affably; "for even I, who have made Latin my study, am daily warned of my mistakes by the natives of this country. It is even possible that a savant carefully on the watch for solecisms might find such in my discourses. Indeed, I have met with persons who accuse Cicero of having perpetrated such. And as for incorrect idioms, they are so frequently used, that even the oration on the preservation of Rome is full of them. You, my mother, doubtless care little for those purities of style, but so well do you understand the genius and almost divine power of language, that the true savant will perceive that if you have disregarded the outward form, you have retained the spirit."†

Therefore, for these two reasons, and because Monica loved the truth so deeply that she was ready to lay down her life in its behalf, and because she was endowed with a lofty, penetrating intellect, Augustine insisted on her being present at his philosophical conferences. Also for another reason. A woman's presence is useful even at the most serious

---

* *De Ordine*, lib. II., cap. xvii., n. 45.   † Ibid.

and elevated discourses of the other sex. It necessitates a certain degree of reserve, and imparts an atmosphere of delicacy and grace. Where men, especially learned ones, are tempted to use their minds only, she rouses the heart, thus preventing science from becoming that dry science of which Bossuet speaks. And when these discourses on God, the soul, the infinite, conclude, as they always should do,—with hymns and prayers,—she it is who lends wings to these hymns and force to these prayers.

A fine instance of this occurred at Cassiacum. Augustine had discoursed on Divine Providence as worthy of admiration in its distribution of happiness and its permission of evil. Having at last reached the moment when the light with which the soul is illumined, and the emotion which oppresses the heart, are merged in adoration and in love, he suddenly stopped, and turning to his mother, addresses to her these words, so characteristic of himself, and which alone would suffice to win St. Monica eternal honour: " In order that these supplications and vows may be enunciated with additional fervour, we entrust them, O my mother, to thee, to whose tears I am indebted for my present sentiments and for my love of truth. Yes, if it is the prime object of my thoughts, if I yearn for and love it with a love surpassing all other affection, to thee, O mother, do I owe it. How, then, can I doubt that after having won for me grace ardently to desire the truth, thou wilt fail to obtain for me by your prayers grace to possess it in its fulness ?"*

Moreover, not only was St. Monica present at these conferences, but she sometimes spoke, and as God grants singular light to purity and love, there fell from her lips many words which Augustine had at once transcribed on his tablets, and which we in our turn will peruse, in order to become more intimately acquainted with the mother of Plato the Christian.

The most noteworthy of the conferences held at Cassiacum, that most irradiated by St. Monica's beautiful mind, took place on the 13th of November, 386. As it was Augustine's thirty-second birthday, Monica had assembled all her son's friends around her table, entertaining them with that Christian sobriety and cheerful gaiety wholly compatible with noble sentiments and freedom of thought. During the repast the conversation naturally turned upon life, (since it was the anniversary of the day on which Augustine had known its first smiles and tears,) and the life of the blessed, (inasmuch as happiness is our being's end and aim.) Dinner ended, they retired to the baths, (for the weather was cold and wet,) continuing the same conversation, which was led by Augustine, who himself proposed the questions, urging his young friends to reply, like the eagle, who, taking her little ones on her wings, soars upwards with them to the sun.

What, then, is life? In what does it consist? Where is the hearth which renews and feeds it? They

* *De Ordine,* lib. II., cap. xx., n. 52.

soon ceased discussing, as unworthy of their notice, this poor dying, grovelling life of the body, which is indebted to earthly aliments for its duration, passing on to that which alone deserves the name of life, that is, the life of the soul. Augustine asked what was the soul's food. " Only one, to know and love the truth," replied St. Monica.* Trigetius would not allow this: he admitted two aliments for the soul, one good and one evil, asserting that if there are souls who feed on truth, there are others who feed on error, vanity, and deception. St. Augustine instantly rejoined that Trigetius was wrong, for, far from nourishing the soul, error, vanity, and illusions do but increase her hunger, and render her empty, sterile, and weak; that his mother was therefore right in saying that truth was the sole aliment worthy of the soul, and which alone could still her hunger. But whither does life tend? Life consists in activity and movement. What is its goal? On this sad earth, in this vale of tears, where we drink the bitter stream called life, what do we desire or demand save happiness? These words were applauded by all.†

And indeed, such is the aim of life. Scarcely is man born than he is conscious of a longing for happiness, and so long as life lasts not a thought, feeling, wish, or breath, but craves for this. But where is happiness to be found? How attain it? What are its conditions? Thus did St. Augustine propound this sovereign question. " Tell me, who is the

* De Beat. Vita, n. 8.   † De Beat. Vita, n. 10.

happy man? Is it not he who has all that he desires?" "Oh no," replied St. Monica, with vivacity;
" if he desires and possesses what is good, then truly
he is happy, but if he desires what is evil, even should
his wish be granted, how unhappy is he!" Augustine, much impressed, smiling, replied, " Oh, my
mother, you have attained one of the highest truths
of philosophy."* In proof of which he recited the
following truly admirable extract from the *Hortensius*:
"The majority, not of philosophers, but of dispu-
tants, says Cicero, declare those happy who have all
that they desire. This is a mistake, for to wish for
what is evil is the very height of misery. Far better
not to have what we desire than to have what is
injurious. Therefore the injury done to the soul by
desiring that which is evil is far greater than the
happiness which the greatest good fortune could
bestow."† Monica listened attentively to these noble
words; she reverted to them, explained them, and
so admirably displayed their excellence, that all
present, forgetting her sex, "thought," so says
Augustine, "that we were listening to some eminent
doctor. As for me, ravished with delight, I contemplated the divine source whence flowed such
beauteous thoughts."‡

Proceeding with the conversation, Augustine wished
to fathom the question of happiness. Having rejected all that was bad as incapable of rendering man
happy, they arrived at that which, without being
really reprehensible, is simply transitory, fleeting, and

* *De Beat. Vita,* n. 10.   † Ibid.   ‡ Ibid.

perishing: riches, health, glory, beauty. Can these render man happy? "No," replied St. Augustine, "for how can we possess that which is but transitory. unstable, and fleeting? Or, how, having obtained it, can we prevent its eluding our grasp?" All applaused. "And yet," said Trigetius, "there are some who possess these fleeting, perishable things in such rich abundance that they have not a single wish ungratified. *

To this Augustine rejoined. "Tell me, Trigetius, can he who fears be happy?"

"No," said Trigetius.

"He who loves, if he can be robbed of the object of his affection, can he be free from fear?"

"He cannot," replied Trigetius.

"Is not all that is perishable and fleeting liable to be lost?"

"It is."

"Then," concluded St. Augustine, "he who loves and possesses perishing things can never be happy."

"Certainly not," replied Monica; "but I will go farther than that. Even were he sure of never losing them, I should still count him unhappy, because nothing transitory can ever satisfy the heart of man, and the more he seeks his happiness therein, the more miserable and indigent will he be."

"What!" said St. Augustine, "if he possessed all terrestrial things in abundance, knew how to moderate his desires, and enjoy worldly gifts wisely, would he not be happy?"

* *De Beat. Vita.*, n. 11.

"No, no," replied St. Monica, "nought terrestrial can ever render the soul happy."

"Oh, how beautiful!" said St. Augustine. "What better answer could possibly be given! Yes, whoever desires to be happy, let him live superior to all transitory things, seek that which is eternal and which no reverse of fortune can ever take away. Only God is eternal; therefore in Him alone is happiness to be found."*

To this remark the hearts of all readily and piously assented.

But if no human or created thing, how beautiful soever it may be, can appease the hunger of the soul, which God alone can still, how can man possess Him? For knowing, as we do, that happiness is our aim, and that in God alone can it be found, we must be able to attain it, and, within certain limits, find there wherewith to satisfy our desires and dissipate our fears. This new question was started and proposed by St. Augustine as follows: "Only he is happy in whom God dwells. But, tell me in whom does God dwell?"

"For my part," said Licentius, "I think the Divinity dwells in him who acts aright."

"And I," eagerly replied Trigetius, "think God dwells with him who does His will."

Then Adeodatus, opening his lips, uttered the beautiful words we have already cited: "God dwells in him whose heart is not impure." St. Monica applauded this reply.

* *De Beat. Vita,* n. 11.   † *De Beat. Vita,* n. 12.

"And what kind of man is he whose heart is not impure?" asked St. Augustine, wishing to make Adeodatus explain himself more fully.

"He," replied the child, " who lives chastely."

"And what do you mean by that? Avoiding grave faults only ?"

"Oh, no," replied Adeodatus; "no soul is really pure save that which loves God and clings to Him alone."*

Thus, in three short phrases did this child, St. Augustine's son and St. Monica's grandson, it is true, attain the highest truth of philosophy and of religion too. Nought human or terrestrial can suffice the soul. She can find no happiness save in possessing God; and on earth, as in heaven, only by loving God can we possess God. For love sets distance at defiance, space is nothing to her, she links soul to soul no matter how far apart they are, and in uniting beatifies and transfigures them. And if it be true, that when the object of her attachment is an earthly being, love renders the soul indifferent to fatigue, sorrow, and privation; imparting to her peace, security, and invincible courage; not only filling her with joy, but rapture, what must it be when the object of her love is God? Therefore all the saints have been happy, even on the cross; and if the world cannot comprehend their joy, it is because the world knows not what love is!

The conversation was resumed on the following day; the subject was still the same, namely, those who seek

* *De Beat. Vita,* n. 18.

20   S. M.

after God. It had been asserted that only they who possess God are happy. What of those who do not possess, but seek Him? This question was started by Augustine, whose mind was filled with sadness in thinking of those who were still a prey to the doubts he had known so well.

They soon ceased to discuss the case of the Academics, viz., those philosophers who, not having yet succeeded in finding truth, despair of ever doing so, and end by universal doubt. "Happy they," said St. Monica, smiling, and playing on the two Latin words, *Caducarii sunt!* words capable of the two-fold meaning, *they cling to perishable things*, and, *they are epileptic*, that is, miserable view them as you will. The company smiled at, and applauded, this "*jeu d'esprit.*"[*]

Having set these on one side, they came to those who are seeking God. "Given, a man who does not despair of finding the truth, who has sufficient confidence in God to feel sure that He has not left man without light to guide him, and who is seeking this light: is such a one happy or not?"

"Unhappy," said the young man, "for he does not possess God."

"Are you so very sure of that?" rejoined St. Augustine, who throughout the conversation ever pleaded the cause of those whose doubts he had shared. "You, Licentius, say that he who does God's will has God dwelling with him: is not the seeker after God doing God's will? You also say that God

[*] *De Beat. Vita*, n. 17.

dwells in him who does what is right: is not he who seeks God included in this category? And I ask you, Adeodatus, whether he who is impure in heart can seek God?"

The three young men, finding themselves powerless to reply, regarded Augustine half smiling, half confused, not knowing what to say. Monica came to their rescue, and with admirable tact and skill unravelled Augustine's rather subtle arguments; she showed that, in order to be happy, it was not enough that God dwelt in us, for He dwells in all, in those who seek and in those who possess Him; but to be happy, we must have God for our friend, which is the case only with the latter.

It was now the young men's turn to speak, and Licentius said: "If they who are seeking God have not God for their friend, He must be their enemy, and this I will never admit."

"Nor I, either," said Trigetius; "but there must be something between the two."

"Yes," rejoined Monica, quoting a text from the Holy Scriptures, "he who leads a holy life has God within, God is his friend; he who lives an evil life has God within, but as his enemy; he who is seeking God and has not yet found Him, has God neither for his enemy nor for his friend; but God is not far from such a one. Do you admit this?"

"Yes," they replied unanimously.

"Wait a moment," said Augustine, who was not content with the lot assigned to the seekers after

God. "Is not God the friend of those to whom He is favourable?"

"Yes," they answered.

"Is not God favourable to those who seek Him?"

"Yes," they again replied.

"Therefore, he who seeks and finds God, has God for his friend, and is happy. He who seeks, but has not yet found God, has God for his friend, but is not yet happy. He who wanders from, and refuses to acknowledge God, who is drawn away by his vicious passions, is neither happy, nor has he God for his friend."*

Admirable doctrine, though expressed somewhat subtly; well worthy of him who had known all these conditions, and knew by his own experience how near God is to those who seek Him, and how sweet to those who have found Him.

The conversation only ended on the third day. The rain clouds, which for the two preceding days had compelled the little company to retire to the bath-room, had now dispersed. The sky having cleared, they went down into the garden and seated themselves beneath a tree. Having treated, on the first day, of those who possess God; the second day, of those who seek Him; they were now about to discourse of the sad condition of those who do not possess Him, of their misery, indigence and sterility. Trigetius had just asked a rather subtle question, whether all they who are miserable are indigent. He cited as an example, the rich man of whom Cicero speaks, who

* *De Beat. Vita,* n. 21.

possessed all that heart can wish, a noble name, a vast fortune, fine reputation, was held in much esteem and honour, and yet his enjoyment was entirely marred by the fear of losing all these things. " He was miserable," said Trigetius, " but not indigent."

On this Monica spoke. " I do not well understand all these distinctions, neither do I see how you can separate indigence from misery, nor misery from indigence. Shall we call a person indigent who has neither gold nor silver, and not indigent when he does not possess wisdom ?"

All lauded this remark, which included spiritual gifts among the elements of fortune, and St. Augustine was delighted that it was his mother who had found this solution, than which, he considered, none more beautiful could be found in any of the philosophical writings. " You see," he remarked to his young friends, " the difference between studying a multiplicity of books, and remaining in constant and intimate union with God, which union gives rise to those beautiful thoughts which we admire in my mother."*

Augustine terminated these conversations by the following words, full of faith and quiet enthusiasm. " Let us think of God, seek Him, and thirst for Him, who is the light of the soul. Even when our eyes, too weak, or too lately opened, cannot discern His full splendour, every truth we utter proceeds from Him. True, until we have found Him and drunk at the fountain of light, we have not yet reached our

* *De Beat. Vita,* n. 27

final goal. We are neither wise nor happy, neither shall we be so until we fully know and love the Triune God; the Father, the source of truth; the Son, who is the truth; and the Holy Ghost, by whom we are united to the truth."

On hearing these words, already so deeply graven in her memory, for they were those of her spiritual father, the great illustrious St. Ambrose, which words she had often heard sung in the church of Milan, she exclaimed with transport:

"Holy Trinity, receive our prayers."*

And after having recited the whole verse with the deepest emotion, she exclaimed: "Yes! that is blissful life, perfect felicity, which we must seek for with unswerving faith, and ardent hope and charity." These beautiful words concluded this important conversation, which had lasted for three days.

Thus, at times, more light emanates from woman's humble heart than from man's intellect, no matter how brilliant it may be. Purity and love soar heavenwards with more rapid flight than genius, and thus will it ever be. Those who best know what love is, will best understand these virtues, which have their seat in the divine heart.

* *De Beat. Vita, n. 35.*

CHAPTER XIV.

ST. AUGUSTINE'S BAPTISM.—MONICA'S HAPPINESS ON THAT
OCCASION.—THE RESULTS, AS TO MOTHER AND SON.

25th April, 387.

Nearly six months elapsed in the intimate converse
and pleasant life at Cassiacum; a portion of the day
was consecrated to study, another, and the larger part,
set aside for prayer and meditation on the Holy
Scriptures. During the interval Augustine antici-
pated, as it were, his baptism, laved and purified his
soul beforehand from her stains, and at the fount of
divine love acquired an innocence greater than that
which he had lost. "How I blush," said he to his
young friends, "when I look at the wounds and impurities of my soul! Each day I bathe them with my
tears. I pray God to heal them, but I feel how little I
merit such a favour." Then he added, sighing: "But
these images, which my mind has been so in the
habit of dwelling on, still live in my memory. Pale
and feeble when I am awake, but when I am asleep
they are more vivid, striving to captivate my senses,
and wring from me a shadow of consent. Wretched
illusions, still too powerful! But Thy hand, my God,
can heal my wounds. Therefore I humbly confess
all my misery to Thee."*

* *Confess.*, lib. X., cap. xxx.

Having bewailed his sins and humbled himself in the dust, Augustine turned to God, whose love was now beginning to consume him. "Now am I certain that I love Thee, O my Lord. No sooner hadst Thou wounded my heart with Thy word, than I loved Thee. What then did I love in loving Thee? Was it the beauty of the body, glory, the brightness of light, so pleasant to the eyes, the sweet melody of music, the fragrance of flowers, manna, honey, or voluptuous pleasures? None of these things do I love when I love my God. And yet I love a certain light, voice, fragrancy, food, embrace, when I love my God. The light, voice, fragrancy, food, and embrace of my inward man, a light which is boundless, sounds which no time can measure, a perfume which no blast can disperse, a food of which the appetite never tires, and an embrace that never wearies: this it is that I love, when I love my God."*

In order to quicken his love, he took delight, when wandering beneath the lofty trees at Cassiacum, in interrogating created things, and his soul was filled with joy, and his meditations aided by this beautiful solitude, where all breathed peace and liberty; where man was absent, and God was present. "What do I love when I love my God? I asked the earth, and it said, 'It is not I.' And all things therein confessed the same; I asked the sea, and the deeps, and the living things therein, and they replied, 'We are not thy God, seek higher above us.' I asked the fleeting air above, and the whole region thereof, with its in-

* *Confess.*, lib. X., cap. vi.

habitants, cried out: 'Anaximeus is mistaken, I am not God.' I asked the heavens, the sun, the moon, and the stars: 'Neither are we,' said they, 'the God whom thou seekest.' And I said to all those things which are about the doors of my senses: You have told me concerning my God that you are not He, give me at least some tidings concerning Him. And they all cried out with a loud voice: " It is He that made us."*

But as soon as he began to learn what God is, overwhelmed by his own wretchedness, sins, and the opposition he experienced within, he began to weep anew: " Alas, alas! have pity on me, O Lord. Again my evil sorrows contend with my holy joys, and which are victorious I know not. Alas, O Lord, have pity on me! behold, I hide not my wounds; Thou art my physician, I am sick. Thou art merciful, I am miserable."†

Then, raising his eyes to the cross of Jesus, the sinner's refuge, remedy, hope, and comfort, he exclaimed: " O good Father, who hast not spared Thy only Son, but hast delivered Him up for us sinners, how hast Thou loved us, for whom He who thought it no robbery to be equal to Thee was made subject unto death, even to the death of the cross. He offered Himself to Thee in our behalf, both a victor and a victim, therefore a victor because a victim; both priest and sacrifice, and therefore a priest because a sacrifice. On our behalf He took on Himself the form of a servant, that of servants He might make us sons.

---

* *Confess.*, lib. X., cap. vi.   † *Confess.*, lib. X., cap. xxviii.

Therefore, strong in hope, I trust in Him that Thou wilt heal all my maladies, else I should despair, so many and great are these my maladies: great and many though they be, Thy medicine can heal them all."

Then, with admirable confidence he adds: "Alarmed at the enormity of my sins, and bowed down by the weight of my misery, I had resolved to flee away and hide me in the wilderness. But Thou didst stay me by these consoling words: Christ died for all, that they that live, henceforth may not live to themselves, but to Him who died for them. " Therefore, O my God, I cast all my iniquities into Thy bosom, that I may taste and see the wonders of Thy grace. Thou knowest my ignorance, teach Thou me! Thou knowest my weakness, heal Thou me. Let not the proud essay to discourage me by calling my sins to my remembrance. I know the price of the ransom offered on my behalf: it is the blood of Thine only Son, in whom lie hid all treasures."*

In order to participate in some measure in the sufferings of our divine Lord, Augustine would fain have added corporal mortifications to his tears and to his prayers of hope and love. He envied Alipius, "that valiant subduer of his body, that prodigy of austerity, who, as an act of humility and of penance, had walked barefoot on the frozen ground of Italy.† But St. Augustine's health precluded him from carrying out this wish; so delicate was he that he could not even fast, and although the quiet of Cassia-

---

* *Confess.*, lib. X., cap. xliii.   † *Ibid.*, lib. IX., cap. vi.

cum had proved beneficial, he was constantly suffering from inflammation of the chest. He was worn out with excitement and hard work, and consumed by a slow fever. At times the mere act of speaking gave him pain, and he was often incapable of writing. More than once, the evening conversations had to be suspended, so weak was he. The soul had exhausted the body, and many a long year of quietude, rest, and care, were needed to restore his vigour.

At times he suffered from severe pains in the head, teeth, and ears. On one occasion, so violent was his tooth-ache, that " when it had increased to that degree that I could not speak, it came into my mind to request my friends who were there present to pray for me to Thee, the God of health. I wrote my request on wax and gave it to them to read, and as soon as we knelt down to humble prayer the pain was gone. But what a pain it was! And how strangely did it cease, filling me with admiration of Thy goodness !"*

We know of those who prayed for the alleviation of Augustine's pain, none prayed with greater fervour than did St. Monica. She entreated God to grant him this favour, in order to fill his heart with deeper gratitude, and her prayer was answered; for Augustine, then, and ever after, regarding this cure as miraculous, felt his love to God augmented thereby. He could no longer endure his own misery; the sight of his soul all covered with wounds, " exhausted, blighted, and dead," made him yearn for the cleansing

* *Confess.*, lib. IX., cap. iv.

waters of Baptism. "Too late have I loved Thee, **O** beauty ever ancient, ever new! Thou wast within me, but I sought Thee abroad, and lost my own beauty in running after those beauties which Thou hast made. They kept me far from Thee, who art the source of their existence. But Thou hast called, and pierced my deafness; Thou hast lightened, shone forth, and dispelled my blindness. Thou hast sent forth Thy fragrance, and I have inhaled it, and pant after Thee. I have tasted Thee, and therefore after Thee do I hunger, O my God."*

And again : "O truth, illumine my heart that I may understand Thy word. The night of earthly darkness has obscured my intellect, but Thy love draws me towards Thyself. Whilst I wandered far from Thee, Thou didst call me, though the tumult of sin scarcely permitted me to discern Thy voice. Now, breathless with haste, I return to Thy Sacred Fount. Let me not be rejected! But there let me quench my thirst and live!"†

"O Love, ever-burning and never consumed, kindle and consume my heart. Command me what Thou wilt, but," he humbly adds, "give me what Thou commandest."‡

"I grieve at my remaining imperfections, (he adds, thinking of holy Baptism,) but I hope that Thou wilt perfect Thy mercies in me, till I arrive at that full peace which my whole being shall then enjoy, when death shall be swallowed up in victory."§

---

* *Confess.*, lib , X., cap. xxvii.   † *Confess.*, lib, XII., cap. x.

‡ *Confess.*, lib. X., cap. xxix.   § *Confess.*, lib. X., cap. xxx.

Monica sympathized in each holy aspiration, desire, grief, regret, and deep emotion that filled Augustine's heart. Long had she prayed that God would be pleased to pierce her son's heart with the arrow of His word. And now that her prayer was granted, and the arrow planted in his flesh, she entreated God to let it pierce to the very quick, and so the wound might never heal. She who had watched so anxiously and so sadly by the dying embers of that heart, having at last re-illumined the flame of Divine Love, assiduously tended this flame, so that her son's heart might be consumed thereby. Burn then, O sacred fire, twice kindled by a mother's breath! purify, transform, consume Augustine's heart! Change this young wanderer into a Christian, priest, doctor, martyr, and restore him his virginity; consume his heart, until the earthly tabernacle giving way beneath the ardour of Thy flame, Thou unitest the mother and the son in those regions of endless love and joy, far removed from this sad world.

Meanwhile Lent was drawing near, and it was customary that all who desired to be baptized at Easter should give in their names on Ash Wednesday, and also attend the instructions specially given on their behalf during the forty days of Lent. Therefore Augustine left Cassiacum and returned to Milan with his mother. Although he could easily have been dispensed from attending these preparatory instructions, he would not do so. And this eloquent young man, already so renowned, who equalled and surpassed the most learned savants, was to be seen attending these instructions with child-like assiduity, and an attention, piety, modesty, and humility, truly edifying. He received from God a rich spiritual reward for the grand example he thus gave the Church, and after the lapse of twenty years, the remembrance of the sweet emotions he had experienced still filled him with joy.*

At last the moment of Holy Baptism arrived. In conformity with ancient usage it was fixed for Easter-Eve, which was observed by all as a vigil, and the sacrament of Baptism was administered after the evening Office and before the Mass at daybreak. This celebrated night, destined to witness the spiritual birth of the Church's greatest doctor, was the night of April 24th, A.D. 387.†

The traveller still visits with emotion the little Church in Milan, which was the baptistery at the period to which we allude, and which has not yet wholly perished. It bore the name of St. John Baptist, and has since then been dedicated to the saintly young man whose spiritual birth it witnessed that night.‡

At the appointed hour, Augustine repairs to the church, accompanied by his mother. Adeodatus is with them, replete with innocence, purity and joy, his genius rendering him worthy of Augustine, his faith of Monica. Alipius, penitent and much affected; Trigetius, ardent and joyous, and a few others, follow in Augustine's train and range themselves with him

* August., *De Fide et Operibus*, cap. vi.

† Possidius, *Vita August.*, cap. 1. ‡ Mabillon, *Iter Ital.*, p. 16.

around the baptismal font. A few favoured Christians have been able to gain admission to the sacred spot. All eyes are riveted on this young man, to whom the Church, rent by so many heresies, could now look for most potent aid, and whose brow was crowned by faith, genius, repentance, and love. As for Monica, she, robed in the widow's purple-bordered garb, and enveloped in long veils, vainly strove to hide the joy which filled her soul.*

Ambrose arrives, kneels an instant in prayer, and then the ceremony commences. Augustine was seated near the baptismal font, his face turned westward. At a signal from the saintly bishop, he arises, and turns towards the east to salute that light which had so long been hidden from him, and which at last arose within his soul.† He then approaches the sacred font, thrice he plunges therein, and thrice emerges therefrom, as from a tomb, at the first time uttering these words of faith, "I believe in God;" at the second time, "I believe in Jesus Christ;" and the third time, "I believe in the Holy Ghost."‡

After this the saintly bishop of Milan ascends the altar, and with outstretched arms prays aloud; then, pouring the holy water on the meekly bowed head of the young man, who strikes his breast, says; "I baptize thee in the name of the Father, of the Son, and of the Holy Ghost."§ And Augustine is born anew to God and to the Church, and becomes a blessing to others, and to himself.

* *Brev. Prædicat., in Festo Convers. B. August.,* 15 *Maii , lect.* vi.
† Ambros., *De Init.,* lib. I., cap. ii.
‡ Ambros., *De Sacram.,* lib II., cap. vii.   § *Id., ibid.*

Then, according to the usage of the Church of Milan, Ambrose girds himself with a linen girdle, and kneeling, washes Augustine's feet;* after this, they robe the newly baptized in a long white tunic, symbolical of the purity that has just been restored to him.† This garment had been woven by his mother, with whose tears of joy it still glistened.‡ Then Augustine takes in his hand a lighted taper, type of the pure and gentle flame by which, henceforth, his soul will be consumed; and thus, his heart burning with the purest love, crowned by the lilies of a newly recovered chastity, encircled, though invisibly, by the doctor's aureola, he advances to the altar, there to receive for the first time the God who makes glad and renews his youth.

No pencil can depict such scenes as these, where the purest joys are mingled with the most sublime presentiments; that young man oppressed by deep emotion, approaching the altar with a penitent's humble yet triumphant joy; that aged prelate, that invincible athlete, who, at the moment when his own sun is on the point of setting, beholds the rise of another luminary, more brilliant than himself, and now joyously says within himself, that death may come when it will, that Ambrose may be silent now that Augustine is about to speak; that mother, too, who veils her tear-stained countenance, vainly essaying to conceal the greatness of her joy.

It is said, that at the conclusion of the ceremony,

---

* Ambros., *De Sacram.,* lib. III., cap. i.

† Ambros., *Ad Virgin. laps.,* cap. v.   ‡ *Brev. Rom. Aug., die 5 Maii.*

the enthusiasm was so general that St. Ambrose arose as one inspired, and, with arms and heart raised heavenwards, exclaimed:

"We bless and praise Thee, O my God and Lord!"

And St. Augustine, thrilling with holy rapture, also arose, saying:

"O my Father, let all the earth worship Thee!"

To which St. Ambrose rejoined:

"Let all the Angels, and the heavens, **and the** Powers celestial bless Thee!"

And St. Augustine:

"Let the Cherubim and Seraphim proclaim with ceaseless voice: Holy, Holy, Holy!"

Thus inciting each other, like enraptured Seraphim, they improvised the beautiful canticle of the *Te Deum.*

Its opening sentences are full of ardour and sublime daring, fervent as the enthusiasm of those two saints. In three bounds they reach the gates of heaven; there they stop for a brief instant, and rest awhile, listening to the angels. With them they hymn the Father, Son, and Holy Ghost, in whose names Augustine had just been regenerated. Then, as if suddenly called back to earth, they change their key, and their pæan is for a moment saddened by a sigh. But, anon, they raise their eyes to heaven once more, their enthusiasm springs up afresh, and the hymn ends in a long cry of hope and trust in God.

St. Monica was standing there, singing in her heart, whilst the two saints sang with their lips. She was overwhelmed with happiness, and fervent must have been the response awakened within her soul by the voice of faith, love, and gratitude, with which that wondrous prayer concludes. *

Thus transfigured, Augustine emerged from the little chapel where he had been baptised, and where he had first received the Holy Eucharist. So humble, so detached from the world, and so full of Divine Love was he, that he was scarcely recognized. All his sorrow and anxiety at thought of his past transgressions had wholly vanished. One sole thought engrossed his soul: the silent contemplation of Divine Mercy, and the wondrous manner in which he had been rescued from his evil ways. In order that he might make a fitting return for these many favours, Augustine felt his need of all the succour the Church could afford him. "Like one exhausted by prolonged thirst, I eagerly betook myself to the breasts of Holy

---

* In the Liturgy of the Church this hymn is called *Hymnus sancti Ambrosii et sancti Augustini.* And, although it is impossible to cite proofs of the authenticity of these verses, which go back as far as St. Ambrose's time, this belief rests on a tradition so ancient and trustworthy that we cannot doubt its correctness, unless we had strong proof to the contrary, and such proof is still wanting. "The title *Ambrosian Hymn,*" says M. de Maistre, "would encourage the supposition that this beautiful prayer owes its existence exclusively to St. Ambrose; and yet the general belief, grounded on a simple tradition, is, that the *Te Deum* was, if I may be allowed the expression, improvised at Milan by the two saintly doctors, Ambrose and Augustine, in a transport of religious fervour; a supposition highly probable. Indeed this inimitable Canticle bears not the faintest trace of premeditation. It is not a *composition*, but an *effusion*; an ardent poem in blank verse; a divine dithyrambic, born of enthusiasm, soaring on its own wings, despising all the resources of art. I doubt whether faith, love, and gratitude have ever uttered words more true and more impressive." (*Soirées de Saint Pétersbourg*, tome II., Entretien vii.)

Church, and groaning over my misery, and bewailing my past life, I sucked and pressed them with all my might, in order to find the spiritual nourishment, strength, and vigour, of which I stood in need."*

So great was his fervour, that he could not enter a church, nor listen to the hymns which ascended to God from the lips of the faithful, nor behold a holy picture, without feeling the fount of his tears flow forth afresh, as at the moment of his conversion. "O how much did I weep," he says, "in hearing Thy hymns and canticles, being exceedingly moved by the voices of Thy harmonious Church! Whilst those voices entered in at my ears, Thy truth gently distilled into my heart, awaking the deepest affection, and drawing from my eyes many tears, in which I found much comfort."†

His tears redoubled when he thought of the time in which these same hymns had fallen lifeless on his ear.‡ In spirit, he already dwelt within that eternal abode of which the Church of his baptism was but a type, and at thought of those beauteous canticles, celestial harmonies of that heaven of which he had just been made an heir, his heart overflowed with tears of gratitude, love, and holy longing. "O wondrous abode, all radiant with light, where dwells the glory of my God, how dear is Thy beauty to me! How, in this my exile, do I sigh after Thee! Alas! I had strayed like a lost sheep, but I trust myself to the shoulders of the Good Shepherd, Thy Divine

* *De Utilitate credendi*, cap. i.
† *Confess.*, lib. IX., cap. vi.　　‡ *Confess.*, lib. IX., cap. vii.

Architect, that He may bring me safely within Thy walls. Till then, my canticles shall tell Thee of my love, and my sighs shall reveal to Thee all the weariness and pain I endure in this my pilgrimage; and my heart, weaned from earth by the dear thought of Thee, shall sigh but for Jerusalem, my country and my mother; nought shall I desire save thee, O Jerusalem, and Thee, who art her king, her sun, protector, spouse, source of all her chaste and lasting pleasure, and her eternal joy! No, never shall I cease my sighs till Thou in Thy mercy hast welcomed me with the kiss of peace, and clothed my soul in undying beauty, O my God." *

Great as were the blessings which Augustine reaped from his baptism, they were perhaps exceeded by those which fell to his mother's share. It seemed as if the final stroke had just been given to the picture. This venerable woman, who had but a few months to live, had reached that moment when all the divine graces with which God had enriched her soul, and all the treasures of faith, humility, purity, devotedness, and divine love, with which her victories over self had been rewarded, attained their highest degree. The close of a saint's life resembles a warm and fruitful summer. This period St Monica had just attained, and all her virtues were yielding an abundant harvest.

We call to mind the ardent faith of her childhood and early youth. Where the heart is sincere, there is nothing that has a more rapid and luxuriant growth

* *Confess.*, lib. XII., cap. xvi.

than faith. At first we are surrounded by twilight; then the light becomes visible and increases as we advance. God, who remained concealed from our infant gaze, soon reveals Himself; in the hour of peril, sorrow, and temptation, we are conscious of His presence; when all the world abandons us He comes to console us, and saves us when all seems lost. Who but remembers such moments in his past life? Thus the shadows flee away, and the closing years of the Christian's life are years of almost cloudless splendour. Thus was it with St. Monica. In days gone by she had walked in faith, now faith was lost in sight. Sooner would she have doubted self, than have doubted Him who so often, and so efficaciously, came to her rescue.

As her faith grew, so did her hope. She knew that God was faithful. He had granted all her requests. She had earnestly desired her husband's conversion, and, in spite of the apparent obstacles, Patricius became a Christian. Long and ardently had she prayed for the salvation of Augustine's soul; she obtained even more than she asked for, inasmuch as she now saw him pious, chaste, fervent, and on the road to sanctity. She had but one wish more: it was, that they might enjoy heaven together, and there feast on Divine Love; and this she was sure of obtaining. Nought could shake the confidence which during so many years had silently ripened within her soul.

Therefore her heart was filled with a deep, ineffable peace, compared with which that she had known in early youth was but as a phantom. As on a beautiful evening in summer-time, at a certain moment all becomes hushed, and a ravishing silence ascends from the depths of the vales; so in the evening of that beautiful life, all St. Monica's desires ceased; all her anxieties and vague apprehensions sank to rest, and her soul was full of an unalterable serenity, proceeding from her absolute trust in God. A ray of this peace and divine confidence illuminated her brow, and imparted a celestial expression to her countenance.

Of all the Christian virtues, none had increased so rapidly as had love in St. Monica's heart. How paint its growth? As a young girl she loved our Divine Lord with that naïve, delicate, confiding affection, which, since it has power to move the cold heart of man, cannot fail to touch the Divine Heart. As a young woman, oppressed with grief, betrayed and deserted, she had poured forth her tears at His feet; and perceiving the instability of all human affections, and that God is the only friend who never betrays and never forsakes, she felt her love to Him augment, as her sorrows multiplied, and earthly illusions melted away. As a young mother, rejoicing for a brief moment in her maternity, but soon filled with anxiety as regarded Augustine's spiritual condition; unable to look to Patricius for aid, she clung to God as her sole hope; and during thirty years made Him the sole confidant of her fears, anxieties, hopes, and painful presentiments. For thirty years she ceased not to beseech Heaven with an ever growing fervour, striving to love God more ardently, that by so doing she might move him to compassion. Now that success had crowned her efforts, this happy mother shed at His feet tears such as she had never shed before. Ah! what tongue shall tell the depth of her love to our Lord Jesus Christ! Not a sorrow, anguish, hope, fear, or joy, but increased the intensity of that love. She spent whole hours at the foot of the altar. She communicated daily, and with redoubled fervour; and now that the fount of her bitter tears had for ever ceased to flow, she poured forth at her Saviour's feet those sweet tears which would never stay their course, because from love they flow, and by love they are treasured up.

What rendered St. Monica's love so ineffably beautiful, was that her love for Jesus Christ and her love for Augustine formed but one. They had grown up simultaneously, and had interwoven their tendrils together. Never did she think of Jesus Christ without thinking of Augustine; never did she gaze at Augustine without gazing at Jesus Christ. If her sufferings had been acutely painful, it was because the sole objects of her love, Jesus Christ and Augustine, were divided. Therefore, now that she beheld Jesus Christ loved by Augustine, and Augustine beloved by Jesus Christ, her joy transcended all bounds. She had risen superior to sorrow; it seemed as if she would now die of happiness.

During prayer, she had already often been rapt in ecstasy, that is, she had known some of those moments of grace in which God takes possession of the soul, raises her to Him, allowing her only to retain the faculty of contemplation, adoration, and love. It was remarked that these hours of ecstatic rapture had become more frequent since Augustine's baptism. At times, so profound was her happiness, that she would remain for an entire day perfectly absorbed, speechless, unconscious of what was going on around, wholly lost in Divine contemplation. At others, so profound was her ecstasy, that she became quite unconscious, and her friends tried in vain to wake her from that sweet sleep.*

This occurred most frequently after Holy Communion, and on the day of Pentecost, especially, just fifty days subsequent to Augustine's baptism, so deep was her joy that during that day, and the following night, she was incapable of taking any nourishment.† Those with whom she lived observed that, since her son's conversion, the whole current of her ideas had undergone a total transformation. Heaven had become the sole object of her thoughts, and it was easy to see that she would not long remain a denizen of earth.

We remember the project formed by Augustine in the early days, when grace first began to operate within his soul. Not yet a Christian, but already weary of the world and his aimless life, he pictured to himself a solitude where, far from this sad world, in the society of a few chosen friends of his own age, and sharing his exalted sentiments, he should spend the remainder of life in seeking for and contemplating

* *Boll., die 4 Maii* † Ibid.

truth. But when he wished to realize this dream, he was conscious of the fetters chaining him to earth; his heart was not free, neither were the hearts of his friends, so he renounced his project with a bitter smile.

The same ideal presented itself to his mind in the days immediately following his baptism. The gravest obstacles had disappeared. " Had they offered him in marriage a young girl, ornamented with all the graces of youth, beauty, and intellect, he would not have bestowed even a glance upon her."* His heart, henceforth, should be for ever God's alone! His friends, inspired by the same spirit, shared his sentiments. Wherefore, then, should they not now essay to realize their former dream? Augustine broached the subject to Alipius, who thrilled with joy on hearing of the project. Navigius gave his approval, Evodius was of the same opinion. Adeodatus would not desert his father. St. Monica was therefore the only one who might prove an obstacle. But this was utterly impossible: she would be their mother, the model, spur, intercessor, and permanent providence of the little community. There was no dissentient voice; and thus originated the religious life, destined to give birth to the immortal *Rule* of St. Augustine.

The sole remaining question was as to the locality where they should establish their community. Why hesitate on this point? Monica, Augustine, Navigius, Adeodatus, Evodius, and Alipius, were all natives of Africa, belonging to Tagaste or its environs. What

* *Solil.*, lib. I., cap. x.

tie had they to Italy? Why not return to their families and friends, and, novices though they might be, give their native land the first fruits of their new found faith, and the earliest ardour of their apostolate? They decided at once, and towards the close of October, 387, set out for Ostia, where they hoped to find an early opportunity of returning to Africa.

How different were the two voyages! Three years prior to this, they had arrived separately, each lonely and anxious. Augustine first, fleeing from his mother, whom he had deceived, his heart more restless than the ocean he traversed. Then Monica' arrived, pursuing her son, in spite of the tempest allowing neither storms nor distance to retain her, and watering with her tears the road he had traversed. Now they returned together, peaceful, happy, hand clasped in hand, both their countenances irradiated by the same peace and the same light.

And Monica had been so opposed to this voyage! had wept so bitterly in St. Cyprian's little chapel! had prayed God so fervently not to let Augustine leave Africa! And now she sees clearly that it was love which actuated God when He denied her request, that Infinite Goodness had directed all. Such thoughts as these ravish the soul, and sooner or later elicit an act of perfect confidence in God, to whom we entrust children, friends, projects, and the future, saying: "Do with me, Lord, as seems best in Thy sight; Thou art wiser than I am, and Thy heart more tender than mine!

St. Ambrose had a final interview with the travellers, gave them a parting benediction, and clasping Augustine in his arms, entreated heaven to bless his journey, which prayer was fully answered.

CHAPTER XV.

ST. MONICA DIES OF JOY AT HER SON'S CONVERSION.

387.

Shortly before their departure, or perhaps even on the journey, for the exact date of their quitting Milan is unknown, St. Monica fell into an ecstasy, which plainly revealed whither her thoughts were constantly tending more and more. It was St. Cyprian's Day.* She had received Holy Communion that morning, and returned home, absorbed and rapt in the profound meditation usual to her at such times. Perhaps she remembered, in a transport of gratitude, St. Cyprian's little chapel, and the night she passed within its walls three years before. (A.D. 384.) However this may be, suddenly she appeared to soar from earth, and in ecstatic rapture, exclaimed: "Let us fly to heaven, let us fly to heaven!" The spectators were surprised, for Monica was very gentle, and such impetuosity wholly foreign to her nature. Augustine, Adeodatus, and Alipius, hastened to her side, but she made no reply to their questions. Her countenance

* 16th September.

was irradiated with holy joy, and she was unable to do more than to reiterate David's words: "My heart and my flesh have rejoiced in God my Saviour."*

Thenceforth all her thoughts were fixed on heaven. Not that she had ever clung to earth, but until Augustine was converted, she could not dream of leaving him in darkness and danger, to enjoy heaven's repose herself. Had such a thought presented itself, she would instantly have chased it from her mind. She desired to convert her son, and until that work was effected there was no place in her mind for any other thought. Therefore, now that she beheld Augustine a fervent Christian, no longer needing her protection, heaven regained the ascendant. She spoke of it incessantly; contemplated it with ardour; and as it is said of certain exiles that they are home-sick, it might be said of St. Monica that she was pining for heaven.

The journey did not interrupt the current of her thoughts; on the contrary, it aided her contemplations, the instability of all terrestrial things making her yearn more and more for that world where change is unknown. Calm, contemplative, her heart raised God-wards, her mind full of the thought of eternity, though she was apparently travelling to Africa, in reality she was soaring heavenwards.

If the voyage failed to interrupt St. Monica's contemplations, it also failed to interrupt her son's devotions and studies. Since his conversion, Augustine had divided his days into two equal parts. The

* Boll., die 4 Maii.

first he consecrated to prayer, recitation of the psalms, the perusal of Holy Scripture, to that intimate union with God which is true bliss, and in which alone the soul can find repose. The remainder of his time he devoted to the most profound theological and philosophical researches. At Milan, he had just concluded his treatise on the errors of Manicheism, was meditating his treatise on religion, and, already soaring higher still, was beginning to fix his searching gaze on the mysteries of the Blessed Trinity, and on the Incarnation; and all this while continuing his journey.

Also, in concert with his mother, he completed the plan of that community life, so serious, simple retired, and hidden in God, which he had already essayed at Cassiacum, and which he had found so delightful that he resolved never to abandon it. Therefore, on approaching Pisa, St. Monica and her son swerved a little from their route, in order to behold a sight deeply interesting to them both. The deep forest-shades of the Apennines had afforded an asylum to some pious hermits, who there renewed the wonders of the Thebaïd. St. Augustine and St. Monica, who, before leaving Milan, had visited the religious and the virgins under St. Ambrose's direction, in order to gather from their conversation and holy life some information which might prove useful to themselves in furthering the project they had in view, were now desirous of seeing and conversing with these hermits. Unfortunately, we have no details of this visit, which is one of the many facts of which Augustine said: "I omit much because I am pressed for time. Blessed be Thy holy name for all Thy favours! recorded or unrecorded, I would praise Thee alike by my silence and by my pen."*

The next place we meet with our travellers is at Cività-Vecchia. Tradition has preserved the memory of a celebrated occurrence which took place there, and which confirms our previous statements as to the lofty philosophical and religious speculations which St. Augustine pursued, even while travelling. During one of those long intervals of leisure, so frequent in the mode of travelling then general in Italy, St. Augustine was pacing up and down the sea-shore at Cività-Vecchia, his mind occupied with the somewhat daring desire of fathoming the mystery of the Blessed Trinity. Suddenly he perceived a charming child who, having made a little hollow in the sand, brought water from the sea in a shell, in order to fill it. The saint stood still, and smilingly regarding the child, asked whether it thought that tiny hollow capable of containing the ocean. "And why not?" replied the child with pleasing gravity; "it would be far easier for it to do so, than for thy mind to contain the incomprehensible ocean of the Blessed Trinity." The spot where this charming incident occurred is still pointed out, and is the site of a primitive church, dedicated to St. Augustine.

From Cività-Vecchia our travellers journeyed on to Rome. How, at the moment when they were about to bid an eternal adieu to Italy, could they re-

* *Confess.*, lib. XI., cap. viii.

frain from visiting the tombs of St. Peter and St. Paul ? Augustine, to offer the tribute of his grateful joy, and the ardour of his new-born faith; Monica, her joyous gratitude for her son's conversion. Also, as regarded the religious life, which was then the subject of their thoughts, Rome, possessed as she was of many a band of virgins and monks, the purity and spotless beauty of whose lives Augustine had so highly extolled, must have possessed great attractions for St. Monica and her son. They entered Rome, this we know : but remained there only a few days, on account of the near approach of winter, which she dreaded on Augustine's account. The Apennines were already snow-capped, therefore she hurried him away to Ostia, where she hoped to find a vessel ready to transport them to Africa.

During the few days of their tarrying at Ostia, Monica again fell into a state of ecstatic rapture, which, though less impetuous, was more sublime than the preceding one.

She was sitting at a window overlooking the sea on one of those beautiful autumnal afternoons, no-where so splendid as in Italy. The deep clear bosom of the sea glittered in the rays of the setting sun. Augustine seated himself at his mother's side, in order to enjoy this magnificent spectacle. The silence of the evening, the beauty of the heavens, the bound-less expanse of sea, the vaster horizon of Augustine's and Monica's mental vision, the peace around, exceeded by that within, gradually raised their souls upwards, and gave rise to the following dialogue, so redolent of heaven.

"Alone at this window, we began to discourse with ineffable delight. Oblivious of all save the future, we were inquiring between ourselves what the eternal life of the saints shall be, which neither eye hath seen, nor ear hath heard, nor hath mortal mind conceived. Then the mouths of our hearts opened with avidity for the celestial waters of that fountain of life which is in Thee, that bedewed and strengthened thereby we might in some sort comprehend such a transcendent subject.

"We soon concluded that the most vivid joy of the senses in any corporeal light and beauty were not only unworthy to be compared with the felicities of heaven, but unworthy even of being mentioned.

"Rising on the wings of love towards this immutable felicity with a yearning past description, we ascended by several steps through all corporeal things, and through that heaven itself, from whence the sun, moon, and stars illuminate the earth. Considering Thee, my God, speaking of Thee, and admiring Thy works, we mounted higher still, to arrive at that happy region where truth is the sole nourishment, wisdom the only life; and having arrived there, as it were, with one whole spring and beat of the heart, our souls were filled with ineffable rapture."*

This sudden soaring of the soul to God, borne on the wings of love, is termed an ecstasy. How long St. Augustine and St. Monica remained in this silent

---

* *Confess.*, lib. IX., cap. x.

rapture it would have been impossible for them to tell, for when every faculty is thus in suspense, the blissful soul takes no heed of the flight of time. A century would have seemed but a second, so swiftly would it have passed away. The soul awakes from such a state with a sigh of deep regret. "We sighed, and leaving our hearts and minds captive there, we returned to the realm of speech, where our word hath its beginning and its ending."*

After this interval of silent rapture, during which St. Monica and St. Augustine were wholly absorbed in the contemplation of God, they resumed their conversation almost in the following words: "If a soul were to be still, and in perfect silence, in whom the voice of passion, the vain tumults of earth, sea, air, and heaven were hushed; if dreams and all imaginary revelations were silent, and every tongue, sign, and transitory thing were hushed; and the voice that issues from created things, and which proclaims, 'We did not make ourselves, but He made us who lives for ever:' supposing this voice, too, were silent, that we might hear His word, not by the tongue of the flesh, nor by the voice of an angel, nor by the voice of thunder, nor by the obscurity of a similitude, but that we should hear His very voice, as now with a swift thought we have touched upon that eternal and immutable wisdom; if such a thing were to be continued to us, and all other sights of an inferior kind were to be withdrawn and swallowed up, and engulph the beholders into its interior joys, so that

* *Confess.*, lib. IX., cap. x.

our life for ever should be such a moment of rapture, would not such bliss be that of which it is written, ' Enter into the joy of thy Lord ?' "*

Such were the thoughts of the mother and the son, whose hearts overflowed with celestial joy. Seated at that window in Ostia, hand in hand, hearts and eyes raised heavenwards, they contemplated in turn earth, sea, stars, all created things, and finding them too transitory and insignificant, they soared together far above this sad vale of tears, to the realm of imperishable beauty and of eternal love. " Son," said Monica, gravely and tenderly, in terminating her conversation, " I have now no tie to earth ; what I have to do here any longer, or why I am here, I know not, since I have nothing more to hope for in this world. One thing there was for which I did desire to tarry a little longer in this life, which was that I might see thee a Christian Catholic before I died. And my God hath granted me more than this, in that I see thee now despising all earthly felicity, entirely devoted to His service. Why, therefore, do I tarry here ?"†

On another occasion, taking advantage of St. Augustine's momentary absence, she expressed in the most ardent terms her contempt for this mortal life, and spoke of the happiness of dying. And as Alipius, Navigius, and the others, surprised at beholding a frail woman possessed of such courage, asked her if she did not fear dying far from her native land, she replied, " Oh, no; we are never far from God: no

* *Confess.*, lib. IX., cap. x.   † Ibid.

fear but at the day of judgment God will know where to find my body to resuscitate it."[*]

This wondrous detachment from earth was not remarked until the close of her life: its choicest and latest bloom. For until then, says St. Augustine, " she had always felt much concern about the place of her sepulture, which she had provided for herself at Tagaste, near the body of her husband, by whose side she had desired to be interred, even in the days when she endured much suffering at his hands, much more so now that she could look back on his conversion, in effecting which she had been so instrumental. Therefore, before quitting Africa she had made all necessary arrangements, so that her body might be conveyed to Tagaste, and that she might have the happiness of affording the world this proof of her fidelity, and that it might be commemorated, that it was granted her, after crossing the seas and living so long abroad, to mingle her ashes with those of Patricius."[†]

But the nearer she drew to heaven, the fainter grew these thoughts, beautiful though they were. What did it signify where she slept, in Italy or in Africa, provided she awaked in heaven? If hearts are united in an eternal union, what matters it where the ashes lie? Patricius slept in God: it was now her turn to do so, and Augustine would rejoin them later on. All else was unworthy a single regret.

Thus detached from earth, her work completed, with her wonted patience and courage she awaited

[*] *Confess.*, lib. IX., cap. xi. [†] Ibid.

the signal for her departure. It did not tarry long. Scarcely five days had passed after this before she was seized with fever, and was compelled to keep her bed. It was at first supposed that she was suffering from over-fatigue, consequent on her long voyage. But she was not deceived, she knew that the Divine Spouse was calling her, and was only anxious to prepare herself for His coming.

This conviction was strengthened shortly after, for, whilst lying in bed, praying and meditating, she swooned away, again lost in sweet and extatic rapture. They thought her dead, and Augustine, Adeodatus, and Navigius hastened to her side, and whilst seeking for some remedies whereby to recall her to life, she opened her eyes gently, asking, with a tone of surprise, "Where have I been?" Then, in order to reveal to them from what sublime regions she had descended, and what she had there learnt, added, "Here you shall bury your mother."*

On hearing these significant words, Augustine felt his heart overwhelmed with grief, but had strength to refrain from weeping. This Navigius was unable to do, and broke out in lamentations, regretting that she should die abroad, and not in her own country; which Monica hearing, checked him with a reproachful gaze. Then, looking upon Augustine as the stronger of the two, said, "Do you hear what he says?" Then, regarding both of them so that there might be no doubt as to her wishes, she added, "Lay this body anywhere, be not concerned about

* *Confess.*, lib. IX., cap. xi.

that ; only this I beg of you, that wheresoever you be you make remembrance of me at the Lord's altar."[*]

From that moment Monica was silent, wholly absorbed in preparing herself for the advent of the heavenly Bridegroom. She carefully inspected her soul, so that she might cleanse it from those imperceptible particles of dust which cling even to the most brilliant flowers ; and she roused all the ardour of her soul, so that faith, love, hope, humility, and detachment might attain their highest perfection within her heart ere the advent of Him for whom she waited.

Her sufferings were very acute ; but pain is no obstacle to the transfiguration of souls, but, on the contrary, aids it effectually. Only love is stronger than pain and death, and when these three co-operate to purify and adorn the soul, a few hours suffice to render her incomparably beautiful.

This transformation Augustine watched in silence. A year earlier such a scene would have been incomprehensible to him, and would have overwhelmed him with grief ; but now he was not only a son, but a Christian, and something of the future priest was already discernible. Full of love and fortitude, he remained by his mother ; though alternately lost in wondering admiration, and overcome by sorrow, with his prayers and ardent love he aided St. Monica in this last painful struggle.

She, whose fortitude even exceeded Augustine's, encouraged him by her look. Her sufferings were

* *Confess.*, lib. IX., cap. xi.

great, but feeling that the end was near, she thanked him for his aid, calling him her dutiful son; and noting Augustine's brow overclouded by regret for the tears and sorrow he had caused her through so many a long year, she pressed him to her heart, assuring him that she had never once heard from his lips any harsh or reproachful word towards her.*

On the tenth day the hour of deliverance sounded.

God willed that a heavy trial should be superadded to the rest. Monica desired to receive the Holy Eucharist to strengthen her for her long journey. But she suffered from such intense pains in the stomach that this consolation had to be withheld, and as she could not receive the Viaticum, a cross was placed in her hands, which until her last sigh she gazed at fixedly. Engaged in silent prayer, full of faith, detached from all below, and happy in the consciousness that she was about to precede Augustine to that home where he would rejoin her, her brow was irradiated by a glow of light, joy, and peace.

It is said that at the last moment, when with augmented fervour she again entreated to receive her Lord, a little child was seen to enter her room, similar to the one whom Augustine met a few days before on the sea shore at Cività-Vecchia. He approached the saint's couch, kissed her on the breast, and instantly, as if responding to his summons, she bowed her head and breathed forth her last sigh.†

Augustine, Adeodatus, Navigius, Alipius, and Evodius were kneeling near her bed "at the moment

---

* *Confess.*, lib. IX., cap. ix.   † *Boll.*, May 4.

when that holy soul was loosed from the body."
This occurred on the ninth day of her illness, the
fifty-sixth year of her age, and the thirty-third of
Augustine's.*

As soon as Monica had expired, Adeodatus broke
out into a loud lamentation, and throwing himself on
his grandmother's corpse, bathed it with his tears.
They checked his grief, for so like a triumph was that
death, they were loath to mar it by a single tear. The
boy having held his peace, they again knelt down to
pray in silence. But soon Augustine could no longer
restrain his feelings, and feeling the flood of grief
within his soul, yet forcibly restraining his tears, he
arises, approaches the bed, and after one last long
look, with grateful hand closes those eyes which had
shed so many tears on his behalf, then flees hastily
away, for he was unwilling that even his lamentations
as a son should mar a scene where, as a Christian, he
felt that all should be characteristic of joy.†

When the tidings of the saint's death had spread
abroad, a number of Christians hastened to the house.
It was only a few days since St. Monica's arrival at
Ostia; but whether Augustine's reputation and the
fact of his conversion and baptism had preceded him,
or rather whether the wonders which had attended
St. Monica's last days had transpired; also whether,
as in the instance of so many saints, God had revealed
to certain souls the mystery of piety which had just
taken place, the little chamber where St. Monica died

* *Confess.*, lib. IX., cap. xi.   † *Confess.*, lib. IX., cap. xii.

was crowded with Christians praising God for her happy death.

Meanwhile, Navigius, Evodius, Alipius, and Adeo-datus, recited aloud the Psalms of David. Augustine was seated in their midst, a prey to a twofold agony. Acutely feeling the wrench which severed him from his mother, (whose life till now had been so intimately united to his as to form but one) tears of poignant sorrow flooded his eyes; but rejoicing in the wonders of grace which had been vouchsafed his mother, per-suaded that the hour of her death was the hour of her triumph, he restrained his tears. He says: "A very great grief came flowing into my heart ready to flow out into tears; but my eyes, by the forcible com-mand of my soul, drank them up again, even unto dryness, and in this inward conflict I suffered much."

The less he wept, the more he suffered: the tears he repressed did but increase his suffering. "I restrained the flood of my grief, and sometimes it yielded to me a little, and then again with violence it rushed upon me, not so far as to discover itself by bursting out into tears, nor yet so far as to be dis-cernible in my countenance, but I alone know what I kept close in my heart. Thus was I afflicted with a double sorrow."*

He spent the day on which his mother died and the following one in praying at her side, or in reciting the psalms of David, and even conversing with his friends in the adjoining room. He followed his mother's bier, pale, silent, overwhelmed with grief,

* *Confess.*, lib. IX., cap. xii.

still violently repressing his tears. "And now the body is carried out to be buried, and I both go and return without tears. Neither did I shed any in those prayers which we poured out before Thee, when the sacrifice of our redemption was offered to Thee for her, the body being set down by the grave, before interment therein. But sorrow overwhelmed me, and with a troubled spirit I begged of Thee, as well as I could, that Thou wouldst heal my grief."*

On the evening of the same day he essayed some of the remedies prescribed by the ancients, for being as yet but a novice in the Faith, he had not wholly freed himself from his old stoic fancies. In bathing, walking, and sleep, he sought for an alleviation of his woe, for he was resolved not to weep.

But all in vain, for on awaking the next morning, missing his mother, and calling to mind her kindness, gentleness, and deep and unchanging love to him, the many loving services she had lavished on him for more than thirty years, his heart melted within him. "I let go my tears, which I had kept in before, that they might flow as much as they pleased, and found rest to my soul in weeping for her who so long had wept for me."†

To the very day of his death Augustine ceased not to mourn his mother. He never forgot her. In compliance with her dying request, he daily remembered her in his prayers and at the holy altar. Her gentle presence seemed ever to surround him, inciting him to virtue, courage, and fidelity. He often spoke

---

* Confess., lib, IX., cap. xii.　　　　† Ibid.

of her to his friends; and sometimes mentioned her in his sermons. For instance, one day, more than thirty years after St. Monica's death, Augustine was speaking of the departed, of the respect due to their memory, of praying on their behalf, of the superstitions to be avoided, such for example, as believing they can return to earth and reappear to us. Suddenly, the sweet memory of his mother filling his mind, he exclaimed: " Oh! no, the dead return not; for could they do so, not a night would pass without my dear mother re-visiting me whom she loved so tenderly, whom she followed by sea and land, even into foreign lands. For God forbid that she, whose love for me passes words, on entering a happier state should love me less, and not hasten to comfort me in my sorrow!"*

His *Confessions* prove still more clearly than this passionate outburst, the depth of his affection for his mother. In that immortal book, written by Augustine to silence the admiration of which he was the object, and which has but increased that admiration, we see how great was his affection for his mother; and although he has left her in partial shade, lest the aureola on her brow should illumine his, it is in those writings that, in spite of all his reticence and faint allusions, we discern, as through a transparent veil, this admirable woman's gentleness, piety, virginal modesty, chastity, maternal heroism, and divine ardour. In a word, there we behold the type of a Christian mother, there we learn what she has power

* *Serm.* 68.

to do for her children, and after saving, healing, and restoring them to life by her prayers, what pious memories and tender, undying gratitude she kindles within their hearts.

In order to give a crowning proof of this, and also to conclude the description of that wondrous death, we will cite Augustine's own words, (taken from his *Confessions,)* so classical in their beauty, redolent of the deepest affection, and stamped with the impress of filial grief, which time has been powerless to heal, and a love which separation has but strengthened and purified.

"And now," writes St. Augustine, (that is thirty years after his mother's decease,) "my heart being healed of that wound, in which a carnal affection may have had too great a share, I pour out to Thee, Lord, in behalf of that servant of Thine, a far different sort of tears, flowing from a spirit freighted with the consideration of the perils of every soul that dies in Adam. For although she, being revived in Christ even before being set free from the flesh, had lived in such a manner as that she glorified Thy name by her faith and the purity of her manners; yet I dare not say that from the time that Thou didst regenerate her by baptism no word contrary to Thy command issued from her lips. Therefore, O God of my heart, my glory and my life, setting aside her good deeds, for which I give Thee thanks, I entreat Thee at present for my mother's sins. Hear me now, I beseech Thee, through that Physician of our souls who hung upon the Cross, and who now intercedeth for us at Thy right Hand. I know that mercifully and from her heart she forgave her debtors their trespasses; do Thou likewise forgive her her debts, if she has contracted any during those many years she lived after her Baptism. Forgive them, O Lord, forgive them, I beseech Thee; enter not with her into judgment, O my God!

"But hast Thou not already done this? Yes, I believe Thou hast; but these free-offerings of my mouth approve, O Lord. Let none separate her from Thy protection. Let not the lion and dragon by force or fraud interpose himself. Because she will not plead that she owes nothing, lest she should be convicted by that crafty accuser. But she will plead that her debts have been discharged by Him, to whom no one can repay what He, who owed nothing for Himself, laid down for us.*

"Let her therefore rest in peace, together with her husband her only spouse, whom she dutifully served that she might be worthy of gaining him to Thee. And do Thou inspire, O Lord my God! do Thou inspire Thy servants, my brothers, Thy children, my masters, whom I wish to serve with my voice, heart, and writings, that as many as shall read this may remember at Thy altar Thy handmaid Monica, with Patricius, formerly her husband, by whom (after what manner I know not) Thou broughtest me into this life. Let them remember with a pious affection

* *Confess.*, lib. IX., cap. xiii.

those who were my parents in this transitory life, that so my mother's last request to me on her death-bed may be more abundantly performed for her by the prayers of many than by mine alone."*

CHAPTER XVI.

THE SON OF MANY TEARS.

387-430.

If St. Monica's last moments were illumined with joy on account of her son's conversion, what would she not have experienced could she have contemplated the results, and witnessed the wondrous development of his sanctity and genius, (but dimly shadowed forth in those days of retirement spent at Cassiacum)? It was not God's will that she should enjoy such happiness; it would have been too perfect for earth, therefore it was reserved for eternity. But to us, who grope amid the clouds enveloping her history for a clearer insight into the character of this holy woman, it is permitted to study this marvellous spectacle awhile, and if it be true that her mission was not only to convert her son, but to prepare and present to the Church the greatest of her doctors, we shall but continue the study of her character, by contemplating the striking genius and sanctity of the son whom she left on earth. Should we succeed in portraying Augustine's mind and heart, such work may prove

* *Confess.*, lib. IX., cap. xiii.

"a golden back-ground," on which St. Monica's beauty will stand forth in high relief.

As soon as his mother was interred, Augustine's first thought was to return to Rome. He had not courage to tear himself from his mother's tomb, and desired to remain in Italy that he might be able to resort often to that much loved spot, offer his prayers there, and seek those holy inspirations and that light, which a mother, even when dead, never refuses her son. He remained in Rome for a twelvemonth, continuing to lead the same kind of life which he had led at Cassiacum, devoting the morning to prayer, the study of the Holy Scriptures, (a study which he never discontinued,) and composing many works, of which we shall soon speak. The evenings he spent in visiting the churches and holy spots so numerous in Rome, the Catacombs, where, weeping, he kissed the martyrs' sacred relics; and especially the monasteries, where he was a constant visitor, and where he gradually initiated himself in that religious life which, after his conversion, had been his heart's earliest aspiration, and which he proposed to introduce into Africa. In perusing the letters, (too rare, alas!) written by him at this epoch, we note the ever-growing ardour of his soul. His whole demeanour was expressive of silence, poverty, and humility; he yearned for solitude, which, he says, is more favourable than aught else to growth in holiness, and to self-sanctification. Death he termed the companion of love, who opens the door and admits us to the presence of our beloved ones. His visits to his mother's tomp must have greatly deepened these sentiments, weaning him ever more and more from earth, and drawing his affections heavenwards.

When the year of mourning was completed, Augustine started for Africa, accompanied by Adeodatus, Alipius, Evodius, and a few others; he sold his small patrimony and distributed the proceeds among the poor, selected for his own dress and that of his companions a black tunic, girt about the reins with a leathern girdle, wore a large tonsure, resembling that of the monks of Egypt, and, aided by his friends, inaugurated at the gates of Tagaste that life of prayer, poverty, and obedience, which had so long been his cherished dream. " He remained there nearly three years," says his biographer, " withdrawn from the world, he and his companions living for God alone, in fasting, prayer, and the exercise of good works; meditating day and night on the mysteries of the faith, and by conversation or letter, communicating to others the extraordinary light which God imparted to him in his hours of contemplation."* Apart from this, he wrote but little, rarely went out, and carefully avoided appearing in public, especially in those cities standing in need of priests and bishops. For now that his name was beginning to be spread abroad, he feared lest that which had happened to St. Ambrose and to many others, (whom the populace had laid hold of and compelled to become priests or bishops,) should also happen to him.

But the hour having arrived when this light was no

* Possidius, cap. iii.

longer to be hidden, his humility and all his pre-cautions were unavailing. One day that he was in Hippo, whither he had gone in the hope of winning to the religious life a noble soul whom he thought worthy of such a vocation, as he was assisting at the Holy Sacrifice, absorbed and fearing nothing, for there was a bishop at Hippo; this latter, a venerable old man, ascended the pulpit, and by chance began to speak of his onerous duties and the need in which he stood of some young priest to aid him. At these words, all eyes turned to Augustine, who was seized and forcibly led to the bishop's feet, and all present with loud cries demanded that Augustine should be ordained priest. The saintly young man, taken by surprise, burst into tears and began sobbing. His biographer says that, "Some, to whom Augustine was unknown, thinking to console him, whispered in his ear that though he was worthy of a higher dignity, priesthood was a stepping-stone to the episcopacy; words these which only augmented the sorrow of this godly man." * He called to mind his past life, and wept at the thought of the responsibilities of the priestly office.

Hardly was he ordained priest, when, instead of abandoning the mode of life he had led at Tagaste, he resolved to live in greater poverty and humility than before. With the bishop's permission the early com-panions of his solitude joined him at the gates of Hippo, as also did several others, and in a retired and tranquil spot Augustine founded a monastery which

* Possidius, cap. iv.

speedily became a school of sanctity, and whence issued all the eminent African bishops of that time: St. Alipius, Bishop of Tagaste; St. Evodius, Bishop of Uzales; St. Severus, Bishop of Milevius; St. Possidius, Bishop of Calamus, who has bequeathed us a precious, but far too brief life of Augustine; St. Profuturus, Bishop of Cyrthea; and more than ten others eminent for sanctity, who, in their turn, were founders of monasteries, and, says Possidius of these zealous workers in the spread of Divine truth, "they everywhere furthered the peace and unity of the Church." In their midst, Augustine, as a star, began to shed abroad the light he had amassed during the five years, so full of fruit, that had elapsed since his conversion, preaching every Sunday in the church at Hippo, inviting the heretics to public conferences, writing innumerable letters, planning works, "ever ready to preach the word," says Possidius, "whether in public or in private, at home or in church. His writings and sermons transported the faithful with admiration and joy. And his books, which, by the singular grace of God, succeeded one another with marvellous rapidity, were eagerly welcomed by heretics and Catholics, who vied with each other in the ardour with which they perused them, and both alike were anxious to obtain copies of the same. Thus, after her prolonged humiliation, did the African Church raise her head once more, and the Church of the West proudly rejoiced at the sight."*

There was one sight even more beautiful than this

* Possidius, cap. vii.

23   S.M.

unexpected display of genius and sanctity in so young a man (since whose baptism five years had elapsed, and who had been ordained priest only a few days before,) that of the aged bishop, "rejoicing so exultingly, and with tears thanking God for sending him such help," remonstrating with those envious ones who desired, on what legal grounds I know not, that Augustine should not be allowed to teach, and smiling at those who essayed to inspire him with jealousy also; and who, in order that the other churches might not rob him of the treasure he possessed in such a powerful auxiliary, hid him away in a retired spot, until he had received permission from the primate of Africa to associate him with himself as coadjutor. As soon as this permission was granted, a noble contest was seen; the aged bishop ascending the pulpit and announcing, amid the enthusiastic outcries of the faithful, his intention of consecrating Augustine bishop; and Augustine,—though refusing with tears, bringing forward the canons of the Church, the African custom, and his own unworthiness, as excuses,—commanded and almost forced to accept the dignity, regretting it all through life, ever confessing his unworthiness of such an honour, but with augmented zeal and fervour using his episcopal authority for the extension and defence of the faith.

Thus was this luminary exalted, whose splendour God was about to render so brilliant. Thus, after fifteen years of irregularities and errors, permitted by God in order that Augustine might the better know the impotence of man's intellect, and the still greater weakness of his heart; after spending five years (the first at Cassiacum, the second in Rome, and the three others at Tagaste) in almost perpetual silence, continual prayer, and profound study of Holy Scripture, Augustine entered on the post assigned him by Providence, whence he was about to illuminate the Church and the world.

To fit him for this grand work, he had been endowed by God with a sublime reason, powerful imagination, the keenest, loftiest, and most penetrating intellect, metaphysical powers of the highest order, enabling him to go straight to the very root of things, and seize first principles. With these God had associated a most tender and loving heart, so that he might not only possess the clear perceptions arising from genius, but the deep intuitions which have their home in the heart and the affections. Thanks to his estimable mother, sanctity completed the work. And, inasmuch as genius is indebted for its awakening to outward circumstances, God willed Augustine's birth to take place at the moment when heresies of all kinds were rampant, and Arians, Manicheans, Donatists, and Pelagians, were multiplying in the field of the Church, in order that, by professing each heresy he might be able to explain all dogmas, scrutinize all mysteries, defend all the principles of morality, and to erect, on the eve of the barbaric invasions, and at the very moment when darkness was about to cover the world, a religious edifice so beautiful, vast, luminous, and strong, that it should defy both time and change.

Such a work was not the work of a moment, and this Augustine knew full well. The hour was still far distant when it would be possible to a single individual, (as to St. Thomas for instance,) to attempt to unfold the Divine plan fully. Born in the world's earlier age, Augustine pursued a different method. At different times and in different ways he handled all the parts of this vast edifice, surrounding himself with all its magnificent materials. But by arranging the diverse subjects, of which he treated at different times and in different manners, we can reconstruct the temple. It is almost perfect, and perhaps the most sublime which mortal hand has ever erected in honour of the Deity. In order that our readers may have some idea of the same, we will endeavour to classify the chefs-d'œuvre of the collection.

It seems to me right to award the foremost place to all those works composed at Cassiacum: the treatise on the *Blessed Life,* the two books on *Order* or *Providence,* and the three books *Against the Academicians;* to these we must add the *Soliloquies,* not alluded to by us, the book *of the Master,* consisting of a dialogue between Augustine and his son Adeodatus; the works *on Music,* and especially the last volume containing a theory respecting God and creation, singularly original and profound; the book of *The Soul and its Origin,* the treatise on *The Immortality of the Soul,* and another small treatise on *The Greatness of the Soul,* which he composed during his walks with Evodius. Throughout this first series of works, written or projected at Cassiacum during the poetic season of his early youth and that of his conversion, St. Augustine approaches, examines under a thousand different aspects, and solves these three great questions: God; the soul, and the bond uniting them to each other.

What is God? What is the soul? What are the relations subsisting between them? What the harmony, and what the diversity between them? Such is the portico of the edifice.

Laden as Augustine still was with the spoils of ancient philosophy and the teachings of the " divine Plato," of the " venerable and all but divine Pythagoras," and of " Aristotle the master," Augustine ornaments this portico therewith, but illuminates it with a light wholly unknown to them. How profoundly does he examine into the mysterious depths of the Divine Being, of His existence, nature, essence, and attributes! He is by turns both poet and metaphysician; rather a subtle metaphysician sometimes, but original, deep, vigorous, and always eloquent. And, besides this searching investigation into the nature of the divinity, how profoundly has he studied the soul! " Nothing is so precious as the soul," he exclaims, " neither earth, sea, nor stars."* " But whence does the soul proceed? What is her nature? Of what do her faculties consist, and in what manner do they perish? Why is she wedded to a body? What befalls her on the death of the latter?" &c.† Fenelon asserted that if an intelligent man were to cull from Augustine's writings the sublime truths scattered hither and thither by this great man, as if by hazard,

---

* *De Quantitate animæ*, cap. xxxiv.   † *De Duabus animabus*, cap. iv.

this extract, if carefully made, would be far superior to Descartes' *Meditations,* although the latter are the grandest work of that philosophical mind.*

But nowhere is Augustine's genius so striking as when he approaches the sublime question of the relation in which the soul stands to God. Here Augustine's heart speaks, and when his heart and mind unite their radiance, their brilliance is incomparable. No one has better described the abyss of separation between God and the soul; but no one has better shown in what manner that abyss can be filled up. "The soul is made for God. The soul is an open eye which is fixed on God. The soul is love aspiring after the Infinite; God is the soul's home."† He takes all the faculties of the soul one by one, and reveals them all as terminating in God. As a rising tide all the faculties of the soul ascend to God by successive and ever deeper waves. Even this does not content him. It is not only the soul that is made for God, a little more and Augustine would say that God is made for the soul. How grandly does he depict the heart of God ready (as a full ocean) to pour out its plenitude upon man, and man by his very indigence aspiring to God, even as an arid land thirsts for the life-giving waves! What precision and delicacy in his analysis of the degrees by which the soul ascends to God! "For," he says, "it is not all at once, but by degrees that the purified soul can attain to God." "Let the soul," he eloquently remarks, "reflect on the

---

* *Lettres sur divers sujets de métaphysique et de religion,* lettre **iv.**
† St. August., *Op.,* tom. I., p. 401.

power and virtue of numbers, and she will see how supremely unworthy of herself, and how deplorable it is that she should be able to construct harmonious verses and extract sweet sounds from the lyre, whilst her own life is so wanting in order, and, a prey to passion, resounds with the discordant tumult of vice. Let her compose herself, restore order within, render herself harmonious and beauteous, and then will she spontaneously and readily soar upwards to the fount of beauty, harmony, and light.*

"We must ascend the steps of our hearts, and sing the *Song of Degrees.*" †

Then Augustine hymns this canticle, and indicates the seven degrees which the soul must ascend. After the three first, which are of minor import, he reaches the fourth, having attained which, the soul sets a higher value on herself, not only than on her own body, but than on all created bodies; values spiritual things above temporal ones, despising the latter, when compared with her own beauty and power; and the more she disengages herself from the slime into which she was cast, the purer, freer and more perfect does she become. Then by a sublime ascent the soul attains God, and this is the fifth degree; she begins to contemplate Him, and aspires after the joy of His Presence. The sixth consists in action. Contemplation is nothing, action is necessary; it is nothing to see the truth, we must deserve to become united to her. Then, and this is the seventh and last degree, contemplation, allied to virtue, opens up that life

* *De Ordine*, lib. II., cap. xix.   † *Confess.*, lib. XIII., cap. ix.

which knows no end. It is a state of perfect serenity, the foretaste of eternal joy. "Shall I attempt to describe that happy state?" he exclaims. "No! certain lofty, incomparable souls have revealed so much of their own experience with regard to it as they considered necessary for us to know. But what I can unhesitatingly affirm, is, that by God's grace we too shall attain that blissful state. Then we shall see the vanity and nothingness of all terrestrial things. Then will those grand and marvellous changes awaiting our corporal nature be so clearly understood by us, that even the resurrection of the flesh, difficult as it is to realize, will appear to us more certain than the rise of to-morrow's sun. Then shall we regard those foolish ones, who make sport of the mysteries of eternity, with feelings similar to those with which we regard a child who, on seeing but the faint outline sketched in, cannot believe it possible that a picture can emanate from the artist's pencil. So absorbing and delightful is the contemplation of truth, that the soul, in her holy zeal to attain the object of her contemplation, loses all dread of death, and regards it as the greatest boon."*

But if God and the soul are in harmony and united to each other, *(religio)* where is the bond which joins them? Where find that religion, which must have existed from the very beginning of time, and always have revealed itself to men of good will so clearly that all who seek may find? Such is the question which at once presents itself to the mind of Augus-

---

* *De Quantitate animæ,* cap. xxx.-xxxiii.

tine, but not for the first time, seeing that on leaving Cassiacum and traversing the Apennines it had already engrossed his thoughts, and to solve which, on reaching Rome, he penned his *Treatise on the true Religion;* a work tinged with that Platonic philosophy which he was about to abandon for a more theological style. This book is the latest chef d'œuvre of the former class of writings.

The exordium is remarkable for its beauty and amplitude. "Were Plato still living, and permitted me to interrogate him; or if, during his life any one of his disciples had asked him what he would think of a man such as Jesus Christ, who would succeed in winning esteem for a doctrine so exalted as that of His gospel, and succeed in spreading it throughout the world, so that even those who could not comprehend it would nevertheless believe it, and that those who would have sufficient mental vigour to shake off the yoke of error and vulgar prejudice would go so far as to practice it; what, I ask, would his reply be? Assuredly, such a one would seem to him super-human. For thus wise Plato would say: it is not given to man to operate such a wonderful change in the world, unless God, by a miracle of His wisdom and power, had raised him above the ordinary condition of mankind, in order to unite him intimately to Himself, enlightened him from his cradle, not by instructions such as man is capable of imparting, but by a secret effusion of the clear light of truth; and finally, enriched him with so many graces, armed him with so much courage, and raised him to such a degree of excellence and majesty, that, despising all which, through his natural depravity, man seeks after with avidity, exposing himself to everything which inspires men with the greatest dread, and performing in their sight the works most fitted to excite their admiration, he compels them to enlist themselves among the ranks of his followers, as much by the attraction of love as by the weight of authority.

" If, then, all these marvels have really taken place, if the writings and the monuments in which they are recorded have rendered their celebrity world-wide; if certain individuals, selected from among their brethren and sent out from the only spot in the world where the true God was worshipped, and which spot was therefore the fitting birth-place for such a man, have throughout the whole earth kindled the fire of divine love by the force of their language and the renown of their miracles; if in quitting the earth, after thus firmly establishing the doctrine of salvation, they have bequeathed the knowledge of these divine truths to posterity at large; and if, omitting all those past events which some may hesitate to believe, the same gospel is everywhere preached at the present day; if the people receive it with respect and love; if, in spite of temporal opposition, martyrdom, fire, and torture, the Church still increases; if no one is surprised to see thousands of youths and maidens renounce marriage and profess perpetual virginity; if the universe has become a vast temple resounding on all sides with the cry of *Sursum corda:* I again ask, what would Plato say? And with what admiration would he exclaim: Behold the realization of our dream; that which we should not have dared to propose to the nations of the earth, that with which we could never have inspired them, is believed, practised, and loved throughout the world!"*

After this magnificent introduction, and after having demonstrated, on the one hand, the inanity of Plato, that is the inanity of ancient philosophy to bring men to the knowledge of virtue, and on the other hand, the omnipotence of Jesus Christ, St. Augustine examines in turn all the bases of religion: that of history, by which we trace it back even to the world's cradle; that of prophecy, by which we see that it will exist till the world shall have an end; that of miracles, which are a manifest sign of the Divine Presence; the transforming power of religion: for, if we cannot associate with a clever or a virtuous man without increasing in virtue and knowledge, must not religion, by drawing men near to God, render them more divine? Then follows the celebrated portrait of a good man, by the side of which the just man delineated by Plato grows dim; he then speaks of the incomparable beauty of the life of Christ, the ideal type of the regenerated man. "Men pursue earthly riches with insatiable ardour; Jesus Christ chose to be born in poverty. Our pride makes us shrink from enduring the slightest outrage: He endured the most terrible ones. We revolt against injustice; He suffered injustice even to death. Pain is insupportable to us; He was scourged, and pierced with nails and thorns.

* *De Vera religion,* cap. iii. et iv.

Men shun death; He embraced it voluntarily. Nothing is so ignominious as the death of the Cross: He chose it. By despising the world, He has taught us to overcome the world. Therefore we see that there is nothing in the life of Jesus Christ but is a lesson for us, containing a complete epitome of morality."

We cannot agree with M. de Villemain, that "this treatise, revealing Augustine's heart, was destined to mark an epoch in his religious life, rather than serve as a proof of the Truth which he had embraced."[*] On the contrary, we assert with Arnauld,[†] Villemont,[‡] Bossuet,[§] and with the whole of the seventeenth century, that "this book, as much or more than any other, fills us with admiration of the mighty intellect and wondrous wisdom of this incomparable man. For who, (remembering how recently he had begun to study the mysteries of Christianity, and that he was but a simple layman,) but must be struck with surprise at the noble and sublime terms in which he speaks of that divine religion, and admire that lofty genius whose eagle-flight, sound arguments, and sublime propositions, it is difficult to follow without being dazzled by the brightness of his splendour!"

The completion of the subject treated of in this beautiful work, (addressed to Romanianus, whose conversion it effected) is found, first, in the four books on Christian Doctrine, in which St. Augustine

---

[*] *Les Pères du iv. siècle*, St. Augustine.
[†] *Préface* du *Traité de la vraie religion*, traduit par lui.
[‡] *Mémoires*, etc., tome XIII., p. 139.
[§] A. Floquet, *Études*, tome II., p. 517.

proves that religion is love, and in which, says Bossuet, "he has furnished us with more grounds for listening to the voice of Holy Writ, than all the other doctors put together;" and especially in the magnificent *letter to Volusian,* which filled the Church with astonishment and enthusiastic admiration. In this, Augustine, no longer soaring on the wings of Plato, but on those of the prophets, reaches that inaccessible light where the Word dwells. He bids us remember the eternal existence of that Word, begotten before all time. He speaks of His Incarnation, poverty, and sufferings; His works of light, holiness, and love; His incomparable superiority to the rest of mankind. Then draws our attention to the Hebrew nation, a nation called into existence in order that it might look for, announce, and desire the Messiah, and cherish within the hearts of men the expectation of His advent. Then alludes to the Church, indebted to His Blood for her very existence, spreading throughout the world, proclaiming His name, winning men's hearts to Him, and transforming them by the knowledge and love of Him. All this he treated of with an eloquence, profundity, and vigour, so striking that it filled Bossuet with admiration, who, roused to emulation by the perusal of this work, wrote, and he does not deny the fact, and which a single glance at his book suffices to establish, the second part of his *Discours sur l'histoire universelle.* Thus light kindled light, and genius awoke genius.

But that religion whose birth dates from the commencement of the world, and whose existence shall know no end; that Church of the Lord Jesus Christ, whose mission is to announce His truth, sanctity, and love, throughout all time, and throughout all lands, by what signs are they recognizable? This was precisely the very question which was agitating and engrossing Africa at the moment of Augustine's arrival. Having been led by the course of his studies, and still more by his controversy with the Donatists, to examine minutely that grand edifice called the Catholic Church, it was with passionate enthusiasm that Augustine entered on a subject affording such full scope to the exercise of his lofty and sublime genius. Absorbed in contemplation, roused to action, deeply affected by the light he discovers, but more deeply affected by the sad condition of those who discern not that light, he multiplied his discourses,* conferences,† letters,‡ and treatises,§ that he might manifest to every eye the divine beauty of the Church. He draws attention to her origin, her miraculous establishment, God's ever watchful care of her, the miracle of her unity, the

---

* *Serm.* 37, 45, 62, 75, 78, 79, 91, 116, 129, 138, 144, 267.

† St. Augustine's conferences with Felix the Manichean; with the Donatists, at Carthage; with Emeritus, in the presence of several bishops, &c. &c.

‡ *Epist.* 23, 33, 34, 35, 43, 44, 49, 51, 70, 76, 87, 93, 185, etc.

§ Liber de Utilitate credendi.—De moribus Ecclesiæ catholicæ et de moribus Manichæorum, lib. II.—Libri XXXIII. contra Faustum manichæum.—Psalmus contra partem Donati.—Contra Epistolam Parmeniani, libri III.—Contra litteras Petiliani, libri III.—Libri IV. contra Cresconium.—Epistola ad catholicos contra Donatistas.—Breviculus collationis cum Donatistis.—Liber ad Donatistas post collationem.—Sermo ad Cæsareensis Ecclesiæ plebem.—Libri II. contra Gaudentium.

historic evidence we possess, her catholicity, (in con-
tradistinction to the Donatists, who were to be found
only in one small portion of the globe); her holiness,
which not only transforms individuals, but laws,
manners, nations, and this despite the strong opposition of evil passions. And when in open controversy he floored and worsted his adversaries, and
compelled them to avow themselves defeated, or
with his pen crushed their vain objections, the giant
lays down his weapon, and allows the pent-up voice
of love to issue from his soul, never has such a
tender heart been seen in conjunction with so logical
an intellect. Then, after a conflict of twenty years
duration, in order to confound heresy and give it a
mortal blow, he urges the reunion of all the Catholic
and the schismatic bishops of Africa, obtains from the
former a promise that they will resign their sees, if
such a step be advantageous to the unity of the
Church, and opens that renowned assembly, consisting
of more than four hundred prelates, by a discourse on
peace, in which each word breathes of the love with
which his heart was full; then he descends into the
arena of conflict and for several days sustains the discussion alone, obliges his adversaries to confess themselves vanquished, and amid the applause of the
whole Church terminates that grand struggle by restoring peace and unity to Africa. *

The following are the sublime themes with which
Augustine's work commences, and our readers will
note the grandeur of the subjects and the links of

* Cfr. *Lib. de Gestis cum Emerito.*

union between them. He begins with God and the soul; religion, the tie that unites the soul to God; religion centering in Christ; the Church, His representative on earth; and yet these are but the mere outlines of the edifice.

Having proceeded thus far, and grounded his work on that immoveable rock, Augustine enters the temple, and taking courage as he advances, examines its lowest depths and most exalted summits.

He commences with the mystery of God, no longer studying it, as at Cassiacum, in the light of Christian reason, but illuminated by the more brilliant light of revelation, which light revealed to him the Triune God: God the Father; God the Son, eternally begotten of the Father; and God the Holy Ghost, proceeding from the Father and the Son; these adorable mysteries are treated of in succession in the fifteen books of the sublime *Treatise on the Trinity,* "commenced in early life, and completed in old age."* Until Augustine's day none of the Fathers had made deeper researches into these divine mysteries than Tertullian had done, but in the work to which we allude, the thoughts are loftier, more philosophic, and if I may be allowed the expression, more ethereal though not less grand. Perhaps nothing more sublime than this treatise, and Bossuet's *Elévations,* has ever been written respecting that unapproachable Light, where He dwells whom no mortal eye has ever seen.

But God speaks; the universe starts to life. How?

* Cfr *Lib. contra sermonem Arianorum.—Collatio cum Maximino Arianorum episcopo.—Libri II. contra Maximinum.*

and f what purpose did God create? This is the second mystery of which Augustine treats, a mystery formidable even to the mind which has been essaying to fathom the depths of the Blessed Trinity, a mystery which the greatest philosophers of antiquity have been unable to solve. Augustine views it with the eye of a metaphysician and the eye of a poet. He has devoted twelve books to the explanation of the three first chapters of Genesis, treating not only of general principles, but of the minutest details of natural history, with erudition, amplitude, eloquence, and remarkable perspicuity; he discards the literal theory, substituting those longer epochs which modern science demands; treats of the creation of light, water, air, and specially of man, in a wondrous manner, developing in countless ways that theory of the creation to be met with at the close of his treatise *De Musica:* "Surprising intuition," says Father Gratry, "and in full harmony with the reply science is now preparing to that important question: 'What is matter?'"* In every page of this treatise we discern the metaphysician and the poet. The three last books of the *Confessions* contain a poem on creation in three cantos, an epopee of singular grandeur, in which, one after the other, all the worlds hymn the glory of their Creator.

But in the midst of this beautiful creation evil exists, and intellectual, moral, and physical disorder. Whence comes it? Was it created by God? If not, how came it into being? We remember that in early

* *De la Connaissance de l'ame.* tome I., page 251.

life this formidable question tormented Augustine, caused him to fall into the errors of Manicheism, and tortured his mighty intellect for the space of nineteen years: on it he sheds new and startling light. Scarcely had his conversion taken place, than he lays hold of this problem, never more to qu't it. He developes, in fifteen treatises,* his theory, so profound and so correct, that evil is only a negation, a weakness of will, a non-observance of the laws of equity and justice, just as night is nothing more than an absence of light, that God did not create darkness any more than He created death or evil, but that vil owes its existence, in the first place, to the fallen angels, then to sinful man; that God permits its existence because He will punish it, and because the very punishment of evil will be as glorious a sight as the recompense bestowed on righteousness. He reverts incessantly to this origin of evil, chanting it in varying cadence throughout that sad poem, which presents to view the fallen angel causing the fall of our first parents, and with them that of all their posterity, a sight that would indeed be mournful in the

* Liber contra Epistolam Manichæi quam vocant fundamenti.—De Actis cum Felice Manichæo, lib. II.—Liber de natura boni.—Liber de duabus animabus.—Acta seu disputatio contra Fortunatum Manichæum—Libri III. de libero arbitrio.—Liber contra Secundinum.—Serm. 1, 2, 12, 50, 153, 182, 237.—Enarratio in Psalm. 140, Nos. 10, 12.—Libri IV. de anima et ejus origine—De peccatorum meritis et remissione libri III.—Liber de spiritu et littera.—Liber de natura et gratia—Liber de gestis Pelagi.—Liber II. de gratia Christi et de peccato originali.—Libri II. de nuptiis et de concupiscentiis. Contra duas epistolas Pelagianorum libri IV.—Libri VI. contra Julianum Pelagianum. Opus imperfectum contra Julianum Pelagianum.

extreme, did not a ray of light gleam athwart the scene and reveal the glorious spectacle of the redemption.

Having reached the point when Adam, guilty but penitent; and Eve, fallen, yet sustained by one great hope, quit Eden, bearing in their loins the whole human race, St. Augustine exclaims: "Two cities have been erected by love, but not by the same love. The love of God, a love so intense that it defies self, has built the first, which is the city of God; self-love, so intense that it defies God, has built the second, which is the city of the evil one. These two cities are now mingled and confounded one with another, and will remain so unto the end of the world. They wage perpetual war with each other, the one striving in behalf of iniquity, the other in behalf of justice. Tolerate the one, and sigh yearningly after the other."

Full of this grand idea, Augustine pens *The City of God.* In the first book, which serves as an introduction, he begins to show the two cities mingled together in the course of ages, subject to the same catastrophes, to the same trials, struck by the same blows, but the sufferings which befall the city of evil are sent in chastisement, those which the city of God endures, but embellish, purify, and transfigure her. Thus, in a few pages, he presents us with those beautiful and profound reflections, which, fifteen centuries subsequently, M. de Maistre developed amid similar catastrophes, scandals, and alarms.

After these preliminary considerations, St. Augustine commences to attack the city of evil, with the arms and with the vigour of an athlete, who has been fitted for this grand encounter by twenty years of training. Its lying divinities, its system of philosophy, false or imperfect, and always proud and obstinately sterile; its fables, either ridiculous or corrupt; its licentious manners, impure theatres, false honour, pompous assumption of virtue, its senseless hostility to the city of God: all these he lashes with severe irony, probes each stone in the city of evil and hurls it to the ground.

Then, after replying, in the first ten books, to the enemies of the holy city, he begins treating of the rise, progress, and ultimate fate of the city of God, and of its being intermingled with the city of evil; its commencement in heaven with the different ranks of the angelic hierarchy; its apparition on earth with man; Abel, a citizen and type of the celestial city; Cain, a citizen and type of the terrestrial one; the promises made to Abraham, Isaac, and Jacob; David, the victorious king of the holy city, and type of Jesus Christ; the prophets arising one after the other to hymn the Messiah's Advent; the Assyrians, Persians, Greeks, Romans, succeeding and over-throwing each other; Jesus Christ appearing at the hour predicted, and dying for man by man; the Church, born of Jesus Christ and sharing His fate, a prey to terrors, sorrows, labours, and temptations; knowing no joy save that of hope; the tares mingled with the wheat; both the reprobate and the elect enclosed in the Gospel net, where they swim together in the world's ocean, until they reach the shore, when the wicked will be severed from the good; the wicked useful to the good by affording them opportunities of exercising virtue; heresy useful, inasmuch as heresy gives rise to dogmas; the ten fierce persecutions waged against the Church, but which neither destroyed her nor prevented her from leading her elect ones to heaven; heaven open, containing a portion of the Church, the Church triumphant, and yearning to possess the other; God, the all in all; then the final separation of the two cities, God as much glorified by the punishment of the one as by the triumph of the other. All this did Augustine hymn with almost superhuman energy, in the twenty-two books of *The City of God.* The whole of theology is there developed in one vast epopee, that of humanity.

The appearance of this marvellous work threw Africa and the whole Church into transports of enthusiasm. In his previous works, on the Trinity, and original sin, Augustine had had predecessors, who, though they did not rise to his level, had prepared the way for him; here all was new, and no Christian pen had hitherto enriched the Church with such a work.

And whilst Augustine was uttering these things to the wise and learned in chosen language, for he devoted ten years to this one book, he sang the same poem, in more moving strains, to the boatmen and to the poor women of Hippo, who never wearied of listening to him. In twelve books on Genesis, to which I have just alluded, the *Questions* on the Old Testament, the *Commentary on the Psalms,* the hundred and twenty-four *Treatises on St. John's Gospel,* and the twelve *Treatises on the first Epistle of St. John,* you have, in the form of Sunday discourses, marked by spirit, boldness, familiarity of style, tenderness, and eloquence, the same grand poem of which I have so lately spoken, and which embraces all, from eternity to eternity, *ab æterno in æternum.* The grand musician has changed his instrument; but the harmonies are as sweet and full.

And yet, astounding as these labours are, they form but a portion (barely half) of the edifice raised by Augustine's genius to the divine honour.

He has shown us the Church built by Jesus Christ, the holy city descending from, and returning to heaven. But how shall man gain entrance there? Where find strength to live as becomes a citizen of heaven, and a stranger upon earth? Who is the mysterious agent that will enable him to live up to this high divine vocation? It is grace. At this word a fresh series of writings starts to life; those immortal works on grace, which threw Bossuet into such raptures of admiration that he could find no words in which to laud Augustine, "that master-intellect,"[*] "that eagle among the Fathers,"[†] "that doctor of doctors,"[‡] "Augustine the incomparable,"

---

[*] *Œuvres complètes,* tome III. p. 424; *Défense de la Tradition,* etc liv. IV., ch. xvi.

[†] *Ib., ibid.,* liv. IX., ch. xiv.

[‡] Sermon preached at the habiting of a Bernardine postulant at Metz.

"the loftiest of intellects, the grandest of human intelligences, the apostle of grace, the preacher of predestination."* As the latter, Augustine is entitled to the gratitude and admiration of posterity. His highest glory is that of having, throughout ten years of undying efforts, and in twenty-two chefs-d'œuvre,† proved the need, defined the nature, and explained the mysterious operations of grace. He was attaining the zenith of his genius and of his sanctity, when Pelagius appeared, teaching that man has no need of grace, that his will suffices; that his will is good and stands in no need of illumination, but is omnipotent for good. Alas! who knew the falseness of these assertions so well as did Augustine? For how many a year had his lofty intellect been seeking, in vain, to find the truth? How far away from God had his noble heart strayed! To what shameless excesses had he descended, who was formed for such sublime virtues! Afflicted at such ingratitude on his part towards Jesus Christ, the redeemer of his soul and of all the souls of the human race, Augustine seized his pen and entered the lists. The Church, too, demanded this much at his hands. "The laity, episcopacy, councils, popes, in fine, the whole world," says Bossuet,

* *Défense de la Tradition*, liv. IV., ch. ix.

† *Libri III. de peccatorum meritis et remissione.—Liber de spiritu et littera—Liber de natura et gratia.—Liber de perfectione justitiæ hominis.—Liber de gestis Pelagii.—Libri II. de gratia Christi et de peccato originali.—Liber de gratia et libero arbitrio.—Liber de correptione et gratia.—Liber de prædestinatione.—Liber de dono perseverantiæ.—* See also all the other works on Sin, cited above.—See also *Serm.* 2 and 169.—*Epist.* 140, and the 26th *Traité sur l'Evangile de saint Jean,* and the *Enchiridion,* etc. etc.

" both eastern and western, turned their eyes towards this father, as being the sole one capable of unmasking the Pelagian heresy, which had attained the highest degree of subtlety and malice to which depraved reason can attain !"*   To this add the importance of the union of free will and grace, that of merit and predestination, original sin and final perseverance; grave and formidable problems, which caused St. Paul to exclaim: *O altitudo divitiarum sapientiæ et scientiæ Dei!*† Augustine entered on the subject with indomitable ardour, and a perspicacity that was proof against all subtlety. He consecrated the remainder of his life and his latest and highest energies to the task, and was still writing, even on his death-bed.   But how wondrous and potent are the mysteries of grace! No sooner had his works appeared, than their celestial doctrine was at once acknowledged. All weapons were laid down, and all tongues were silent. Even the aged Jerome, bending beneath the weight of his labours, throws aside his pen, fatal to so many a heresy, and only breaks silence to declare that now Augustine has spoken there is nothing farther to say. The Church proclaims him the doctor of grace, and in the ardour of her admiration assigns him the title of divine: *Divus Augustinus.*

And whilst studying, as a skilled theologian and a philosopher, the nature of grace, and defining the exact relations subsisting between it and free-will, as he had formerly defined those of reason and of faith, for the question is the same, he examines and studies

---

* *Défénse de la Tradition.*   † Rom., cap. **xi.**

the different channels by which grace pours her living waters into the human heart. Those channels are the Sacraments. St. Augustine has made nearly every one of them his study, has taken up arms in their defence, or hymned them! Baptism, which, intimately allied with the doctrine of original sin, has also been the subject of his most serious and crushing controversies;[*] Confirmation, administered in those days immediately after baptism, and which Augustine treated of in his writings on baptism;[†] Penance he wrote of in its two-fold character as a sacrament[‡] and a virtue; in the former character handling it with wondrous vigour and logical precision, in the latter, discoursing of it with superhuman tenderness, bequeathing to penitents, so long as the world shall last, the most sublime effusions of repentance, surpassed by none save David; the Holy Eucharist, for which his love was so intense, and for the reception of which he prepared himself by using those prayers, of such deep and touching theology that the Church employs them even at the present day.[§]

---

* *Libri VII. de Baptismo.—Liber de unico Baptismo.*—See also the majority of St. Augustine's works against the Pelagians.

† *Expositio in Psalm.* 132, n. 2.—*Libri II. contra Petilianum,* n. 239. *Contra Epistolam Petiliani,* lib. II., n. 28.

‡ *Serm* 275, n. 2.—*Serm.* 278, n. 12.—*Serm.* 149, n. 7.—*Serm.* 99, n. 9. —*Serm.* 351, n. 9.—*Serm.* 98, n. 6, 7.—*Liber de natura boni et mali,* n. 48.—*Contra adversarium Legis et Prophetarum,* lib. I., n. 3-6.—*De Civitate Dei,* lib. XX., c. ix.—*Epist.* 185, etc.

§ *De Trinitate,* lib. III., n. 10; lib. X., n. 20.—*Contra Faustum,* lib. XX., n. 18.—*De Civitate Dei,* lib. XX.—*Epist.* 2, 13.—*Serm.* 59 et 95.— *Opus imperfectum contra Julianum,* lib. II., n. 30.—*Contra Faustum,* lib. XII., n. 10.—*Explanatio Psalmi* 33.—*Serm.* 1, n. 10; *Serm.* 2, n. 2; *Serm.* 3 et 6, published by Denis; *Serm.* 35, published by Caillau; *Serm.*

Marriage, the unity, indissolubility, and sanctity of which he maintained in opposition to the Manicheans, the affection, purity, and peace of which he has so lauded in several beautiful letters ;* Extreme Unction† and Preparation for Death,‡ on both of which he often treated, explaining them in language bearing the impress of ineffable sadness, serenity, and sublimity. In glancing through these works we regret that we can make no extracts. But time presses, and much of our task is, as yet, unaccomplished.

Such life-giving streams gave birth to virtues wholly unknown to antiquity, which, flourishing in the sacred ground of the Church, and flourishing only there, for ever testify to the fertilizing influences of those streams. St. Augustine has made each lovely flower of faith, hope, and love, the object of his care, specially the latter, which was his chosen theme, for with him the gospel was synonymous with love, and so sublimely has he hymned it, that the middle ages always represented Augustine as bearing a heart in his hand ; also the higher virtues of chastity, poverty, and obedience, the mystery of souls enamoured with the noble beauty of the Saviour, and aspiring to thé cross, whence proceeds redeeming and transfiguring

143 et 193, published by Mai.—*Epist.* 140, n. 48.—*De Trinitate,* n. 21, etc. etc.

* *De Bono Matrimonii,* lib. II.—*De Matrimoniis adulterinis,* lib. I.— *De Matrimonio et Concupiscentia,* lib. II.—*Epist.* 200, 262, 137, 150.

† *Unctionis Sacramentum, unctio invisibilis,* tome XXXV., Patrologie Migne, p. 201.—*De Sacramentis ab infirmo suscipiendis; Il.,* XL. 1154.

‡ *Liber de cura gerenda pro mortuis,* n. 1-3.—*Enchirﬕion,* n. 29.— *Serm.* 31, 32, 38, 96, 124, 345.—*Epist.* 22, 92, 263.—*Epistolæ consolatoriæ ad Probum, de obitu filiæ.*

grace. Augustine shows us the commencement of this transfiguration; the individual restored to his primitive dignity; the family reconstituted; society becoming more obedient to the eternal laws of truth; pagan vices hiding themselves away, unwilling to die; the increasing sympathy of class with class; and although the world, in those years of evil omen, commencing with Alaric and ending with Genseric, was convulsed on every side, though the whole social fabric tottered to its very centre, and men were in daily expectation of their last hour, Augustine energetically refused to believe that the end of the world was at hand, and convinced that Christianity is possessed of boundless resources, and has a remedy for every wound, beyond the intervening ruins he discerned and hailed a brighter future, and beheld posterity, peaceful and transformed, obedient to the voice of the Good Shepherd.*

We have thus sketched in rapid outline the edifice Augustine's genius erected in honour of his God. All is marvellous; the vast proportions of the plan, the beauty of its leading features, the abundance of the materials, the perfection of certain portions, bearing the impress of the master, of "such a master," as Bossuet says. Nothing is lacking, unless it be that the style betrays the epoch at which the edifice was

---

* *Liber de fide et operibus.—Liber de agone christiano.—De Doctrina christiana,* lib. III.—*Liber de moribus Ecclesiæ catholicæ.—Libri II. de Sermone Domini in monte.— Speculum seu collectio præceptorum moralium.—Liber de Patientia.—Liber de Continentia.—Liber de bono conjugali.— Liber de sancta Virginitate.—Liber de bono Viduitatis.—Liber de opere monachorum.—Liber de catechizandis rudibus.*—And the majority of his sermons and a great number of his letters.

designed. But in face of such genius, eloquence, logic, and erudition, we must not insist too much on what after all is but of secondary import, lest we should hear Bossuet exclaiming to us: " After that let who will tell me that Augustine has his faults, even as the sun has spots; I will neither admit, deny, excuse, nor defend them. All that I really know, is that whoever is capable of fathoming and appreciating his theology, sublime as it is sound, will but contemn and pity those who, devoid of all taste for, and sympathy with what is noble and grand, take umbrage at trifles, and think themselves authorized to speak lightly of St. Augustine, whom they do not understand."*

We can readily picture the delight of the Catholics, vexed as they were by so many heresies, and alarmed at the ominous signs which seemed to denote that the end of the world was near at hand, as they beheld this edifice growing before their very eyes; to-day saw one stone added, to-morrow another, and each day witnessed the accomplishment of some chef-d'œuvre. Eleven hundred and thirty works in the space of forty years! Their surprise was augmented daily, and betrayed itself in language that has been transmitted even to our own day. And whilst a species of Christian pride filled every heart, the world was moved to tears on learning that this great man, this extraordinary genius, was the most gentle, humble, poor, and the purest and holiest of Christians. The splendour of his mighty intellect waxed pale before the ardent flames which issued

* *Défense de la Tradition,* liv. IV., ch. xviii.

from his heart. So intense was his love of God that he despised all terrestrial things, longed for death, and lived a life of poverty. His dwelling was humble, his couch hard, his table frugal, and his garments such as were worn only by the poorest of his priests. "That may be all very well for a bishop," he said, gracefully thanking some persons who offered him rich vestments, "but it is too beautiful for Augustine, who is a poor man and born of poor parents."* And another time: "I should blush to wear a splendid garb; it would be unsuited to my position and to my vocation, as also to an infirm and aged body, and hoary hairs such as mine." To this inflexible rule he made but one exception, and then his affections gained the victory. A young girl, having embroidered a tunic for her brother, who was a priest, carried it with joyous heart to Hippo; but on arriving there, her brother fell ill, and died without having even so much as tried on his new garb. Overwhelmed by grief, the poor girl gave it to Augustine, and, to console her, this gentle and affectionate old man put it on at once, and consented to wear it constantly. Within this heart, new born, and weaned from earth, there sprang up an angelic purity, inspiring him with great reserve, with modesty and prudence, touching in the extreme. In remembrance of his past transgressions, and always believing himself the weakest of men, he would never permit a woman to enter his house, not even his sister and his nieces, and this, from no want of affec-

---

* *Serm.* 356.

tion to them, for he loved them tenderly, but on account of the female friends who would come to visit them, and which, he said, would not be becoming in Augustine's dwelling. He was wont to lay such a touching emphasis on the word Augustine, that it suffused with tears the eyes of those who heard him.

His humility was God-like. Perhaps no mortal has ever been the object of such admiration as was lavished on him; but the more others exalted him, the deeper did he abase himself. " You do not know Augustine," was his incessant remark. And in order that he might be known, and this admiration cease, he published his *Confessions,* which first startled the world, and then filled it with rapturous enthusiasm. Ah! there is a mode of public confession which costs but little. But when I note the accents in which Augustine speaks of his faults, when, in lieu of confining himself to the irregularities of his youth, to the gentle liaison which existed between him and the mother of Adeodatus, all of which was pretty well-known, and would have furnished materials for a romance, he penetrates into the inmost recesses of conscience, that he may drag to light its most secret and shameful secrets. When I remember a certain page in the *Confessions,* a certain relapse, when, not only faith, conscience, but honour and delicacy are betrayed and trampled under foot, when, in spite of oneself, one blushes for Augustine's sake, when I remember that this page was written by a Bishop, an aged man who had attained the pinnacle of glory,

that it was sown broadcast among his priests, among
the faithful, and throughout the whole Church, in
order to silence the applause that, to him, was
unendurable: ah! such humility is indeed sublime,
and stands unrivalled in the annals of history!

But this humility and purity did not weaken his
vigilant exercise of authority, nor interfere with
the tenderness of his zeal. We must go to St.
Paul, or to St. Francis of Sales, to find a love for
souls as tender and as strong as that which filled
Augustine's heart. With the former, he did not
desire heaven for himself, unless his dear friends,
for whom he was ready to suffer anathema, entered
there also. "I do not wish to be saved without you,"
he exclaimed. "No, my God, I will not be saved
without my flock! Grant me the lowest place in
heaven, so that I but behold all my children there!
Ah, what is the aim of my every wish and word? why
am I a bishop? Why do I exist, save to live a life
hidden in Christ Jesus, and to share that life with
you? That is my earnest desire, my honour, glory,
and treasure." And whilst his love and devotion
manifested themselves in those cries of love which remind us of St. Paul, he was filled with a tenderness,
delicate attention, and patience towards the souls of
his fellow-creatures, never equalled save in the case
of St. Francis of Sales. As the holy Bishop of
Geneva, so he too reproved at times, but gently and
sweetly, ever fearing to quench the smoking flax; and
whatever the circumstances of the case might be,
ever tender as a mother. "Sometimes," he said, in

words resembling those of St. Francis of Sales, "in traversing narrow paths the hen tramples, but not with her whole weight, on the little ones whom she shelters, but she is still a mother in spite of that." He evinced the same affection for sinners, and for heretics. Many a time he interceded with the governors in order to obtain their pardon. He offered his own life, his blood. He was ready to resign his own see, and induced all the African bishops to take the same resolve, in order to further the salvation of souls. "Let us agree, let us agree, my well-beloved," he repeated incessantly to the heretics. "We love you, we desire your salvation, and are ready to treat you as ourselves." "There is no necessity for us to be bishops," he exclaimed to the three hundred African bishops; "but it does behove us to save our people, even at the expense of ease and life itself."

And yet all this detachment, purity, humility, love for souls, was nothing by the side of the deep, strong, intimate, and confiding yet ever reverent love he bore to God. He would spend whole hours kneeling, or seated, motionless and absorbed, paying no heed to those around; it was at the termination of these prolonged meditations that he seized his pen, and that there issued from his soul those groans and plaints over the duration of his exile, those aspirations towards the celestial country, those ardent effusions of love, with which his works abound. "I love Thee, O my God," he exclaimed; "yes, I know it, I feel it, I am sure of it. No servile fears, no selfish hopes, are mine. Extinguish the flames of hell; I fear, but only because I love. Annihilate Thy paradise; my joy, my hope, and my felicity consist but in loving Thee." The following words, ever on his lips, were the expression of his inmost heart: "While here below let us prepare for the heavenly life that knows no end, where our sole occupation will be to love."

Such was Augustine. His seventy-sixth year was near at hand; he was vigorous in body as in mind, his sight and hearing were good, and all his faculties most perfect, when the terrible woes which burst on Africa overwhelmed him with grief and shortened his life.

The host of barbarians, who had devastated the whole empire during more than a century, suddenly appeared in Africa; they committed the most dreadful ravages, pillaging, massacreing, sparing neither women, children, nor priests, and burning the churches to the ground. "This man of God," says Possidius, "beheld the commencement and the progress of this scourge with emotions far different to those which filled the breasts of others. He discerned far direr evils than they did: he foresaw spiritual dangers and the ruin of souls, and as it is said in Holy Writ *that much knowledge and great discernment rob their possessor of ease of mind,* he passed the closing days of his life in the deepest sorrow and anguish. Wherever his eye turned there were churches burnt to the ground and destitute of priests, consecrated virgins a prey to the sword, or robbed of their purity; bishops and priests stripped of all their possessions, and sunk

in the lowest poverty; altars desecrated, **no sacra-**
ments possible, and a host of Christians demanding
baptism, penance, and absolution, and dying without
their request being granted. Inflamed with love to
God and man, this saintly old man spent his days and
nights in the deepest sorrow, consumed by grief."

Having ravaged and destroyed all the African
cities, save Carthage, Cirtha, and Hippo, the barbarians
began to lay siege to the latter, whither a number of
bishops, priests, and religious had fled for refuge. It
seemed to be God's will to assemble the whole of the
African Church there, in order that she might learn
from Augustine how to endure misfortune, and with
what resignation Christian nations should await their
downfall. He mingled his tears and groans with
those of the other bishops; but his lofty reason
soared higher that theirs. "We should indeed be
very foolish to lament the destruction of wood and
stone, and to mourn the death of the body." His
tears flowed for much greater woes than these.

At last, worn out with sorrow, and incapable of
further effort, he said to his bishops : "Brethren and
fathers, let us pray that these woes may cease, or that
it may please God to call me hence." Some time after
this, he retired to his couch, a prey to a violent fever,
caused by the intense grief that filled his soul, and it
soon became visible to all that death was near at
hand. All hearts were filled with alarm. Then that
brave and loving heart became even more tender and
affectionate. He spent his remaining strength in dic-
tating an admirable letter to the bishops of Africa,

in which he urged them not to forsake their flocks, but to give them an example of resignation and patience, and to suffer and die with them and for them. This was his last work, sweet as the song of the dying swan; such loving strains were worthy of the noble heart of the dying Augustine.

Meanwhile the people of Hippo learn that Augustine's end is fast approaching. His house is besieged, for the faithful desire to see their bishop for the last time. The sick crowd around his bed. Mothers present their little children that he may bless them. Moved by these proofs of affection, the dying man offers his tears and prayers to God in their behalf. A father having entreated him to lay his hands on his child's head, in order that he might be healed, the gentle old man, smiling, said: "Had I the power of healing, I should begin with healing myself." But on the father persisting in his request, he placed his hand on the head of the child, and the infant was healed.

But Augustine's moments were numbered, soon his people would cease to behold their much-loved bishop. Borne upwards on the wings of love, yet weighed down by the remembrance of his sins, which forty years of penance had failed to obliterate from his memory, he employed his last hours in completing the purification of his soul. He had caused the Penitential Psalms to be written on broad pieces of cloth, fastened to the walls of his chamber, and during the final days of his sufferings, as he lay in bed, he read those verses amid abundant and continual tears. "And in order," says

Possidius, "that none might disturb his final meditation, about ten days prior to his death he entreated us to allow no one to enter his chamber save at the hours when his medical attendants visited him." This command was religiously obeyed, and that great man passed those ten last days in absolute silence, alone with God, his heart full of repentance mingled with love.

As the last hour drew near, all the bishops re-assembled once more around his bed; and, amid their embraces and sighs, the soul of the saintly old man winged her flight to the bosom of her God. Seventy-six years had elapsed since St. Monica gave him birth, forty-three since she had converted him by her tears, and forty-two years had she waited for him in heaven. His old friend Alipius closed his eyes and interred his body, and none can doubt but that Monica herself received and bore his parting soul to heaven.

It has been vouchsafed to a great saint of modern days to contemplate in a vision the union of two souls who, while on earth, were bound by the ties of a strong and pure affection. St. Vincent de Paul beheld the soul of St. Francis of Sales descend from heaven in the form of a ball of fire, whilst the soul of St. Chantal was ascending from earth in a similar form; as the two luminous globes of fire approached each other they united, forming but one single flame, which vanished heavenwards.

Surely something similar must have occurred at St. Augustine's death. The soul of the son and that of the mother must have mounted together until they attained the Divine centre of their mutual love, to abide there for ever, and know no parting such as Ostia witnessed. But no mortal eye beheld that sight. Why should God reveal that which the heart already knows? He whose heart fails to picture such . a scene does not deserve to have it revealed to him.

O Augustine, blessed is the womb that bore thee! Ineffable the rapture which filled thy mother's soul that day. O Monica, open thy arms to welcome that son who is doubly thine, and rejoice for ever in the bliss thy tears have purchased for him.

CHAPTER XVII.

COMMENCEMENT OF THE CULTUS OF ST. MONICA.—FINDING OF HER RELICS.—THEIR TRANSLATION TO ROME, WHERE THEY ARE AUTHENTICATED BY POPE MARTIN V.

430-1586.

Whilst Alipius, Possidius, and the other African bishops were interring the body of St. Augustine in the church of St. Stephen at Hippo, where he was destined to remain for the space of fifty-six years, and then to be borne to Sardinia, and later on to Pavia, in which place he still reposes, Monica was sleeping on in the tomb her son had prepared for her on the sea-shore at Ostia. Even in most remote ages, those who examined that revered ₁tomb observed a small marble monument, of which the origin is unknown, but which monument is assigned by many to St. Augustine himself. What doubt but that he often made a pilgrimage to his mother's tomb during that first year of mourning, spent by him in Rome? Who can doubt but that he would have transported those precious relics to Tagaste, that they might repose side by side with those of Patricius, his father, had not Monica strictly enjoined him not to do so. At least, as Monica had said, "Here will you bury your mother," he did not quit Italy, nor take a last farewell of those venerated remains, without evincing some care and respect for the tomb which guarded them.

Whatever may be the origin of the marble monument, Monica remained many centuries in the stone sarcophagus for which she was indebted to her son's filial affection. Her name was revered in Ostia, and after the publication of the *Confessions*, throughout the entire world. But we have no proofs of any cultus being rendered to her. Her feast has no place in the universal Martyrologies of Usuard, Ado, Venerable Bede, nor in the special calendars of the African Church. It had been decreed by God that more than a thousand years should elapse before St. Monica was honoured by being the object of a special cultus. And why this? Why, too, was St. Philomena, martyred in early times, not thus honoured until the nineteenth century, she whose aureola is now so brilliant? Why was the glorious mystery of the Immaculate Conception reserved for our own day? And why are there other stars in heaven whose light, the learned tell us, has not yet reached us? These are God's secrets.

But in the case of our saint the mystery is transparent; and, if we examine it a little closely, we shall easily see why it behoved St. Monica to sleep (the object of admiration, but not yet of honour,) in the humble tomb Augustine had prepared for her. Monica was to become the patroness of mothers who have Augustines for their sons. Her sweet image had been created by God, that it might at a future day, encourage, sustain, and console those unhappy ones, whose children stray away far from their childhood's faith. This is why the Christian centuries of the middle ages beheld, but did not understand St. Monica. They admired her, but no beseeching hands were raised to her for help. In order to understand that sweet and consoling face, it must be seen through eyes suffused with tears, and as in those days maternal eyes were not so filled with tears, therefore St. Monica was not understood.

Thus elapsed a thousand years, during which period God alone kept watch over those precious relics. "Therefore," a great pope has said, " St. Monica died in Italy, and was left there by Augustine; for had those sacred remains been transported to Africa, they would inevitably have disappeared amid those successive invasions, which, after destroying churches, altars, and the bodies of saints, destroyed even the very cities, and rendered desert the whole of that vast and fertile country."* And for the same reason, later on, and at an epoch of which but little is known, but which must have coincided with the invasion of the Lombards, about the close of the sixth or seventh century, St. Monica's remains were quietly removed to the church of St. Aurea, at Ostia, and buried beneath the altar in a vault, the secret of which was known to none save to the priests of that church. In His great mercy God was reserving those holy relics for other days, days in which they would be sorely needed.

At last, about the middle of the fifteenth century, on the eve of Protestantism, which would break the unity of the Faith, and usher in those sad days of which St. Monica was destined to be the light and the consolation, Providence unsealed her tomb, as we shall see, and a place is assigned her among the saints.

But as early as the twelfth and thirteenth centuries she began to emerge from obscurity. Her feast was observed in many localities, and always celebrated on the fourth of May, the eve of the day when the Church commemorates the conversion of her son; as if to assure the faithful that if, after so many errors and wanderings, faith, conscience, and affection re-awoke to life within Augustine's breast, and even his genius, freeing itself from the mists that had obscured it, irradiated the world and the Church, we owe this to St. Monica. Altars were erected to her honour in

* Vide Sermon of Pope Martin V.

the ancient mediæval cathedrals; hymns were composed in her praise, and her beautiful countenance began to appear on the frescoes and windows of the churches. A disciple of the Blessed Angelico de Fiésole, Benozzo Gozzoli, had depicted a few of the most beautiful incidents of her life, and specially her death, in the choir of the church of San Gimignano, and later on, a hand, unknown, but inspired by a grand soul, portrayed her sweet features over the altar of the ruined church at Ostia.

This was but the dawn of a cultus impatient to start to life. It was now time for the supreme head of the Church to intervene and enrol St. Monica on the list of saints.

Martin V. was chosen of God to effect this important work. Few popes have suffered as much as this pontiff. For although his exaltation to the holy see terminated the grand schism of the west, and he had the ineffable joy of beholding the re-union of the severed members of the Church, and the mystery of unity, for an instant veiled, shone forth in brighter splendour, he had also before his eyes the painful scene of the Council of Constance, which paved the way for those enacted at Basle. He saw the rise of Wycliffe, John Huss, and Jerome of Prague, witnessed the horrors of the Hussite war, and, from the height of St. Peter's throne, where the light of genius and of human experience pale in presence of that wisdom bestowed by the Holy Ghost, he had the bitter presentiment of the sad and wretched course on which, in defiance of God and of His Church, the world was about to enter. At this very moment, in which the Church experienced those throes which but presaged sufferings acuter still, in obedience to one of those divine impulses which the sovereign pontiffs obey albeit they know not always what the result is to be, Martin V. authorized a search to be made for St. Monica's relics, in order that they might be brought to Rome.

The execution of these commands was entrusted by him to his own confessor, one of the most venerable men of the day, Brother Peter Assalbizi, of the Order of the Hermits of St. Augustine, and Bishop of Aleth, universally reputed a saint. He, happy at receiving such a commission, associated with hims.lf a monk of the same Order, the Blessed Augustine Favaroni, Prior-General, who afterwards died in the odour of sanctity, and, in company with a certain number of priests and monks, they started at once for Ostia, for Palm Sunday was at hand, and was the day appointed for the translation of the precious relics.

At a very early epoch, the date of which was uncertain, the saint's remains had been removed, and interred in the sanctuary of St. Aurea, at Ostia. Thither the apostolic commissioners proceeded, accompanied by the priests of the town; and after having knelt in fervent prayer, they commenced by making an excavation at the right-hand side of the altar. There, at about eight feet below the surface, they found some long, broad stones, strewn with a few bones, possibly the saint's relics, but of this there was no proof. They proceeded no further, feeling convinced that this was a sepulchral chamber, that had perhaps been desecrated and robbed of its contents. They then examined the other parts of the sanctuary, sounding them one after the other; but the heavy iron instruments with which they tested the walls revealed no cavities within. Therefore they resumed their examination of the above-mentioned stones, and, after removing them with difficulty, discovered a small aperture beneath one of them, which opening was adroitly concealed, and led to a secret vault much deeper than the first. Full of lively hope, the apostolical commissioners were let down into the crypt, which was of ample proportions, and contained many sarcophagi of various dimensions. Three on the right, contained the bodies of St. Linus, pope and martyr; St. Felix, also pope and martyr; and that of St. Astera, who also suffered martyrdom.

The tombs on the left were eagerly examined. The first was the large tomb in which St. Constantia had been interred with St. Aurea; the second was more a shrine than a tomb, containing the bones of the last-named saint, which remains had at some earlier period, (date unknown,) been removed thither from St. Constantia's tomb. Above these was a large stone sarcophagus, resembling those used by the Romans for the burial of the dead. The apostolical commissioners turned the light of the lamp upon it, and, with eyes suffused with tears, read on a leaden plate the name of St. Monica.

The moment was a solemn one. After twelve centuries of obscurity and of silence, St. Augustine's mother again saw the light of day, as also did all the relics of the town of Ostia. In a moment of alarm, on the eve of one of those Lombard invasions which spread desolation around, when churches, and specially the bodies of the saints, were exposed to destruction, these sacred relics had been hidden, with trembling hand, more than eight feet below the surface of the ground, in a carefully concealed crypt, which relics now emerged from their obscurity, to rejoice Christendom, for they were deemed lost for ever, and to encourage by their immortal examples the new martyrs whom God was about to demand from His Church.

After all the monks and the priests had prostrated themselves in adoration to Him who is glorified in His saints, by the aid of the torch-light, with hands quivering with emotion, they opened the stone sarcophagus in which the most eminent of doctors and the most loving of sons had enclosed his mother's body. There were only dry bones, but they were full of those odours of life and immortality which are generally emitted by the relics of the saints. An eye-witness says: " From those relics issued an indescribable aroma, which clung to the hands and vestments, and which never disappeared. This aroma was unlike all other perfumes, even the most exquisite ones could not compare with it; it raised the soul to God."

When the happy spectators of this scene had spent some long time in contemplation and prayer, and had kissed the venerated relics, they enclosed them in a wooden shrine which they had brought with them, and hastened to return to Rome.

No preparations had been made for a solemn translation of the relics. It had even been arranged to bring them privately to Rome, and allow the sovereign pontiff to fix the day for the public ceremony. But in the case of a saint who has lived a life of self-immolation for his Lord's sake, there issues from his purified remains, as formerly from the Sacred Body of our Redeemer, a healing virtue, an indescribably celestial charm, which attracts souls in order to console them, wean them from earth, and raise them up to God. Soon an ever-growing crowd formed a cortège to that humble chariot which bore St. Monica's remains. On entering the city, another scene awaited them. Palm Sunday is one of the great fairs of Rome. The roads were thronged with crowds of peasants, farmers, and traders from the surrounding country; "who on beholding the cortège began to ask its meaning, and hearing that it was St. Monica's body, some did not understand the reply; but when they learnt that it was 'Augustine's mother,' the air resounded with joyous acclamations."* Everyone wished to see, touch, and kiss the shrine, so that the apostolic commissioners, the monks and the priests from Ostia, who surrounded the chariot, forming a guard of honour, found it impossible to proceed.

* Sermon of Martin V.

A miracle that took place augmented the enthusiasm, and proclaimed to all who was this incomparable woman now entering Rome. Whilst those
who guided the chariot vainly tried to make their
way through the crowd, it suddenly and respectfully
made way for a woman who was hastening onwards,
carrying a sick child in her arms. Impelled by some
deep presentiment of faith, they made room for the
afflicted mother, who, with a countenance revealing
the intensity of her faith, approaches and touches
the shrine with her child. Suddenly a deep thrill
runs through every member of the crowd: the child
was healed. From that moment the enthusiasm was
boundless.

Meanwhile the church is reached, but when they
have entered and deposited on the altar the wooden
shrine in which they had enclosed the relics of St.
Monica, they are filled with deep regret at having
left behind them in the crypt of St. Aurea the second
relic, consisting of the large stone sarcophagus in
which St. Augustine had deposited his mother's body.
They therefore went back to Ostia, and on the morrow
triumphantly brought back that empty sarcophagus
amid an ever-growing concourse of people.

Another miracle, similar in character, but more
striking than the preceding one, revealed St. Monica's
greatness, and taught what were the special graces
which might be expected from her.

A mother was watching by the bedside of her son,
who had been suffering for about eight months from
an incurable malady. She learns what is going on,

and with one of those impulses of faith and indomitable hope, such as exist in maternal hearts, she takes her child, envelopes him in a shawl, and laying him in the saint's coffin, stands by his side, and with a gaze full of faith waits for St. Monica to show herself a mother indeed. Her expectations were not in vain, for the child quickly arose, and threw himself in his mother's arms, joyous and healed.

"These facts," exclaimed Pope Martin V., in a ceremony which we shall ere long relate, "took place in public. They are renewed daily, and so impressive are they that they should inspire us with a firm confidence in that great servant of God."

Many other miracles occurred during the translation, and will be enumerated further on by Pope Martin V. We will only note one touching fact, exquisite in its delicacy. Besides the children healed in their mothers' arms, the majority of the miracles consisted of the restoration of sight to such as were blind : " whether God," says Pope Martin V., " wished thereby to glorify the mother of that great doctor who illumines the Church, whether He wished thereby to honour the tears that admirable woman shed during twenty years in order that God might open Augustine's eyes."

Thus, from her first appearance in the world, St. Monica desired to teach it two things; first, that she would never turn a deaf ear to the cries of a mother weeping for her child; secondly, that of all the infirm, those who will most readily move her heart to compassion are the blind, not so much those who cannot see the light of the sun as those, most unhappy of all, whose intellects, obscured by passion, are blind to the beauteous sun of faith.

Martin V. was moved to the very heart on learning the manner in which St. Monica's remains had been welcomed to Rome, and as these marks of respect had not been enjoined by himself, but were the spontaneous effusions of public enthusiasm, feeling that he had not fulfilled his duty, he desired that a solemn festival should be celebrated in the church where the saint's relics had been deposited, and announced his wish to officiate thereat.

He went there, surrounded by immense crowds of people, whom the report of the miracles had attracted to the saint's tomb. He offered the Divine Sacrifice, and after Mass, transported by holy joy, he addressed the monks to whom he confided the inestimable treasure of St. Monica's relics, and the populace who thronged the church, in an eloquent and moving discourse, a sketch of which we feel it our duty to present to our readers.

The holy pontiff began as follows: "To-day we celebrate the mother of that great doctor whose virtue, graces, and victories are the glory of Christendom, and whose name is so celebrated above others throughout the whole Catholic Church wherever faith reigns. Now, why should we not allow the mother to participate in the praises we lavish on the son, when we all know that the blessed Monica was not only his mother after the flesh, but after the spirit also, and that his heart and mind were moulded by her? Augustine's salvation was the sole object of her constant prayers and maternal solicitude; he himself tells us in his writings that he heard his mother say incessantly that she desired no other happiness here below save to behold her son inflamed by the desire of heavenly things and despising earthly pleasures. Have I not, then, reason to rejoice, I who am to-day allowed the privilege of touching St. Monica's hallowed relics, and of presenting them to the very sons who owe their existence to St. Augustine and St. Monica? Noble indeed is such a mother, sublime the dignity with which she is invested. Blessed is the womb, blessed are the breasts and arms, and worthy of the deepest homage and veneration is the body of her who gave birth to so illustrious a son.

"Receive it, then, O ye monks, with deep love, handle it with profound respect; for ever holy be those shoulders which shall bear your saintly mother. Henceforth let both Augustine and Monica be the objects of your love and of your praise. Ye also, citizens, magistrates, Romans, rejoice, and give free course to your transports of joy at receiving so great a blessing."

After these first heartfelt effusions, the holy Pontiff commenced recounting St. Monica's virtues, her sweetness, patience, and maternal solicitude, which were rewarded by the creation of such a son.

"For, possessing St. Augustine," he exclaimed, "what need have we of Aristotle's wisdom, Plato's eloquence, Varro's prudence, the gravity of Socrates,

26

the authority of Pythagoras, or the skill of Empedocles? We need none of these men : Augustine suffices us. Prophetic oracles, apostolic teachings, and the obscure passages of holy writ are all explained in his writings. In him are united the genius and the teaching of all the fathers and all the sages. If you seek truth, doctrine, piety, whom will you find more skilled, learned, and, so to speak, more holy than Augustine ?

" And it was the saintly Monica who gave birth to such a man. She is the happy mother, who has given to us and to the whole Church the glory of this illustrious doctor. It would not be giving her her due share of praise to say that she brought him forth, nursed him, trained him, as other mothers do their children. Oh, no; she has done a thousand times more. Who but rejoices to hear Augustine relate his mother's pious custom of teaching his infant lips to pronounce the name of Jesus, a name which, later on, he loved to impress on the lips of little children. Never did she faint or weary of her task. Who may tell the number of the sighs and prayers which night and day ascended heavenwards from her heart, not on behalf of Augustine's bodily health, but in behalf of that of his soul ? Who count her tears and groans ? But God comforted her by the assurance that it was impossible for the son of such tears to perish, and that his faith and piety should equal hers. From that time her only anxiety was to do a mother's part, ever thinking of Augustine, that son promised and vowed to God and religion, ever eager to follow him wherever he went, so that she might snatch him from evil, and restore him to virtue.

"I say nothing of her zealous perseverance and praiseworthy behaviour as a wife, which was rewarded of God by her husband's conversion, so that she saw the fulfilment of St. Paul's words, contained in his first Epistle to the Corinthians: *'The unbelieving husband is sanctified by the believing wife.'* And that, in order that no single member of her family might be missing in the book of life.

"Who but must be filled with admiration at beholding her faith, and the magnitude of the love which induced her to follow Augustine over sea and land? And this against his will, for he himself tells us that he deceived his mother, who on learning that he had started for Milan, set sail for Italy, animated by a courage far beyond that of her sex. O woman, how applicable to thee are the Saviour's words: 'Great is thy faith.' Yes, great indeed was the faith that led thee to brave the sea and its storms, the land and its perils, until thou didst clasp thy astonished son once more within thine arms. How relate the steps taken by this brave and faithful woman, when in Milan, in order to effect her son's conversion? What must have been those merits, what the renown of that virtue, which won her the holy friendship of Ambrose, Simplicianus, and so many other excellent men and holy fathers? In all these relations her only object was to confide the care of her son's salvation to those who were pre-eminent for their sanctity. I could relate many an action, marked by more than womanly courage, having her son's conversion for its aim, but time fails me. She obtained her wish, which was to see Augustine regenerated in holy baptism, and a recipient of the other sacraments. It was as if the court of heaven, yielding to her sighs and groans, could no longer withhold life and salvation from her son; so continual and so fervent were 'hose sighs, that those saintly fathers, Ambrose and Simplicianus, almost weary of them, seemed to entreat heaven that it 'would bid her depart, for she importunes us by her cries.'"

After having related Augustine's conversion, his retreat at Cassiacum, the philosophic conferences in which St. Monica took part, and having exclaimed: " Yes, doubtless that woman's heart was animated by a spirit far different from that which is found in ordinary men," the holy Father continued as follows: " Having accompanied her converted son as far as Rome, and having seen all that was worth seeing in that city, she starts with Augustine for Ostia on Tiber, intending to cross to Carthage. Why did God will her to remain in Italy? for she died at Ostia. And when her end was near we can picture her pointing to Africa, and addressing Augustine in such words as these: 'As for thee, my son, quit these scenes and return to thy native land, ever remembering that heaven alone is the soul's true home. Let it be the goal of all thy desires, the motive of all thy actions. This is the sole heritage I bequeath thee. Hereafter I will welcome thee to my breast, but now it is God's will that I should follow thee no further here below. Here my pilgrimage ends, here my mortal life closes; that is to say, I am about to enter on the immortal life of heaven. Strong in my succour, march safely on beneath my care. Happy the day when thy sons and mine, after recalling thee to Italy, shall guard us both with pious love.'

"Such are the prophetic words I seem to hear her utter. Yes, we have reached those days foretold by her so many ages ago. Who but can discern the goodness, mercy, and providence of God in the events which secured so magnificent a gift to Italy and to the whole world? In fact, had she died in Africa I doubt whether the devastations which ravaged that country would have spared one single atom of those hallowed remains. Never would they have shown mercy to the mother, who would have shown no mercy to the son. What say I? Even in Ostia those holy relics would not have reposed in safety, had not the Lord watched over them. Hence the reason why that blessed body remained concealed for so many years; God willed it thus, in order that you who so honour the son might be enabled to honour the mother also. And I, too, rejoice; I to whom is vouchsafed the happiness of presenting you with so magnificent a gift."

After thus enumerating St. Monica's virtues, the holy Father gave an account of the finding of the relics, and after relating the miracles which had occurred during their transit, concluded as follows:

"Receive the mother with the son; follow their examples, for both are animated by the same spirit.

Ever let this day be kept by you as a solemn feast, for it is our wish that as such it should be handed down by you to remote posterity. May your lives be ever worthy of this holy mother. And in order that the poor, the lame, and sick may flee to her for aid, make known all the wonders that have been wrought at that holy shrine. A woman, named Sylvia, suffered from violent pains in the head; she made a vow, and was at once cured. Another, known as Mariola, sister to one of your own friars, had a cancer in the breast; on merely touching the tomb she recovered from a violent fever, which threatened to prove fatal. A child who had swallowed poison was on the point of death; hardly had its parents recommended it to the saint than all danger ceased. A Roman lady of noble birth, afflicted with paralysis and epilepsy, was also restored to health on touching the tomb. What shall I say of the barren wife of the workman who executed the iron work of the sepulchre? She made a vow at the tomb, and her sterility instantly ceased. Her husband, almost blind, made a similar vow, and wholly recovered his sight. And that young maiden who, though a prey to a fatal malady, was restored to health on promising to enter your order. What need to particularize all those diverse maladies, cured by her intercession, and the numbers of blind persons to whom she restored sight? The latter doubtless easily obtain their cure, either because she is the mother of that doctor who has illumined the Church with the bright light of his teaching, or rather, because of that very son, to

obtain the recovery of whose spiritual vision she shed
such abundant tears for the space of twenty years.
Happy mother! Of old she exclaimed, in accents of
sorrow : ' Alas! I mourn because my son is dead!'
Now she exclaims : ' What bliss is mine! by my son
Augustine I illumine the whole world.' "

After these admirable words, which are equivalent
to a bull of canonization, and by which the holy
Father presented this incomparable mother as an
object of homage and veneration to the Church,
Martin V. proceeded to deposit the precious relics
in the tomb which had been prepared for their reception, which tomb was constructed of white marble, ornamented with valuable sculpture. Matteo
Veggio di Lodi, papal secretary, had piously defrayed
the whole expense of this costly erection. Two noble
Roman ladies had presented three lamps, silver-gilt,
which were suspended before the holy relics, and
kept burning night and day.

But in depositing St. Monica's body in the marble
sarcophagus, Martin V. thought it his duty to reserve the saint's head, which he had enclosed in a
golden reliquary, adorned with crystal, so that the
faithful might be able to see what remained of St.
Monica's venerable features; that brow on which St.
Augustine's lips had rested; those eyes, now dry,
whence fell so many beauteous tears; that tongue
which had sent up to God so many heartfelt and
touching supplications; from which, though now
mute and lifeless, proceed words of consolation,

assuring souls that God never forsakes such as hope in Him.

And in order that the translation of these relics might be had in everlasting remembrance throughout the Church, Martin V. issued a bull, which is in existence even at the present day, and which confirmed the authentic recognition of St. Monica's body, and her canonization also. This bull is dated Rome, 27th April, 1430.

A little while and Luther would appear, rending the breast of the Church, causing iniquity to abound, and by the very evils of which he was the author would afford a clue to the events we have just related. For the reader may observe that as the great doctor's mother, Martin V. and the whole of Christendom then hailed St. Monica; whilst she who is now the hope and stay of maternal hearts is invoked as mother of Augustine the prodigal. In the fifteenth century St. Monica was not yet revealed in her full glory.

But St. Monica had no sanctuary erected to her honour. Martin V. had deposited her close to one of the walls of the little church of St. Trophonius, served by the Hermits of St. Augustine, and so numerous were the pilgrims who resorted there to implore the saint, that there was no room to move. Matteo Veggio di Lodi, inspired by a pious wish to complete the work commenced by him, caused a chapel to be added on one side of the little church, which was dedicated to St. Monica, and in which her remains were laid. Thither thronged crowds of pilgrims, and

as among the number of those who came daily to
cross their hands upon the iron railing of the tomb,
a multitude of mothers, especially afflicted ones, were
to be seen, Eugenius IV. instituted a confraternity
of Christian mothers, under the patronage of St.
Monica; commencement, this, of a noble work, to
which we shall allude in due time, but which, as a
flower that opens its petals too soon, lived but for a
short time. But still this confraternity was the
means of spreading the devotion to our saint through
every hearth and home.

Before the close of the century there was a universal outcry for the erection of a grand basilica
worthy of the treasure with which Rome had so
recently been enriched. And as if France, for whom
more than for any other nation St. Monica had
emerged from her concealment, had a presentiment
of this, and wished already to show her gratitude
for the same, it was a French prelate, Cardinal
d'Estouteville, Archbishop of Rouen, who bestowed
on St. Monica the sole mark of respect wanting to
complete the tribute of honour which was her due.
But, impelled by a feeling of pious regard, instead of
dedicating it to St. Monica, it was dedicated to St.
Augustine, as if to afford this great saint, this loving
son, the joy of sheltering within the walls of his own
church his mother's body and his mother's tomb.

To the right of the high altar are two chapels: that
on the right is dedicated to St. Augustine, that on
the left to St. Monica; both are alike in form, alike

in beauty, as are the souls of those to whom they are consecrated.

There, within the chapel bearing her name, in an urn of ancient glass, shaped in the form of a tomb, and placed beneath the altar, reposes the body of St. Augustine's mother. A brief inscription serves to reveal this fact to the pilgrim:

HIC. JAC. CORPVS. S. MATRIS. MONICÆ.

The ancient tomb which formerly contained St. Monica's remains is religiously preserved in the same chapel, to the right of the altar. It consists of a sarcophagus of white stone, decorated with spiral flutings and ancient carvings, marked by extreme simplicity. Each corner rests on a lion's claw, and it is surmounted by an effigy of the saint, executed in relief, and draped from head to foot. At the base of the tomb is the following inscription:

IC Δ XC
SEPVLCRVM. VBI. B. MONICÆ. CORPVS
APVD. OSTIA. TIBERINA. ANNIS. M. XLI
JACVIT. OB. IN EO. EDITA. IN EJUS
TRANSLATIONE. MIRACVLA. EX
OBSCVRO. LOCO. IN. ILLVSTRIOREM
TRANSPONENDVM. FILII. PIENTISS.
CVRARVNT. ANNO. SALVTIS
MDLXVI.

The end, sidewalls, and vaults of the chapel are ornamented with frescoes descriptive of the life, or rather of the hopes and joys of the saint. First we behold her with tearful eyes, but with a brow on which a gleam of joy is discernible, listening to the aged bishop who predicts the future conversion of *that son of so many tears.* Farther on is the same face, suffused with the same degree of sorrow, but the brow illumined by a brighter ray of joy; she is listening to an angel saying to her: *Ubi tu et ille,** and showing her in the distance the souls of the mother and the son united in one happy embrace. The following representation depicts her with eyes devoid of tears, and full of sweet, pure happiness; it is the moment in which St. Augustine announces to her his conversion. She is next represented on her death-bed, radiant with joy, surrounded by her children, clasping the hand of the converted Augustine, her dying eyes gazing heavenwards, and her lips wreathed with smiles. Twice have I seen these pictures, and though I was then quite young, and know nothing of the sorrows of the times, and therefore was ignorant of the tears suffusing maternal eyes, and knew not that mothers stood in need of hope and consolation, each time I felt, when gazing on those touching scenes, in that quiet, silent sanctuary, which though but partially illumined by the light of day, was yet brilliant with the sun of hope, that it was intended to afford consolation, peace, joy, and sublime encouragement, to such as were bowed down by overwhelming sorrow.

Moreover, as these pictures approached completion,

---

* " Where thou art, he too shall be."

the times were growing more and more evil. It was the year 1566. Luther, having enkindled the flame of heresy and schism in Germany, was no more; Henry VIII., after spreading desolation and corruption throughout England, was also dead; as was also Calvin, the disturber of the peace of France. Except Italy and Spain, who enjoyed peace for a few years longer, all the nations were on the eve of shipwreck, tossed by the waves of heresy and schism, forerunners of impiety and spiritual indifference. Christendom trembled. No mother dared embrace her babes without paling at the thought of the dangers menacing their faith and conscience. It was indeed time for God to send them a consolatory sign to revive their hopes. Hence the reason why St. Monica was daily emerging more and more from her obscurity, shining forth from amid the storm as a peaceful rainbow.

CHAPTER XVIII.

GROWTH OF THE CULTUS OF WHICH ST. MONICA BECAME THE OBJECT—ITS HARMONY WITH OUR NECESSITIES AND WITH OUR GRIEFS.

1576-1866.

Amid the multitudinous apostacies which filled Christian mothers with alarm during the sixteenth century, but especially during the second part of the same, devotion to St. Monica ceased not to increase. Her name, hitherto inscribed in no martyrology, was inserted in that of Baronius, compiled by command of the pope, and from thence it found a place in all modern martyrologies. Her feast, which had been celebrated only in Rome, and in the churches pertaining to the monks following the rule of St. Augustine, now began to be universally observed, and her office was inserted in the Roman Breviary. Her relics, till then concentrated in one spot, were scattered throughout the entire world. In 1576, a portion of the saint's head was sent to Bologna by Pope Gregory XIII. The confraternity of St. Monica in Rome, likewise requested a portion, and obtained its request. Pavia, which glories in possessing St. Augustine's body, also desiring to add to its treasures some part of his mother's relics, through the munificence of the popes, received one of the saint's ribs. The Jesuit Fathers of Munster, and the hermits of St. Augustine at Trèves, were also enabled to enrich their churches with some of the hallowed remains. All the eminent and saintly personages to whom the Church gave birth at that epoch with such marvellous rapidity, as if to show Protestantism that she was still the true spouse of Christ, contributed to spread the cultus and devotion to St. Monica.

We have not time to recount the proofs of piety and veneration wherewith she inspired the noted men and saints of the sixteenth and seventeenth centuries. We beg leave to select but one of these, (St. Francis of Sales,) and trust the reader will pardon us the preference we have shown. This saintly man, whose special mission seems to have been that of speaking to the hearts of Christian women, and winning them for God, at once saw, with his lofty intellect and profound knowledge of souls, that there were few devotions more capable of consoling and strengthening them, of revealing to them the sublimity of their mission, and of endowing them with strength to fulfil the same, than devotion to St. Monica.

In his beautiful book, the " *Devout Life,*" which effected so important a revolution in Christian manners, he makes incessant mention of St. Monica. Does he wish to convince Christian women that there is no condition of life in which we should not strive to attain perfection, and " that it is attainable in all lawful vocations and callings," he holds up St

Monica presiding " in her household."* If speaking to mothers of the necessity of instilling faith and Christian virtues into their children's hearts, even during the days of infancy, he cites the same example. " Before his birth, St. Monica consecrated the great Augustine to God, by frequent dedications of him to the Christian religion, and to the service and glory of God, as he himself testifies of her, when he says that ' he had already tasted the salt of God while in his mother's womb,' adding : ' This is a great lesson for Christian mothers, from which they should learn to offer their offspring, before they are born, to His Divine Majesty.'"†

And when these children begin to grow up, when evil passions begin to manifest themselves, and mothers need a vigilance and firmness wholly divine in order to ward off the peril, does he desire to teach them how to defend, protect, save, and raise their children's souls to life once more, he still cites St. Monica's example. " St. Monica sought with unremitting zeal and constancy to overcome the evil inclinations of her son ; and after having long followed him by sea and land, at length obtained his conversion from God, and thus made him much more the son of her tears than the child of her womb."‡

That which St. Francis says thus in a book intended for publication, he repeats in his letters under a thousand varied forms. For instance, if he met with one of those married women who are as exiles

---

* See the *Introduction to the Devout Life*, part I., chap. iii.

† Ibid., chap. xxxviii.   ‡ Ibid.

here below, who, having given all their heart, and meeting with no return for their love, feel within that immense void which none but God can fill, and who, solely inflamed with love to Him, envy the cloistered nun, he says: " I should prefer your reflecting on the fact that many and many a saint has found himself and herself in a position similar to yours, and that they have borne all with great sweetness and resignation, St. Monica for example. Let this encourage you, and do you recommend yourself to her prayers."* Did he come in contact with a mother who was anxious, troubled, and looking with anxiety on the future (as is the case with all mothers) ; or if he met with any who are oppressed with sorrow, (as many a mother is,) his one word, uttered in that sweet and impressive tone which inspired hope and consolation, was, " Pray, pray ;" adding : " Read the life of St. Monica ; you will see the care she took for her Augustine, and many other things which will console you."†

But it is chiefly in the long, beautiful and instructive counsels addressed to St. Chantal that we must look if we wish to see what he thought of St. Monica.

Madame de Chantal was thirty years of age, the mother of four children, and possessed of a large fortune. She desired to attain perfection, although she had no intention of entering the religious life; on the contrary, her sole desire was to train her children aright, one of whom, in spite of his noble quali-

* St. Francis de Sales' Letters, book III., Letter 26, (ancient edition.)
• Ibid., book II., letter I.

ties, caused her some anxiety on account of the germs of evil which began to manifest themselves in him, as also his violence of temper, originality of character, the dangerous flattery to which he was exposed, and the perils attending his position at court, all of which combined to fill her with disquietude, similar to that experienced by Christian mothers of the present day.

St. Francis de Sales, also of opinion that Madame de Chantal's sphere of duty was to be found in her own home, using every effort to render her a true widow and a true mother, commenced his direction by counselling her to seek retirement and solitude, and to shun worldly society, all of which her sorrow and bereavement rendered congenial to her feelings. He desires her to shut herself up at home with her four children, and that, occupied in caring for them, she should convert her château into a little convent, full of peace and silence, so that she might forget the world, and aspire heavenwards. In this tiny convent there was to be an abbess, the Blessed Virgin, at whose feet and in whose company Madame de Chantal was to work, to whom she was to render filial obedience, whose blessing and orders she was to seek every morning, and present her petitions, prefacing them by kissing the foot of her statue, or lifting her eyes to her image.

All his letters to St. Frances of Chantal are replete with these thoughts. For example : "Courage, my daughter; keep close to your saintly abbess; die, and arise anew to life in her beloved Son."* Again :

* Letter of October 3, 1605.

27

" Beware of quitting your convent; restrain your thoughts, and so prevent distraction of heart. Observe your rule, and rest assured that the Son of your Lady abbess will not forsake you."* Again, on Christmas Day: "My daughter, I desire of God that you may spend this holy day in Bethlehem with your holy abbess. Beg her to allow you to relieve her of her precious burden: she will not refuse it; and having Him in your arms, secretly take possession of one of those tiny tears bedewing His eyelids. It is marvellous how potent a spell that is for every malady of the heart."†

But on entering a convent one not only needs an abbess to whom we render a perfect obedience, but also a mistress who watches over, trains, reproves, and moulds the novices entrusted to her care. Who, then, should be the instructress of Madame de Chantal, who teach her to be a true widow, a true mother, and true woman of the world, fulfilling all her social duties, but centreing her affections elsewhere, ready to quit the world without one shade of of regret, even as did the Christians of those olden times? St. Monica was to teach her this.

And at what epoch of Madame de Chantal's life did St. Francis of Sales present her with this mistress? At the very moment when he saw the first intimation of her desire to quit the world and enter on a religious life, a step which he deemed incapable of being realized. He points to St. Monica, as if to say, " Do

* Letter of July 10th.
† Letter of October 28, 1605.

you seek to attain perfection? Behold St. Monica. Did she forsake her son? And in devoting herself wholly to him, did she not attain the highest degree of virtue? I give her to you as your mistress."

But we must allow him to speak. Nothing equals those charming words, of which we never weary. "Your distaste for all worldly amusements is good, inasmuch as it does not mar your peace of mind. But be patient, we will talk of this in a year hence, if God spares our lives so long. That will be quite time enough. And for the same reason I make no comment on your wish to leave your native land, or enter a noviciate. All of which, my dear daughter, is far too important a subject to be treated of by letter: that also can remain in abeyance for a while. Meanwhile go on using your distaff, not with large heavy spindles, such as are beyond your management, but take such as are suited to your limited capacity, such as humility, patience, the surmounting of difficulties, mildness, resignation, simplicity, tending the sick, and patience under contradiction. With these you will be able to succeed in company with St. Monica and your Abbess."*

From that period St. Francis ever coupled them together. "Rejoice in God," he writes, "and in my name humbly salute your abbess and your mistress." Again, "Live, dear daughter, in union with your mistress, your sweet Lord, and with your abbess, and with whatever be the clouds, thorns, nails, and dere-

* Letter of June 8th, 1605.

lictions which may await you."* And again, "I desire a thousand graces for you and for your children, whom I regard as my children in Jesus Christ. These are the words your mistress addressed to Italica, her spiritual daughter."† And later on, when her son's conduct began to pierce his mother's heart: "Consider your mistress: read her life; it will console you."‡

And when, after the death of St. Francis of Sales, Madame de Chantal grew more and more anxious regarding her son, grieving one day, not that he might perhaps be killed in a duel, but trembling at the thought of his dying in mortal sin, she tells us that on casting herself in prayer at the foot of the altar, and pouring out her soul to God, she heard a voice that filled her with emotion; it was that of St. Francis of Sales, who, issuing from his tomb, or rather, descending from heaven, addressed her in these words: "Read the eighth book of St. Augustine's *Confessions*." She did so, and whilst bedewing with her tears those sublime pages where Augustine is seen saved by his mother's tears, she had the consoling presentiment that by her own prayers, tears, and self-sacrifices she also would save her Celsus-Benignus.§

Thenceforth St. Monica was the object of her fervent love. She counselled this devotion to every one. And we also know that desiring in death to resemble

* Letter of August 30th, 1605.
† Letter of June 29th, 1606.
‡ Letter of July, 1615.
§ Memoirs of Mother de Chaugy, p. 470.

her in death as in life, she desired that the account of the saint's last moments might be read aloud to her. And on arriving at the passage which records that the great saint expressed her readiness to die, though far away from her native land, she pressed Madame de Montmorency's hand, and looking at her sweetly, said: "That is intended for me;" alluding to the fact that she was dying far from her beloved Annecy.*

All the great saints of that day emulated St. Francis of Sales and St. Chantal in inculcating devotion to St. Monica. They all speak in the same strain. As the times grew more evil, and the surging waves of impiety that filled Bossuet with such alarm began to make themselves heard, terrified mothers raised their eyes to St. Monica and crowded to her altars; and truly nothing was so calculated to strengthen, console, and inspire them with hope, as the sight of that happy mother pressing to her heart the son her tears had saved.

But it is especially at the close of the nineteenth century that this devotion was destined to become so popular. Among all its sorrows one stands pre-eminently forth. A fearful phenomenon, which the world had seen but once, and that only for a brief instant, one which would have filled the pagan world with horror, now reappears to view. Men living without God, possessing no altars, observing no prayers or worship of any kind; youths of sixteen abjuring the faith of their childhood, and oftentimes

---

* Memoirs of Mother de Chaugy, p. 286.

descending into the grave without inquiring of themselves if they had a soul, or owed any allegiance to their Creator; intellects, rich as regarded earthly, but poor as regarded heavenly wisdom, devoid of faith, hope, true happiness, and noble aspirations, pursuing their way in sadness, not knowing what awaited them at their journey's end. But there was generally some fellow-traveller, such as a wife, mother, daughter, sister, who both saw and knew the terrible and inevitable abyss, the sight of which overwhelmed them with the deepest sorrow.

During half a century these floods of grief had been accumulating in those hearts; then came the day when, the measure being full, it overflowed and reached even the foot of the altar. It was the first of May, 1850, when a few mothers, either more afflicted, or feeling their grief more acutely than others, met together in a humble chapel in Paris, that of Notre Dame de Sion, just erected by one of the best priests of that day,* and remembering our Lord's words, "Wherever two or three are gathered together in My name, there am I in the midst of them," they resolved to unite their tears in order that they might be the more efficacious. They therefore composed a short prayer for their children, and after binding themselves to recite it daily, promised to reassemble once a month at the foot of the same altar.

It was then seen how deeply in harmony with the

* The Rev. Father Theodore Ratisbonne, Superior-General of the Congregation of Notre Dame de Sion, and First Director of the Christian Mothers.

needs of the age this pious association was. For
hardly had it sprung to life than its growth was most
rapid. Before the expiration of four years, at the
commencement of 1854, it was already established in
Lille, Amiens, Nantes, Versailles, Cambray, and
Valenciennes, and ere the year closed it was flourishing at Belley, Frejus, Toulon, Bordeaux, Tours, Cou-
tances, Rouen, and Bayeux. It even passed the
frontiers, and spread throughout Belgium and England also.*

In 1855 it extended still further; branches of it
were established in Constantinople, Jerusalem, Pondichéry, Mauritius, Martinique, and Sydney, and
whilst spreading beyond the sea, took deep root in
Europe, especially in France. London, Dublin, Liver-
pool, Stockholm, St. Petersburg, Odessa, Vienna,
Stutgard, Fribourg, the Hague, Bologna, Turin,
Madrid, Chambéry, Florence ; and in France, Lyons,
Bordeaux, Orleans, Amiens, Rouen, became centres
whence issued branch associations, established in the
smallest towns and villages even.†

And ere six years had elapsed, six years marked,
it is true, by silence, humility, prayers, and tears,
which, though unobserved, were not shed in vain, the
Holy Father, Pius IX., seeing how rapidly this holy
work had developed, hailed it with gladness, even as
the storm-tossed voyager hails the rainbow that
announces the end of the storm.

* Report of Madame Louise Josson, president of the arch-confrater
nity, at the assembly of March 19th, 1855.

† Report at the assembly-general of March 13th, 1856.

One cannot but feel deeply moved, on considering the humble commencement of a work so important as this. But such is the way in which God effects His purpose at the present day. Had anyone told the ten factory girls of Lyons that the sou they begged from door to door for the propagation of the faith would produce millions, such words would have awaked a smile of incredulity. And had the poor students of the Latin quarter, who had formed themselves into an association for tending the sick, been told that they were the vanguard of an immense army, which would soon spread throughout the world, they would indeed have been surprised, as would also have been the case with the founder of the Little Sisters of the Poor, on hearing that, before she departed hence, her daughters would be innumerable. Thus God accomplishes His work; as if, now that man is intoxicated with his own power, and, because he has constructed railroads and invented the electric telegraph, thinks himself independent of God, God in His turn shows man that He can effect His own purposes without human instrumentality.

It was impossible for this Association of Christian Mothers to meet in prayer on behalf of their erring sons without remembering St. Monica. She was in their thoughts from the very first, but they had selected six or seven patrons, and St. Monica's name was the last on the list. But in the course of time she began gradually to emerge from obscurity; she appeared above the horizon, and so sweet and pure was her light that, after the Blessed Virgin, who stands unrivalled in her sanctity, St. Monica became the chief confidante, patroness, refuge, and grand protectress of Christian mothers.

We have a striking proof that such was the case, for the Sovereign Pontiff having, by an apostolic brief, dated March 11th, 1856, raised the association of Christian mothers to the rank of an arch-confraternity, Mgr. Sibour, at that time Archbishop of Paris, assembling those ladies in the chapel of Notre Dame de Sion, in order to acquaint them with the favour that had been bestowed on them, addressed them in a discourse, some portions of which we beg leave to quote, for the whole of the address may be resumed in this one sentence : " Ladies, if you desire to be truly Christian mothers, let St. Monica be your example."

" Yes, imitate this holy mother, who by her prayers reclaimed her son, and who, aided by divine grace, enabled him to attain so high a degree of sanctity. Alas ! it may be that you also have sons whom you bewail. Do not despair. Invoke St. Monica, and take her for your model. In heaven Augustine's mother will still remember her sufferings here below, and will surely compassionate you, and either obtain your son's conversion, or win him grace to persevere in virtue's path."

And, continuing in the same strain, Mgr. Sibour gave an outline of the saint's life, her anxiety, sorrows, bitter grief, and earnest prayers, which, after her son's conversion, were exchanged for ineffable joy. He spoke of her happy death, and the rapturous bliss awaiting her in heaven. Then, addressing himself to the members of the association, spoke as follows: "Tell me, ladies, who is there that does not understand and participate in sentiments such as those which animated St. Monica's breast? What mother but turns to God to entreat from Him her son's conversion? And on beholding him return to God, and to the paths of faith and virtue, who would not long to quit this sad world, and soar heavenwards with her son, to that realm where sin and sorrow are unknown, where no enemy can invade, and where bliss for ever reigns?" He exhorted them to merit this happiness, so that, their cherished wish fulfilled, earth no longer possessing any charm for them, they might exclaim with St. Monica: "Why tarry I longer here? my task is completed."

Assuredly this was a most appropriate inauguration, and one to which every heart responded.

Since then the association has made great progress, the details of which I need not mention. I will only state that it extended to Geneva, Algiers, Santiago, Buenos-Ayres, Pondichéry, and India.* And wherever the association exists, St. Monica's name, St. Monica's tears, are held in lasting remembrance. Not a single priest or bishop presides in its reunions but St. Monica's hallowed name ascends spontaneously to his lips. I have read many notices regarding this association, and many discourses on the same subject,

---

* See the annual reports, which are replete with interest and information. There is also a notice of considerable length in the *Manuel de la mère Chrétienne*, by Father Ratisbonne. Paris, published by Olmer, Rue Bonaparte, 1850.

all of which express the sentiments of hope and joy awakened by these reunions, of which St. Monica, in her hours of sorrow or of joy, is at once the hope, the comfort, and the stay.

Yes, this gentle star is ascending the horizon. Preceding ages discerned it but faintly, the sun of happiness still shone too brilliantly for that. It was to irradiate our day that God created this luminary, which now, emerging from its obscurity, encircles Christian mothers with its brightness, dries their tears, soothes their sorrows, and fills them with indomitable faith and joyous hope.

Fear not, brighter days are in store. God will be moved to compassion, for it is impossible that the prayers and tears of sixty thousand Christian mothers should fail to touch the heart of Him who of old was so deeply moved by the tears the widow of Naim shed over the bier of her only son! Never will a whole generation of youths bedewed by maternal tears be allowed by Him to perish.

Complete thy work, O Monica, and from the height of that glory where thou claspest within thine arms that son on whom thou didst bestow a second life, look down upon the multitude of Christian women, who are now fulfilling the same noble and difficult mission which thou thyself didst accomplish; support them in those heavy trials through which God wills them to pass, in order that they may insure the salvation of their sons. Sustain their courage. O happy mother, charm away their tears; and in perusing thy life, teach them that the unhallowed fire which at times threatens to destroy their children's souls, is not so potent as the sacred flame which burns within a mother's heart.

As for myself, who have so lovingly sought out the traces,—alas! too faint,—of thy footsteps here below, O incomparable St. Monica, if my attempt prove unsuccessful, I shall not regret having essayed it. In revealing thy heart to me thou hast taught me to know my own. Thanks to thy teaching, I know now, better than I did before, at what cost souls are to be ransomed, and that, if a true mother must possess a priestly heart, the heart of a true priest must be a maternal one. Henceforth, bound by my office to reclaim so many Augustines, no longer will I kneel despairingly at the holy altar's foot. O mother, thou hast taught me how to set about my task! May I profit by thy lessons, and, inflamed by thy example, may I rise superior to my fears, and cheerfully submitting to the sacrifices required at my hands, may I dedicate myself, more entirely than I have ever done before, to the sublime art of saving souls from sin, and restoring them to truth, to virtue, and to God!

APPENDIX.

NOTES AND DOCUMENTARY EVIDENCE

———————

NOTE I.

SOUK-ARRAS (THE ANCIENT TAGASTE).

That Souk-Arras occupies the site of Tagaste appears undoubted. We subjoin the chief documents testifying to this important fact. The following is a letter from Captain Lewal, commander of the circle of Souk-Arras, addressed to the president of the Algerian Historical Society.

"Souk-Arras, Nov. 17th, 1856.

"To the President,

"Sir,

"I have the honour of forwarding you an inscription unearthed a few days back, which may throw some light on the disputed point as to whether Souk-Arras really stands on the site occupied by Tagaste, St. Augustine's birth-place.

"I subjoin a few particulars relative to the question. I take no note of the vast extent of the ruins, and the multiplicity of the tombs, all denoting that this spot was originally one of importance; neither do I allude to the geographical position attributed to Tagaste by ancient authors, and which appears to correspond exactly with the locality where we now are. I simply confine myself to the examination of the inscriptions that have hitherto come to light.

"The one of which I write is the third. The two preceding ones may be thus briefly described. The first, still to be found at Souk-Arras, is on a small stone, and reads thus:

THA
GASI
CHAE
RE

"It has been already mentioned, and the following translation suggested: 'Erected at the cost of Tagaste.' I think it doubtful whether this be the correct interpretation, and, if admissible, the C H remains unsolved.* The word Thagasi can be verified, and certainly bears some analogy, if not resemblance, to Tagaste.

"Secondly, another inscription has been published, the first line of which runs thus:

MAEMILLIVS THAGAS.........ANVS.

* M. Renier has since explained the inscription: "Thagasi Χαίρε."— as "Thagaste, hail."

The second word may perhaps be interpreted *Thagasius*, or *Thagasitanus*. From a grammatical point of view these three forms, *Thagasi, Thagasius,* or *Thagasitanus*, are not entirely satisfactory. Yet the two first syllables, *Thagas*, identical with the two first of Thagaste, naturally lead to the supposition that they belong to the same word, and this in spite of the missing terminations.

" This brings me to the inscription number three, recently disinterred, and which strengthens the supposition that the inductions deduced from the two preceding ones are correct. The stone is in the form of a rectangular parallelopiped. The total height is 4 feet, $5\frac{1}{2}$ inches; its length, $21\frac{2}{3}$ inches; its thickness, $18\frac{1}{8}$ inches. The stone is of a calcareous nature, in colour pale yellow, close, fine, and extremely hard in texture, such as is frequently met with throughout the circle of Souk-Arras. Having been exposed to the air, the exterior has acquired a greyish hue.

" The height of the letters is rather more than $2\frac{1}{8}$ inches; the space between the lines nearly $\frac{1}{3}$ of an inch.

" The inscription is surrounded by two shallow hollow mouldings, surrounded by a narrow fillet; at the two upper angles, between the mouldings and the fillet, two small hearts are discernible. Doubtless there were originally similar ones at the lower angles; but, as the sketch proves, these angles no longer exist. There is no trace of any other ornament or funereal emblem.

" This is the inscription:

```
          MAMVLLIOM
       TIL PAP OPTATO
        CREMENTIANO
         FOR SINGVLA
        RIS FIDEI BONI
        TATIS MVNIFI
        CENTIÆ VI...
        ORDO SPLENDI
        DISSIMVS THA
        GASTENSIVIS
        CONLATA CER
        TATIM PECVNIA
    N CVIVS DEDICATIONE
   Sᵃ-... MILN ADOPVS MV
    NIFICENTIÆ SVÆ PATRI
       Æ DONVIT ETC......S
      PRÆTER FP...VINE
        VD M.QVINCENO
```

" The six first lines can be easily deciphered. At the seventh there are one or two letters wanting after the sixth syllable.

" From the seventh to the thirteenth line, there is no difficulty whatever; in the ninth and tenth is found the word *Thagastensivis* completely perfect, to this I shall revert later on. At line thirteen is an N wholly distinct from the preceding word *Pecunia*, and the succeeding one *Cujus;* possibly it signifies *Nostra.* In the same line, in the word *Dedicatione,* is an I intersected by a transverse line at about two thirds of its height, which evidently stands for a T and an I, since the same thing is met with in the fifteenth line in the word *Munificentiœ,* although in line seven the same word is written with the T and the I separate.

"In line fourteen the head of an S is discernible, although the lower part is uncertain. This is followed by another small S up in the air; this is followed by a line thus —, and beneath it is something resembling the letter C.

"In the same line are four small and very distinct letters, the two last surmounted by a line —; the rest of the line is very legible.

"In line fifteen the last word is effaced; nevertheless a T is discernible, which, being preceded and followed by two letters, with Æ in the succeeding line, is most probably intended for *Patriæ;* which word seems to harmonize with the tenor of the other part of the inscription.

"The end of line sixteen is doubtful; the C of the final word is clear, and the head of the S is almost so; we may then safely presume that the word was *CONS,* the ordinary abbreviation of *Consecravit.*

"Line seventeen is the most obscure; but after careful examination we seem to distinguish the word *Præter.* The P, R, E, and T, seem probable, the rest is doubtful; then follow an E or rather F, a letter resembling a P, then two or three letters wholly undecipherable; respecting the four last there is no doubt.

"The final line appears to contain the date; the end of it is legible, not so the commencement. There seems to be a V and a D, then a letter which I cannot read, perhaps an L; then M or VI, succeeded by an X with a bar across, very legible.

28   ♭ M.

"Whatever be the meaning of this inscription, it undoubtedly contains the word *Thagastensivis.*

"Doubtless, as in the case of the three words above cited, found on the two first stones, these words (though not perfectly correct) are derived from Tagaste, for we find that in the list of bishops present at the councils, that of Tagaste is spoken of as Bishop of *Thagastensis.*

"With regard to this termination, it is difficult to deny that the word Thagastensivis, so legible on the stone to which we allude, is not a derivative of Thagaste.

"This word does not relate to a person whose ashes were contained in this tomb; but has to do with the two preceding words: *Ordo splendidissimus Thagastensivis.*

"This suffices to refute the objection that might arise from the fact of this being the inscription on a tomb; viz., that on the tombs of those who died in their native place it was never customary to state that they were born in that spot.

"Any way, this fresh discovery increases the presumption in favour of the supposition that Souk-Arras occupies the site of the ancient town of Tagaste, a supposition that will perhaps be exchanged for certainty, when you shall have interpreted and completed the inscription I now transmit.

"I remain, &c.,

"CAPTAIN LEWAL,

"Commander-in-Chief

" Of the Circle of Souk-Arras."

In publishing this letter, the *African Review* adds the following observations:

"The rubbing sent by Captain Lewal was obtained by means of black lead, an excellent plan when the stone is unbroken and in good preservation, which was not the case in the present instance. It would have been better to have adopted the process mentioned in p. 78 of the first number of our *Review*.

"There is no doubt as to the following being the correct reading of the inscription we received:

MARCO AMVLIO MARCI

FILIO PAPIRIA OPTATO

CREMENTIANO

EQVITI ROMANO SINGVLA

RIS FIDEI BONI

TATIS MVNIFI

CENTIAE VIRO

ORDO SPLENDI

DISSIMVS THA

GASTENSIVM

COLATA CER

TATIM PECVNIA

IN CVIVS DEDICATIONE

TO MARCUS AMULIUS,

SON OF MARCUS, OF THE

TRIBE OF PAPIRIA,

SURNAMED OPTATUS,

AND CREMENTIANUS,

A ROMAN KNIGHT,

A MAN EMINENT FOR

HIS LOYALTY, BOUNTY,

MUNIFICENCE. THE VERY

ILLUSTRIOUS MUNICIPALITY

OF TAGASTE

HAVING RAISED A SUBSCRIPTION

READILY CONTRIBUTED TO

....

"The remainder of the inscription appears to us to indicate that: 'On the day of the dedication of this municipal monument, Amulius caused bread, wine, and even money to be distributed.'

"The incontestable part of the inscription establishes the following:

"1. That Tagaste stood where Souk-Arras now stands; that the monument above alluded to is essentially *local* in its character; and that, on the other hand, no modern town has been erected at Souk-Arras, which rendered it necessary to utilize the materials of the surrounding ruins.

"2. The true orthography of Tagaste, and of its derivative Thagastensis,* which the savant Morcelli writes without an *h.*

* "On arriving at lines nine and ten, we unhesitatingly read the word as *Thagastensium*. And at the moment of going to press, we received

"3. A new landmark to determine the position of the famous battle-field of Zama. For when once the position of Tagaste has been ascertained, it is easy to find that of Naraggara, which was situated about twenty miles to the east of the former town, on the road to Carthage; it was in the vicinity of Naraggara that the Romans and the Carthaginians met in combat, to decide which of the two nations should be mistress of the world.

"We shall resume this interesting question on receiving a new rubbing of the inscription.

"A. BERBRUGGER."

The following are the unpublished details of the ruins of Souk-Arras.

The following passage is extracted from the *Journal de marche de la colonne expéditionnaire de Tebessa,* under the command of General Randon (June and July, 1846 :)

"SOUK-ARRAS (Tagaste.)—Seventeen miles north of Mdaourouche are the ruins of Souk-Arras, on the banks of a stream bearing the same name. They occupy about twenty-five acres, and are situated on the table-land of a small eminence on the right bank, and testify to the existence of an important Roman colony, which selected this spot on account of its affording them easy communication with the basins of the Seybouse, Medjerda, and Mellaga.

a letter from Captain Lewal, corroborating our supposition, and telling us that the recent rains had so washed the stone as to render all doubt as to this being the correct reading impossible."—*Editor's Note.*

"Water is abundant and excellent in quality, but fodder is scarce.

"On leaving Souk-Arras, an ancient Roman road, traversing foliage-covered hills, leads to the Medjerda."

M. Berbrugger, who visited these ruins in 1850, thus describes them:

"The ruins of Tagaste, St. Augustine's birth-place, are situated on three eminences, stretching from north-east to south-east. The place is called Souk-Arras; a market is held there every Sunday. This locality is an hour's distance from the residence of Mohammed-Salah, the Kadi of Hanencha.

"The greater part of the ruins are situated on the eminence on which stands the Koubba of Sidi M'saoul, a holy Mussulman who died of the plague at the time when Bey Hamouda was reigning in Tunis, and Pacha Ali in Algiers.

"To the east of this eminence lie the ruins of an edifice the foundations of which are forty-four yards broad and ten deep. I read the following inscription on a flag-stone nearly six inches high, the letters being about $1\frac{1}{4}$ inches in height:

......VM VOTIS XXX ET......

"To the left, east of the ruins, is a building, the plan of which denotes a facade twenty-seven yards broad and thirteen yards high. Like the preceding one, it is constructed of rough materials, intersected by tiers of hewn stone placed vertically one above the other.

"In ascending the stream of Souk-Arras, I met with some ruins of considerable magnitude, at a place called Ras-El-Ma (head source of the stream.) A little farther on, below a fountain, is the *Henchir*, or ruins of Mrabta-Fatom (Marabout-Fatma,) a good sized heap of hewn stones.

"Among these ruins I met with the following inscription.*

"The following was found within the Zaouïa of Sidi-M'saoud:

....SA.... TIVS S. F. DATUS P. V. A. LXXI. H. S. E.	THIS INDIVIDUAL, SURNAMED DATUS, LIVED BEYOND THE AGE OF 71.

"In the outer wall of the same, by the side of the entrance, is seen a stone hollowed in the form of a niche, in which niche some artist, if we may thus profane the word, has sculptured an upright figure of most grotesque aspect. The hands are resting on the hips in a fantastic attitude, and the arms are rounded so as to bear an exact resemblance to the handles of a basket. The dress consists of a tight-fitting tunic intersected by folds, which garment, girt round the waist, tightens as it approaches the lower parts so as to render all movement extremely difficult.

"Crosses are to be found on many of the stones; but they are the work of pious visitors of modern

* M. Berbrugger visited these ruins in 1850, many years prior to the French occupation. The works carried on since then have brought fresh inscriptions to light.

times. Mohammed-Salah, then Kadi of Hanencha, told me that he one day accompanied a French marabout, who was going to inter a bone of one of our greatest saints, in the very house where he was born thirty centuries ago! On hearing this I was amused to see how the simplest facts become distorted in passing an Arab's lips."

In his pamphlet, entitled *Excursion to the ruins of Khemissa*, M. le Commandant de la Mare has devoted some pages to Tagaste.

In conclusion, we borrow the following particulars from M. l'abbé Godard:

" SOUK-ARRAS.—I have collected the following inscriptions among the ruins of St. Augustine's native town:

No. 1.

SOLI INVICTO SACR...

PRO SALVTE ET INCO

LVMITATE PERPETVI

IMP. CAES. L. DOMI

TI AVRELIANI PII FELI

AVG. P. M. TR. VI COS.

III P P PROCONSVLI*

* "Monument dedicated to the victorious sun, to obtain health and prosperity for the perpetual Emperor Cæsar Lucius Domitius Aurelianus, the pious, fortunate, august, and great pontiff; Tribune for the sixth time, consul for the third, father of his country, and proconsul."

M. l'abbé Godard mentions the last letter in line three, and the two last in line four, as doubtful.

No. 2.

IOVI OPT. MAX. STATORI ET IVN. AVG. REG.

M. GARGILIVS SYRVS VEL. F. P. P. ET IVL. VICTORIA EIVS

LIBERALITATE ET PECVNIA SVA

POSVERVNT*

" The following inscription is perfectly legible; but I do not understand the CH.—In the *Annuaire Archéologique* of Constantine, it is stated that an inscription had been found containing the word *Thagasius.* Nothing is known a⸱ nt it at Souk-Arras.

No. 3.✝

THA

GASI

CHAE

RE

The third consulate of Aurelian was A.D. 274; we know this from history, and this date does not coincide with the date in which he was elected tribune for the sixth time, as this would bring us down to the year 275, the date of the emperor's death.—*Editor's note.*

* " To Jupiter, the good and great, who arrests fugitives, and to Juno, the august queen.—Marcus Gargilius Syrus, son of Velius (?) president of the provinces, and Julia Victoria, by his liberality and at his own expense, has erected this monument."

At the first line, before the word *Junoni,* we read Et instead of the E given by M. l'abbé Godard, who failed to remark the prolongation to the left of the upper horizontal line of the E, and which denotes the letter T. In line two, we read VEL. F. after *Syrus.*

We think *præses provinciæ* the correct rendering of the abbreviation P. P.—*Editor's note.*

✝ Vide Captain Le wal's letter.

No. 4.

D. M. S.	D. M. S.
O. PRAE	CAECILI
CILIVS	A LIBO
GENIAIS	SA P.V.A.
P. V. A. LXXXI	LXXV
H. S. E.	H. S. E.

PRAECILIV. BATV
RVS PARENTIB*

No. 5.

D. M. S.	No. 6.
CLAVDIA RVF	D. M. S.
NA SACERDOS	B. PRIVATVs
MAGNA PIA VXI	V. A. LXXXX
ANNIS CHI	B. IANVARIA
H. S. E.	PATRI MER.
	S.S. FECIT
	H. S. F.

No. 7.

SEDINI
MVS LIE
BIA VIXI. A
NNIL LVII
H. S. EST

* "*Praecilius Baturus to his parents who lie buried here: Quintus (?, Praecilius Genias, who lived more than eighty-one years; and Caecilia Libosa, who lived more than seventy-five years.*

This name Praecilius has become celebrated since the discovery of the beautiful tomb of Cirta's steward, found at the base of the rock of Constantine.

Above each of these epitaphs is a crescent, supported by a palm on the right hand inscription, and by a kind of flower on the left hand one.—*Editor's note.*

"The epitaph of this Sedinimus Liebia, who lived to the age of fifty-seven, was placed above a crescent; it is defaced and very coarsely sculptured.

No. 8.

" Above the representation of a roughly sculptured female figure, in a niche, we read :

D. M. S.

APRONIA

LAETA PIA

V. AN. LX

H. S. E.

No. 9.

"Above a crescent is the following:

D. M. S.

PAEVI

VS OCTAVIVS

SDATVS P . VL

ANNIS XVII

"In a wall, near the stream in the ravine, is a fragment of a frieze (?) with this mutilated inscription :

No. 10.

......MAMVL....*

"In the same spot is another inscription almost wholly effaced.

* Doubtless the Marcus Amulius mentioned by Captain Lewal.— *Editor's note.*

No. 11.

C. FLAVIO C. FIL
PAPIRIA HILARO
FELICI EQ. ROM. CVI
CVM SPLENDIDISSI
MVS ORD.....
PIIS VII......
MOS V......
PATRI......
ET HON... ..
PRIVM......
QVIIM......
...SDOC......
...IVE......
STATUM LOCO DM
IVXTA PARENTUM
CREVISSET EXEMPLVM
REMISA PECUNIA QVN
MEREBATVR PONI CVRAVI......*

It is a pleasing sight to see French soldiers, young officers, and even generals, at the time when by their swords they are restoring Africa to France, employing their leisure hours in taking rubbings of ancient inscriptions, deciphering their meaning, and illuming their passage with rays of light as well as rays of glory.

* This dedication is made by the municipal (ordo) body of Thagaste Caius.

NOTE II.

TRADITIONS RELATIVE TO ST. MONICA.

St. Augustine has bequeathed us but few details of his mother's youth and early years. Happily, tradition has supplied this void, in acquainting us with a certain number of most interesting facts which reveal St. Monica's character most distinctly. These facts, never varying, are to be met with in very ancient records, and particularly in the divers liturgies of the Orders observing the Augustinian Rule. The Canons Regular, no matter what Congregation they belong to, the Hermits of St. Augustine, the Servites, the Premonstratensians, and the Preaching Friars, cherish and celebrate the memory of these facts with such unanimity that it is impossible to doubt their authenticity. First amongst them are the ancient lessons and antiphons of St. Monica, found in all the liturgies of the Orders following the Augustinian rule. The tones of joy and sorrow are admirably intermingled throughout the whole of the office. The antiphons devoted to St. Monica and her son are most beautiful.

The middle ages dedicated many sequences to St. Monica. The one throwing most light upon her life, commences: "Augustini magni patris." It is attributed to Adam de Saint Victor.

All the liturgies of the Orders following the Augustinian Rule, the Canons Regular, Servites, Hermits of St. Augustine, Preaching Friars, &c., agree not only as regards the traditions to which we have alluded, but also as regards a very ancient document, in the form of a letter addressed to a Spouse of Christ, *dilecta sponsa Christi*, relating the life of St. Monica, to whom the anonymous author gives the name of mother, *caram matrem*. Misled by this word, those who discovered this composition imagined that it was written by St. Augustine, and that this spouse of Christ was probably his sister, (for we know that she entered religion); hence they concluded that Augustine wrote this letter in order to acquaint her with her mother's death. They therefore entitled it: *Ad sororem:* or, *Sorori suæ Perpetuæ Virgini.* And as some not much versed in the art of criticism took the same view of the case, the letter was attributed to St. Augustine.

But this opinion is untenable. The style is wholly unworthy of the great doctor. He relates things which were too well known to his sister for him to dream of recounting them to her. Many of the expressions are borrowed from the *Confessions,* and there are many inaccuracies not to be found in St. Augustine's writings. Moreover, there is no proof that this letter was addressed to St. Augustine's sister. It may have been addressed to an inmate of one of the convents following the Augustinian Rule, for such existed even during the life-time of the saint. And there is no reason why, after St. Augustine's death, and in order to complete his *Confessions*, and reveal those marvels which the great doctor's humility had kept concealed, one of his immediate disciples, or a disciple of those who had personally known Augustine, should not have written this letter, relating all that was known of St. Monica, and addressing it to one of the virgins following her son's rule.

And although we might wish the letter written in a more modern style, and by an author of the seventh or eighth century, who, in order to publish all the traditions relative to St. Monica, resolved to embody them in a letter such as Augustine might have written to his sister, it is none the less true that the subject matter of this letter is excellent and valuable. It is borrowed from records undoubtedly ancient, all the Augustinian liturgies corroborate its authenticity, and many portions of it are supported by the early Roman and Gallican liturgies; therefore it is of great value, in spite of the few inaccuracies by which it is disfigured.

The authentic account of the translation of the relics of St. Monica is carefully preserved in the convent of St. Augustine at Rome.

The discourse of Pope Martin V., in honour of St. Monica, which is, as it were, the Bull of her canonization, is extremely valuable. The Bollandists give only an extract from it, and previous to the publication of this history of the saint it had become extremely rare.

NOTE III.

OPENING OF THE TWO NEW SANCTUARIES OF ST. MONICA, THE ONE AT TAGASTE, THE OTHER AT HIPPO.

The first Bishop of Constantine, Mgr. de Las-Cases, had scarcely ascended the restored Episcopal See, formerly occupied by St. Augustine, when he resolved to open two new sanctuaries, august indeed! for the use of Christian mothers, the one at Tagaste, and the other at Hippo.

He addressed the following letter to the Association of Christian Mothers:

"Ladies,

"I regard your Association as one of the most important of the present day, and am not surprised that it has met with universal approval; that it has spread throughout each portion of the globe, and enlisted one hundred and fifty thousand Christian mothers into its ranks. Mothers, I have the happiness of offering a fresh stimulus to your zeal, by opening to your Association two sanctuaries, whence your maternal supplications will ascend with more potency and greater efficacy.

"Henceforth two chapels are specially consecrated to your use, the one at Tagaste, where St. Monica shed so many tears; the other at Hippo, where her tears bore such an abundant harvest.

"I decree and command, that in both sanctuaries a

Mass shall be said daily for the perseverance, or for the reclaiming of the children in whose salvation you are so deeply and rightly interested.

"All the particular indulgences with which the Holy Father has deigned to enrich these two new sanctuaries I make over to you, to your husbands, and especially to your sons.

"Rest assured, Christian mothers, that from that land formerly so renowned, from that shore of old so fruitful in saints, will be wafted the spirit of innocence, or of regeneration, of fidelity, or of repentance. Augustine will speak, his voice will be heard; Monica will pour forth her sighs, those sighs which always effect conversion."

And after these touching words, the venerable bishop adds, with a modesty and amiability which have affected us deeply:

"The idea just realized by me, has, I am pleased to say, been already suggested by others.

"St. Francis of Sales said to the afflicted mothers of his day: 'Ladies, if you desire to be truly Christian mothers, fix your gaze on St. Monica.' Also: 'Read St. Monica's Life, you will there see the care she bestowed on her Augustine, and find much to console you.'

"In the biography of this illustrious Saint, which M. l'abbé Bougaud has written with such pathos and skill, is one passage which strikes me very forcibly, for is it not, indeed, both a presage and an announcement of that which I have just accomplished? 'It was impossible for this Association of Christian mothers to meet in prayer, on behalf of their erring sons, without remembering St. Monica. She was in their thoughts from the very first, but they had selected six or seven patrons, and St. Monica's name was the last on the list. But in the course of time she began gradually to emerge from obscurity; she appeared above the horizon, and so sweet and pure was her light that, after the Blessed Virgin, who stands unrivalled in her sanctity, St. Monica became *the chief confidante, patroness, refuge, and grand protectress of Christian mothers.*'

"You will therefore doubtless appreciate the value of the gift I bestow on you. I am already assured of this, for several mothers, on learning from me that they would henceforth be able to associate their fears, and mingle their sighs and tears with those of St. Monica, thanked me with effusion of tears, and were unable to find words in which to express the degree of encouragement, strength, and consolation, with which my pious project had inspired them."

These beautiful and touching words, which fall as a benediction on our volume, and which were accompanied by marks of the most delicate kindness, awoke the following grateful and respectful response on our part:

"Paris, March 17th, 1869.

" Monseigneur,

" I much regret being absent from Orleans when you sent M. l'abbé Caussanel to pay me a visit; and more deeply do I regret not having been at home when your grace recently called. I was preaching during Lent at the Madeleine, and therefore had no opportunity of thanking you for your mandatory letter, and the kindness which dictated it.

"For many years, Monseigneur, it well behoved you to take the initiative in presenting the Association of Christian Mothers with those two new sanctuaries, at Tagaste and at Hippo, which sanctuaries will henceforth rank as the most august of all.

"You have lived in the world, Monseigneur; you know whether Christian mothers stand in need of consolation. And, as a bishop, and a successor of St. Augustine, having received at your consecration, among other gifts, grace to appreciate the treasures of your Church, and the benefits accruing therefrom to the Universal Church, you know far better than any one else does what St. Monica was, and the deep wells of consolation and of hope to be found in those two words: Tagaste and Hippo.

"Tagaste! at this word there start to mind the sorrows and disenchantments of marriage in which true unity was wanting; silent tears, untiring prayers, poignant anxiety, as well as the joy of conversion, and the ineffable raptures attending a death-bed. Tagaste means a husband's soul saved by dint of love.

"Hippo! It may be that St. Monica's eyes never beheld thee, save perhaps during her moments of ecstasy when at Ostia; for who can say whether it was not a vision of Hippo which so gladdened that mother's heart that she died of joy? However this may be, Hippo not only recalls the conversion of the lost son, that son of so many tears; but virtue, sanctity, genius, penitence, and love, flourishing where formerly there was naught but evil. It recalls Augustine, the priest, bishop, and doctor. The greatest doctor the Church owns was purchased for her by a mother's tears!

"Monseigneur, wives and mothers will ever bless you for what you have done, and when they turn their tearful eyes to the sanctuaries erected by you at Tagaste and at Hippo, the sight will strengthen and console them; full of faith and fresh energy, they will not forget that land whence came their help; they will not forget your arduous labours, the churches you have built, the souls you have saved, the little ophans whom famine has thrown on your hands, and they will offer their prayers and their alms on behalf of him who reads a mother's heart so well.

"Accept, Monseigneur, the assurance of my deepest respect and devotion.

"Em. Bougaud, Vicar-General."

***

End of Notes and Documentary Evidence.